F. W. (Frederick William) Salem

**Beer**

Its History and Its Economic Value as a National Beverage

F. W. (Frederick William) Salem

**Beer**
*Its History and Its Economic Value as a National Beverage*

ISBN/EAN: 9783337145033

Printed in Europe, USA, Canada, Australia, Japan

Cover: Foto ©Andreas Hilbeck / pixelio.de

More available books at **www.hansebooks.com**

# BEER,

## ITS HISTORY AND ITS ECONOMIC VALUE

AS A

## NATIONAL BEVERAGE.

BY

## F. W. SALEM.

———•—

HARTFORD, CONN.:
F. W. SALEM & COMPANY.
1880.

THE CLARK W. BRYAN COMPANY,
PRINTERS, ELECTROTYPERS AND BOOK-BINDERS,
SPRINGFIELD, MASS.

# DEDICATION.

Thinking as I do, that in the Beer Brewers of the United
States we must recognize real, though perhaps unconscious,
promoters of the great and glorious cause of genuine temperance, and that greater practical results may be attained
through their instrumentality than in any other way, it
seems fitting that this attempt to expound the true nature
and value of beer should be specially dedicated to them as
a body, and accompanied with the assurance of the author's
profound respect and esteem.

FREDERICK WILLIAM SALEM.

HARTFORD, CONN., January, 1880.

# TABLE OF CONTENTS.

# ILLUSTRATIONS.

8    ILLUSTRATIONS.

# PREFACE.

Our object in presenting the following pages to the public, is to call attention to the value of pure beer as a preventive of intemperance. Few persons are aware of the amount of patient investigation this question has received at the hands of eminent social economists and men of science, or of the mass of facts and testimony that has been collected, and lies ready at the hand of any one who is able and willing to work it over into a compact consecutive form, in which it shall be easy of access, and available for use in the further discussion of the subject. This we have attempted to do thoroughly and fairly. Great caution has been used in making statements and no inference has been drawn that could be considered in any way forced or doubtful.

There are doubtless many persons to whom some of the facts and conclusions here presented, may seem strange or even startling, and to such it must be said that the authorities quoted are generally men whose reputation for accuracy and sound judgment stands so high that they cannot afford to make a mistake or a loose assertion.

2

The work has involved much labor and historical research, and the author believes that the information contained in the following pages cannot fail to be of value to those who are interested in any phase of the beer question, whether as brewers, legislators or students of sociology. The end proposed to be served is that of temperance, and the method suggested is one that has been successfully tried in other countries. From the total abstinence party we ask the candid examination of our facts and arguments that is due to a fair statement from all who claim respect for their own opinions, and are honest friends of real temperance.

# BEER,

## ITS HISTORY AND ITS ECONOMIC VALUE

AS A

## NATIONAL BEVERAGE.

————•◦•————

## CHAPTER I.

### PRELIMINARY VIEW OF THE SUBJECT.

As extremes do and must perforce exist, the noblest philosophy of life is *compromise*.

Temperance then is the truest medium between total abstinence and excess, and in the same manner, *beer* occupies the medium position between ardent spirits and water. This fact is of the greatest importance, and until the public thoroughly understands the differences, whether from a moral, social, economic, or sanitary point of view, between distilled and fermented liquors, or in other words, beer and whisky there can be no hope of proper legislation as to the traffic in these articles. This legislation is now greatly influenced by the public advocates of total abstinence, among whom, if their own repeated claims be taken into account we might expect to find only disinterested, high-minded philanthropists. But it is notorious that their ranks are largely swelled by ignorant, ambitious or foolish men, whose vanity or pecuniary interest determines their action, and whose persistence and numerical strength will constitute an effective power until legislative bodies and the people at large are more thoroughly informed as to the actual experience of countries in which the problem has been dispassionately studied and brought to a successful solution. In too many of our states the liquor laws represent the triumph of ignorance and prejudice over reason and the welfare of the community. We hold that the solution of the temperance question is to be found through fermented liquors, and " BEER AGAINST WHISKY " is our motto.

Before coming, as we shall do later in this book, to a detailed examination of the facts in regard to the use of beer, it may be well to declare briefly our position, and give some indication of the kind of testimony that will be more fully displayed under a separate heading.

We hold that the production and sale of beer is so far from being subversive of public morals, that experience in all countries where beer is the national beverage, demonstrates precisely the opposite of this position. We hold too, that the use of beer is not merely indifferent, but, within the limits of temperance (*i. e.* moderation), a good and rational means of developing the mental and bodily powers of man.

We cannot join in the gratulations of those who now—as they say—so enthusiastically enjoy the blessings of total abstinence. During the last thirty years we have seen something of the operation of this enthusiasm, not only in Great Britain, but in the native state of the originator of the movement in this country, and we find it impossible to assent to the famous proposition that a pledged abstainer is a drunkard saved. We have been convinced that a pledged abstainer is too often a man who drinks in secret and thus adds hypocrisy to his other sins.

Notice this passage from evidence given before a state committee appointed to inquire into the action of the restrictive laws. The Hon. James H. Duncan of Haverhill, says :

" My observation and convictions are, that temperance has not been promoted by the prohibitory law ; that the temperance of our people is not so good now as before the passage of the law ; it has no efficacy in checking intemperance and the evils that result from it ; it has been productive of more mischief than good, and I think it an unwise act. It is impossible to make that a crime which is not made a crime by the divine law, and the use of beer, wine and cider cannot by any effort be made a crime *per se*, yet the prohibitory statute makes it a crime to sell either, and worse, it is a crime for a carrier to carry them. No wonder that such a law demoralizes the community, for a vast amount of lying and fraud have been called into existence through its agency."

The Rev. George Putnam, D.D., said ; " I believe and know that the prohibitory law produces demoralization, and disrespect for a law that cannot be enforced. It demoralizes jurors and witnesses. It demoralizes the buyers and sellers of liquors, inducing them to resort to all manner of frauds, tricks and evasions to do that unlawfully which they cannot do lawfully. It is injurious to the conscience of the people to be always violating this law ; and so far as liquor selling is concerned the law has done no good."

These extracts and many others to be given later, go to prove that it is most unwise to interfere with the social habits of a people, that it is dangerous for a state to do so, and that, as a matter of fact, temperance is not promoted by a prohibitory law. Public testimony that such laws are a blunder, or worse, has been given by such men as John Quincy Adams, Professor Agassiz of Cambridge, Rev. Leonard Bacon, D. D., of Connecticut, Professor Bigelow of Boston, Professor Edward Clark of Boston, ex-Governor Clifford, the late Right Rev. M. Eastburn, D. D., the late Governor Andrews, and Oliver Wendell Holmes, all of Boston, ex-Governor Washburn of Massachusetts, Professor Bowen of Cambridge, General Burrell of Roxbury, Hon. Joel Parker of Cambridge, Judge Patch of Lowell, Hon. James H. Duncan of Haverhill, Mass., Rev. George Putnam, D. D., of Mass., Dr. Garcelon, Governor of Maine, Dr. Willard Parker of the Inebriate Asylum at Binghamton, N. Y., A. Schwartz, Esq., the distinguished editor and publisher of the *Americanischer Bierbrauer,* and many others, comprising eminent statesmen, judges, and divines of all the states of the Union.

Our legislators should consider it their solemn duty to protect and foster the manufacture and sale of pure beer, and should frame such laws as will protect the people against imposition and secure the manufacture of an article that shall not only be made from good materials, but be thoroughly well brewed and wholesome, and sold at a moderate price.

Such a course will prove a blessing to mankind, and we do not hesitate to say, that notwithstanding what fools or fanatics may say, preach or write, Americans, and particularly those of the Eastern States, who are probably the most practical people on the face of the globe, will before long adopt beer as their national beverage. In doing so they will but follow the example of the most civilized countries of Europe ; and it will soon be recognized that every brewery and every beer saloon helps to loosen the grasp which alcohol has on any country where distilled liquors are habitually used. Thomas Jefferson, writing Dec. 13, 1818, to M. de Neuville in reference to intemperance and the use of light wines as a substitute for spirits, says, " No nation is drunken where wine is cheap." Beer is yet less alcoholic than wine of any sort and has advantages of its own which will be discussed in due place. Experience shows that sound, wholesome beer at a moderate cost is the best catholicon yet discovered for intemperance. It weans a people gradually but surely from strong drink and brings happiness, content and morality in the place of dissipation and suffering. But it must be good, cheap and accessible, and the responsibility of making it so rests with our lawgivers. The poorer classes are those who need it most and cause most injury and loss to the state when for lack of it they consume ardent spirits—and these cheap and adulterated.

In spite of all difficulties considerable progress has been made, as is shown by a consumption last year of more than nine million (9,473,361) barrels of beer, which is the best evidence of a step in the right direction towards national temperance.

# CHAPTER II.

It is impossible to say where and when the brewing of beer began, for the earliest historical records show its general use.

It is mentioned by Manathos, High Priest of Heliopolis, an Egyptian of Greek education, who lived about 300 B. C. and by command of Ptolemaus Philadelphus translated the old Egyptian history into Greek. He says that the Egyptians, thousands of years before, had beer, and that its invention was attributed to Osiris, a divinity representing all the beneficent principles, also that celebrated breweries existed at that time at El Kahirch, the Cairo of Europeans, and at Pelusinum on the river Nile.

The Greeks had their *zythos* (beer) as also their wine of barley, *ek krithon methu*, and the *oinos krithinos* as mentioned by Sophocles, Æschylus, 470 B. C., Diodorus of Sicily and Pliny. Xenephon in his account of the Retreat of the Ten Thousand, written 400 B. C., mentions that the inhabitants of Armenia used fermented drinks made from barley.

The Romans had their *cerevisia* (beer) but with them it was a special luxury. Julius Cæsar was a noted admirer of it, and Plutarch, 50 A. D., and Suetonius, each of whom wrote of Cæsar, tell us that after he had crossed the Rubicon, 49 B. C., he gave a great feast to his leaders at which the principal beverage used was *cerevisia*, and the biographers of Lucullus tell us that at his magnificent entertainments

VIEW OF AN OLD EGYPTIAN BREWERY,

*As described by Manathas (third century B.C.), High Priest in Heliopolis*

beer was served to his guests in golden goblets of the most costly device. And at that time also the Romans were already accustomed to sing *Cerevisiam bibunt homines, cætera animalia fontes.*

In Germany beer was known about the same time, and Tacitus (54 A. D.,) says, that the Roman general Varius, who was sent by Augustus to conquer the country and subdue the inhabitants, but was defeated by Arminius the leader of the Teutons, attributed the desperate valor of the enemy and their complete success, in great measure to their free use of *bior* (beer).

The Allemanni, a large German tribe who were first mentioned by Dion Cassius, 213 A. D., and who occupied the country between the river Main and the Danube, were formidable enemies both to the Romans and the Gauls. They attached great importance to their beer which was brewed under the supervision of the priests, and before use was blessed with many solemn rites. In an old code of theirs we find that every member of a church (*Gotteshaus*) had to contribute for its maintenance fifteen *seidel* of beer or some equivalent. The Emperor Julian who defeated them in the year 357 A. D., near Strasburg, where all their forces were assembled under seven chiefs, found on the field of battle numerous utensils designed to be employed in brewing.

The old Saxons in the seventh and eighth centuries when sitting in council to consider questions of high importance would only deliberate after drinking beer, which they took in common out of large *Humpen* (stone mugs).

Charlemagne (742–814 A. D.,) himself gave directions how to brew the beer for his court, and was as careful in

3

selecting his brew-masters as in choosing his councilors and
leaders.    A single circumstance, attendant on his defeat of
the Saxons at Paderborn, 777 A. D., illustrates the high respect in which brewing was then held, and in this particular, is suggestive of its semi-sacred character among the
Allemanni as mentioned above.   On that occasion it is
related that the Emperor, surrounded by his chief leaders
and councilors and by the ambassadors of distant nations,
received the homage of the heathen Saxon warriors, caused
many thousands of them to be baptized and then celebrated
the double triumph of his arms and the Christian faith at a
great feast, at which there were seated with him Eginhard,
Paul Warnefried and Alcuin, the Emperor's friends and
advisers, and all drank of beer brewed by Charlemagne
himself, while they discussed the great events that had
just occurred.   The drinking vessels were large mugs of a
peculiar form which are still to be seen among a collection
of relics presented to the Emperor by eastern potentates
and now kept in a tower at the west end of the Cathedral
of Aix-la-Chapelle, and exposed to public view once in
every seven years.   Within a few years numerous relics
have been found in the vicinity of Paderborn which indicate that beer brewing must have been as common and
necessary in both parties as the cooking of food.

The old Danes as far back as 860 A. D. under Gorm the
Old, 936 A. D. under Harold Bluetooth, and 985 A. D. under
Swend Twybeard, were acquainted with the art of brewing, and their old codes mention it as a most honorable
occupation.

In Bohemia, breweries were built at Budweis in the year
1256 A. D. by direction of Ottokar II., King of Bohemia,

and few cities in the world can point to an establishment of such antiquity. Budweis beer is now almost universally known and approved, though it is needless to say that it differs materially from that made six hundred years ago.

In the thirteenth century we see by an old law of France, in the reign of Louis IX., of the year 1268, how highly beer was esteemed and that laws were already made to secure the purity of beer as well as to protect the brewers in their avocation, and for curiosity's sake we give our readers an extract of those laws as mentioned above:

1. No one shall brew beer or remove it in drays or otherwise, on Sundays or on the solemn feasts of the Holy Virgin.

2. No one shall set up in the brewery who has not served a five years' apprenticeship, and been three years a partner with a regular brewer.

3. Nothing shall enter into the composition of beer, but good malt and hops, well gathered, picked, and cured, without any mixture of buckwheat, darnel, etc., and the hops shall be inspected by juries, to see that they are not used after being heated, moldy, damp, or otherwise damaged.

4. No beer yeast shall be hawked about the streets, but shall be all sold in the brew-houses to bakers and pastry-cooks, and to no others.

5. Beer yeast brought by foreigners shall be inspected by a jury before it is exposed to sale.

6. No brewer shall keep in, or about, his brew-house any cows, oxen, hogs, geese, ducks, or poultry, as being inconsistent with cleanliness.

7. There shall not be made in any brew-house more than

one brewing of fifteen septiers at the most, of ground malt in a day.

8.   Casks, barrels, and other vessels made to hold beer, shall be marked with the brewer's mark, in the presence of a jury.

9.   No brewer shall take away from a house he serves with beer any vessels which do not belong to him.

10.   Those who sell beer by retail shall be subject to the inspection of juries.

11.   No one shall be a partner but with a master brewer.

12.   No master brewer shall have more than one apprentice at a time, which apprentice shall not be turned over without the consent of a jury.

13.   No one shall take a partner who has quitted his master without the consent of such master.

14.   A widow may employ servants in brewing, but may not take an apprentice.

15.   Master brewers shall not entice away one another's apprentices nor servants.

16.   There shall be three masters elected for jurymen, two of which shall be changed every two years.

17.   Such jurymen shall have the power to inspect in the city and suburbs.

In addition every brewer had to pay duty, so that the king might not be defrauded, was obliged to give notice of every brewing to a commissioner, stating the day and hour he intended to kindle the fire of his boiler, under a penalty of fine and confiscation.  As brewing necessitates the employment of a large quantity of grain, it was customary, in times of scarcity, for the king to put a stop to the manufacture of beer for a certain number of weeks.   These

JACOB VAN ARTEVELDE,

"Brewer of Ghent," Patrician, Orator and Ruler of the Province of Flanders. Killed July 17, 1345. Taken from the original oil painting in possession of Jan Van Artevelde, in Amsterdam.

rules and regulations, made more than six hundred years since, are interesting and curious to the brewers of to-day.

In the fourteenth century the monks were the ordinary brewers, and one brewery founded by them at Dobraw near Pilsen, Bohemia, and endowed by Charles IV. shortly before his death with a prescriptive right to brew beer, is still in existence and is probably the oldest in the world. Its five hundredth anniversary was lately celebrated with great pomp, by all classes of society in that ancient city. Bohemian beer is to be ranked with the very best known, and an idea of the annual product for home and foreign consumption may be formed from the fact that there are now no less than eight hundred and eighty-seven breweries in actual operation.

In Austria, the first brewery built at Vienna was on the Weidenstrasse and dates back as far as 1384. The oldest standing brewery in the same place is the St. Marx Brewhouse, founded in 1706.

In the Provinces of Flanders and Brabant a beer brewed of malt and hops was the national beverage as early as the fourteenth century, and brewers occupied an important position and were held in high esteem. History tells us that one of them, *Jacob Van Artevelde* the Brewer of Ghent, a nobleman by birth, became a celebrated popular leader who drove Louis I., Count of Flanders, into France, held the government of the province and supported Edward III. of England until his death, July 17, 1345.

His son Philip, who at one time was chosen ruler of the provinces and who died 1382, was as well known as a celebrated brewer as his father.

To Flanders also belongs the celebrated Gambrinus, who

under his real name of Jan Primus, Duke of Flanders,
ruled Flanders and Brabant wisely, and became the pro-
tector of the beer-brewing fraternity.   Under the popular
cognomen, however, (to which many mythical attributes
have ·been attached) he is universally known, and perhaps
held in higher esteem by a greater number of adherents
than all the saints, even including Saint Patrick, who have
been canonized up to the present day.

In England beer was introduced by the Romans.   The
Saxons found it there and improved wonderfully upon the
discovery.   For centuries it received, in the modern literature of England, the constant attention and consideration
of churchmen, historians, poets and political economists.
The churchmen especially were active in the improvement
of malt liquors.   William of Malmsbury says that the best
brewers in England at the time of Henry II. were to be
found in the monasteries, and every reader of early English
literature remembers frequent allusions not only to beer in
general but to that of the holy fathers in particular.   The
monks were the first to discover the peculiar fitness of the
waters of Burton on Trent for brewing purposes, and
may thus be said to have paved the way for the development
of the enormous establishments that now scatter their product over all the world.

According to " Tennant's Guide to London," published
at the beginning of the present century, there were in the
reigns of the Tudors great breweries at London, situated on
the river-side below St. Katherine's.   In 1492 King Henry
VII. licensed a Flemish brewer, John Merchant, to export
a large quantity of the so-called " berre," and that the
beer had to be of good quality and was under the surveil-

lance of the authorities, is proved by the fact that Geffrey
Gate, an officer of the king, twice destroyed the brew-
houses on account of the weakness of the beer.

In the reign of Elizabeth the demand for ale increased
very largely, and we find mention of an export of five hundred tuns of the precious liquor at one time. This was sent
to Amsterdam for the use of the thirsty army in the Netherlands. Mary Queen of Scots in the midst of her troubles
seems not to have been altogether insensible to the attrac-
tions of English beer, for when she was confined in Tutbury
Castle, Walsingham, her secretary asked " At what place
near Tutbury beer may be provided for her majestie's use ? "
To which Sir Ralph Sadler, governor of the castle made
reply, " Beer may be had at Burton, three miles off." This
Burton on Trent began to be famous for its water in the
thirteenth century. There is a document still extant, dated
1295, in which it is stated that Matilda, daughter of Nicholas
Shoben had released to the abbot and convent of Burton on
Trent certain tenements, for which release they granted her
daily for life two white loaves from the monastery, two gallons of conventual beer and one penny, besides seven gallons of beer for the men.

In the fifteenth century the monks in Germany brewed
two kinds of beer in the convents, one kind for the *Patres*,
and an inferior beer for the convents.

In the sixteenth century the breweries in Germany were
already celebrated for their malt beer.

Cities not having good cellars, on account of which good
beer could not be produced, were provided with the beverage through their city fathers from other places, stored
and sold in the cellars of the city hall, hence the origin of

the name Raths-keller.   The most celebrated beer at that time, was the Braunschweiger Mumme, and the beer of Eimbeck, Merseburg and Bamberg.   Beer before it could be sold had to pass a strict examination by a committee con-sisting of brewers of the greatest reputation, appointed by the burgomaster under and by advice of the city fathers ; and a "Brauherr," (proprietor and brew-master of a brew-ery) was a man of importance.   In the principality of Brandenburg—afterwards the kingdom of Prussia—it was thought as early as the seventeenth and eighteenth centuries that beer was the most wholesome of all beverages, and the electors of Brandenburg, later the kings of Prussia, fostered breweries by the concession of numerous privileges which were increased from time to time.   Grants of this character and of no small advantage were held by brewers in Cottbus,* Province of Brandenburg, and were considerably enlarged by Frederick the Great in favor of Huguenots who had at his invitation settled in the kingdom after being forced by the revocation of the edict of Nantes to leave France. These privileges, enjoyed by the Toussaints, Salems and others for many years, were abolished by the declaration of the freedom of trade in 1838.

After the year 1721 coffee began to be extensively used, and at last Frederick the Great in order to check its intro-duction erected large coffee roasting establishments which had a monopoly of the business, and where the coffee was sold at an enormous price, only the nobility, having the right of roasting their coffee beans.   "Coffee smellers " or spies were appointed to look out for evaders of the law, just as

---

*Celebrated for the famous white beer which was at that time largely ex-ported to Upper Silesia, Bohemia, Berlin, Hamburg, etc.

**MYNHER JACOBUS,**
Brewer and First Burgomaster of New Amsterdam (the present New York), 1644.

we have now beer and whisky smellers. On the 13th day of September, 1777, the great king issued his celebrated "coffee and beer manifesto." It was particularly addressed to the provincial members (*Landstande*) of the provinces of Pommerania and Brandenburg, which were called the nurseries of his armies, and read as follows: "It is disgusting to notice the increase in the quantity of coffee used by my subjects and the amount of money that goes out of the country in consequence. Everybody is using coffee. If possible this must be prevented. My people must drink beer. His majesty was brought up on beer and so were his ancestors and his officers and soldiers. Many battles have been fought and won by soldiers nourished on beer, and the king does not believe that coffee-drinking soldiers can be depended on to endure hardship or to beat his enemies in case of the occurrence of another war." This proclamation had the desired effect, and coffee was thenceforth used merely as a luxury, while beer became the usual drink of the people.

In the United States the pioneers in the brewing business were William Penn and Jacobus, a Dutch brewer of whom Irving tells us that he left the States General of Holland to settle on Manhattan Island in company with Hendricks, the Kips and others. It will be remembered that Manhattan Island was discovered by Hendrik Hudson in 1609 when he passed inside Sandy Hook in search of a northwest passage, and that it was granted by charter of the States General to the West India Company to colonize the island. The company was not slow to discover the advantages of such a concession and immediately set at work to build forts, a church, a mill and a bakery while Jacobus, who

4

thoroughly understood the good effects of beer and the benefits that would follow its introduction in the colony, established a brewery ( in 1644 ) and a beer garden on what is now
the corner of Pearl street and Old Slip. He afterwards became the first burgomaster and is said to have dispensed beer
and justice with equal gravity and impartiality, and to the
complete satisfaction of the inhabitants of new Amsterdam.

It may be interesting to some readers to know that while
Jacobus settled near the lower end of the present city the
Kips were established in the neighborhood of Bellevue
Heights, and that on a part of that settlement—in East
38th street—stands now the well known and justly esteemed
lager beer brewery of A. Huepfel's Sons.

Somewhat later the same business was undertaken by
Israel and Timothy Horsfield, who came from England, one
in 1706 and the other in 1720, and settled in Brooklyn,
L. I. Their brewery was near the ferry in what is now
Wallabout.

William Penn, 1644—1718, a man of Dutch extraction on
his mother's side, founder of Pennsylvania and the leading
spirit of its settlement—so justly celebrated for his virtues
—brewed and sold beer at Pennsbury, Bucks County, Pa.

Good Quaker as Penn was, he was no ascetic. He was
a great lover of beer, and accustomed to praise his own
brewing—he was not averse to society, in his house was no
lack of comfort, his table was well provided, and his taste
for good living could never be impeached—dancing did not
shock him, for both he and his family patronized country
dances and country fairs, and William Penn's beer was the
beverage used on such occasions.

Under his proprietary laws he allowed beer to be sold

free of license, and this sensible enactment was continued under the state laws until the year 1847, when a ten dollar license was substituted. Such a tax certainly compares favorably with that of many other states and displays a moderation and reasonableness that does credit to the Quaker community and is in strong contrast to the spirit recently exhibited in some parts of the country.

Another celebrated promoter of early beer brewing in America was Gen. Israel Putnam, known to every child as the hero of the wolf's den and the desperate ride down the rocks, and to an older generation as a brave soldier and marked character, the man who " dared to lead where any dared to follow," and who has gained a higher position in history by virtue of his personal qualities and a touch of romance that clings to his name than might strictly attach to his military services.

Although generally known as a Connecticut man he was born at Salem, Mass., 1718, and in 1739, at the age of twenty-one, removed to Pomfret, Conn., and later to Brooklyn in the same state, with which latter place his name is afterwards associated. Here as a farmer and tavern-keeper he passed the remainder of his life except that considerable part which was given to the active military service of his country. The change from the life of a successful soldier to these commonplace pursuits would seem to many to be near akin to a fall, but Putnam's practical good sense found no difficulty in it. When he returned from the army he resumed his farming, tavern business and beer brewing, and seems to have had no false shame at either of the humbler avocations. Like a wise and self-contained man he did the work nearest to his hand and found honor in it whatever it

might be.   On the other hand, however, it is no small credit
to the beer brewing fraternity to have had such a man in
their ranks, even were it in a more limited and incidental
way than was actually the case.   The tavern sign of General Israel Putnam, which hung before his door in Brooklyn,
(Conn.,) in the year 1768 and later, is now preserved in the
rooms of the Historical Society at Hartford, (Conn.,) and
an illustration representing it will be found on the opposite
page.

The sign is made of yellow pine, painted alike on both
sides.   The device is a full length portrait of General Wolfe,
dressed in scarlet uniform.   The portrait of the young hero
is quite correct.

The sign was presented to the Historical Society by Rufus
S. Mathewson of Woodstock.

Aside from the early public breweries there were doubtless many in which beer was made for family consumption.
"Home brewed" was common in the native homes of most
of the colonists, and there is no reason to suppose that they
voluntarily changed their accustomed manner of living and
dispensed with a wholesome drink to which they had been
used from infancy.

In leaving this branch of the subject it should be noted
that the beer of the earliest periods, like the ale of England
before the seventeenth century, was usually made without
hops, and it is impossible to say when these were first
employed, although the experiment was certainly of no very
modern date.   It was probably the greatest improvement
ever made in the production of beer, since it gives a light,
clear, and elegant product very different from anything that
was produced on the other plan.   The modern demand was

Gen¹ WOLFE.

SIGN OF GENERAL PUTNAM'S TAVERN IN BROOKLYN, CONN.

*The original is now in the Rooms of the Historical Society, at Hartford, Conn.*

for a drink that should be agreeable, refreshing and moderately stimulating, and it is now abundantly recognized that the fermented decoction of malted barley, clarified and preserved by the hops, best fulfills this requirement.

Beer has been considered a necessity in all generations, and only in this, the nineteenth century, have extremists arisen to condemn its use. It is worthy of note that its greatest enemies are among a class who, in the olden times, were its greatest friends. The old abbeys and monasteries were the places where the best malt liquor was brewed; and not least among the benefactors of their species were the Franciscans and Dominicans, who brewed good beer to cheer the hearts of toiling humanity. Bishops have written in its praise; universities have encouraged its production; and kings having the comfort and contentment of their subjects in view have cared for its proper provision. Under date January 27, 1617, it is noted in "Langbaine's Collections" that one John Shurle had a patent from Abraham Lake, Bishop of Bath and Wells and Vice Chancellor of Oxford, for the office of Ale-taster to the university. "The office of Ale-tasting requires that he go to every ale-brewer that day they brew, according to their courses, and taste their ale; for which his ancient fee is one gallon of strong ale and two gallons of strong wort."

Such a fact is enough to make the modern teetotal dominies stand aghast, but it may well be doubted if they are better or wiser men than their predecessors, one of whose distinguishing characteristics was usually a sound common sense in the ordinary affairs of life.

# CHAPTER III.

With the close of the preceding chapter we had intended to leave this branch of the subject, but a paper of Hans von der Planitz, written in German on the same topic, is so interesting that we cannot do better than quote a considerable portion. It is written with genuine enthusiasm and is valuable not merely for its facts regarding the early history of beer, but also as a picture of customs and manners, often given in the words of writers contemporary with the circumstances described. The picturesque or realistic effect of the old German has been as far as possible preserved in the rendering of passages written in that style, and very often the original is added in a note or otherwise, for the enjoyment of readers who are able to appreciate its flavor. Quotation at such length has involved a trifling amount of repetition of matter already stated, but it has seemed better to submit to this than to mutilate an independent account, much of whose effect depends on its manner of developing the subject. Commencing with the ninth century the writer says:

" Beer brewing in England and Flanders is mentioned by Walafried Strabo. (849 A. D.) It had been known from a remote antiquity and continued in use partly, at least, through Celtic influence. In France beer gradually gave place to wine, while in Germany it made good its position, and lager beer was discovered as early as the thirteenth century, that of the Mark being especially celebrated. In

Bohemia the earliest account of beer brewing dates as far back as 1086 A. D. Poland and Prussia were addicted to the barley juice before the time of modern civilization and honored a special god of beer, *Raugunzemapat*, whose name is derived from *rugti*, to ferment, and literally signifies the god of fermentation. In Bavaria, where, under Roman influence, wine growing had attained an important place which it was destined afterwards to lose, beer was commonly known within the first thousand years of the present era and is mentioned by Voehrung, 816, and others. According to Graesse it was a dull brown and reddish drink and soured easily. In the more primitive districts oats were used as the basis, and only "upper-ferment" beer was made. In the latter part of the middle ages the process by "under fermentation" was discovered, its origin, according to Professor Holzner of Weihenstephan, being in one of the monasteries. From this point beer brewing increased vigorously until Bohemian competition and Bohemian hops gave it a staggering check. In the southern countries of Europe beer does not easily give place to wine though hard pushed, while in Asia and Africa the inhabitants use their traditionary drink from one generation to another, and in Egypt especially, the Arabs acquired a taste for the beer of the Copts. Such was the condition of things when the dawn of a new age showed itself on the horizon.

"The characteristic of a period is found essentially in its variation from the adjacent epochs, and that of the one under consideration has been already indicated. But beside the scientific researches, that had very little connection with trade, there grew up a descriptive literature that stands in close relation to the first general empire of beer. To sup-

pose that the present age is the first time of real triumph
for the liquor of Gambrinus, shows a very superficial knowledge of the history of civilization, for apart from the Egyptian and Celtic-Germanic beer epochs, which were somewhat local, we have already long passed the real first period
of success which fell in the time of the *Renaissance.* In
those days the brown flood spread out not merely over Germany, England and Belgium, but into the far corners of
recently discovered countries ; in village taverns and *raths-
kellers* peasants and citizens drank themselves full and
merry.　At the high schools the students already went to
the *kneipen* with their rapiers (*spiessen*) and swords, studied
and rioted behind the tin can, and in the banquet halls of
princes and the cabinets of noble ladies, the barley juice
was a favorite beverage, not swallowed hastily from tum-
blers, but taken with deliberation and full enjoyment from
deep, wide-mouthed mugs or tankards.　Seven maas a day
was the allowance for a lady of high rank.*　About the
end of the seventeenth century the increasing use of brandy
and coffee put a stop to this immoderate consumption, as at
the same time the influence of France and the colonies with
their new dishes and resulting change of tastes, brought
about the progress from middle age cookery to that of modern times, and as the Gustavus Adolphus boots and wide-
brimmed plumed hats gave place to silk stockings and
perukes.　The present age witnesses the second triumph of
Gambrinus, a triumph perhaps even greater than the first,
for though the capacity of individuals is far from equal to
that of the men of the Renaissance, except in the case of
some academic beer soakers and Munich *Danaidenfaesser*

*Sieben Maas Bier per Tag vors graefliche Frauenzimmer war Vorschrift.

(bottomless vessels), yet the distribution of beer is more extensive, more general and more uniform. The consumption in Europe alone has increased tenfold within fifty years and grows constantly. In the first quarter of this century the wave spread from Bavaria farther and farther over the whole map of Europe, and about twenty years ago a new source was opened in Austria, and the Vienna beer flowed through the canals which the Bavarian product had opened.

This first epoch stands in close relation with the general abounding strength of that period of civilization. Adventurous sailors and explorers had broken the bonds of the known earth, plain men had dared to enter the lists with that hierarchy, to attack which had been held profanation ; art had thrown aside the old traditions and brought out the old master-works, the world of scholars had torn itself loose from petrified scholasticism and turned to the ancient classics, and, as in most branches of science, so also in chemistry, there was a genuine revolution, and it was studied in reference to medicine almost as assiduously as it had previously been in the search for the philosopher's stone. New inquiries were set on foot, old problems revived and attacked from a new point of view, and among these the subjects of yeast and fermentation played an important part. Not many decades have passed since the practical brewer found neither interest nor profit in theories of fermentation, and especially all chemical and physical discussion of his work and processes. The purely scientific style which too often had very little reference to the practical man, and the various contradictory views and learned controversies were not calculated to attract the interest of the beer brewer. Scholars discussed and disputed, the man of trade brewed and coopered, and

5

neither paid any attention to the other. Now the case is
very different. Intelligent and thoughtful brewers have
been forced to admit that an insight into the nature of the
materials they use, and the changes these undergo while in
their hands will not merely enlarge their intellectual horizon, but be of great practical use in their business, and in
consequence are found keenly alive to the progress of scientific inquiry.

Some reference has already been made to the empirical
knowledge of the earlier ages. Even Pliny's often quoted
"*Palam est naturam (farinœ) acore fermentari*" is merely
a summary of the result of observation. Noah's wine
making, the leaven* of the Jews and such like may be left
to special history. The word *fermentum* as used by the
alchemists has no very definite meaning; in general their
explanation is to the effect that by means of the ferment a
purifying and refining process is set in action—and hence
many efforts were made to discover a general ferment by
whose instrumentality it would become possible among
other things, to transform the baser metals into gold. For
this reason they often use the word *fermentum* to indicate
the anxiously sought "philosopher's stone."† The indefinite character of the word is mentioned by Petrus Bonus of
Ferrara (1345): "*Apud philosophos fermentum dupliciter
videtur dici: uno modo ipse lapis philosophorum e suis ele-
mentis compositus et completus, in comparatione ad metalla;
alio modo illud quod est perficiens lapidem et ipsum com-
plens*," and Raymond Lull's definition, "*Fili, fermentum est*

---

*\*Galliæ et Hispaniæ frumento in potum resoluto spuma ita concreta pro fer-
mento utuntur; qua de causa levior illis quam ceteris panis est.*

†*De fermento, sine quo ars alchemiæ perfeci et compleri non potest.*

*corpus perfectum, subtiliatum et alteratum per potestatem convertentium,*" has the predicate so indefinite as to give no real information. We add another quotation from the same author merely to show further the jargon these men of learning were accustomed to use. He writes "*Fili, præparatio istius est, quod illud sit transactum primo per naturæ principalia controvertentia, antequam de isto facias fermentationem, quia illud fiat principio pulvis calcinatus per coagulationem et quarto sublimatus per separationem.*" George Ripley's consideration of the subject calls for no special notice, but the views of Basilius Valentinus who wrote in the latter half of the fifteenth century will be found more interesting. He held fermentation to be a purification by means of which the spirit of wine that already existed in a fluid was put in condition to act, unfermented beer being dead, "because existing impurities prevent the spirit from doing its work. Yeast induces in beer an internal quickening that advances of itself and results in a division and segregation of the clear and muddy elements, and after this separation *puri ab impuro* the spirit can accomplish its duty successfully, as appears from the subsequent power of the liquor to produce intoxication." Valentine is the last in the series of scholars who though belonging chronologically to a previous epoch must from the nature and relations of their inquiries be reckoned as belonging to the new era. It is not in the history of progress as in that of politics where two adjacent periods can be sharply defined and their limits assigned to exact dates. Progress goes on gradually, modifying or adding to what has already existed, and we do not clearly notice the transformation until it is complete or at least far advanced. So

it was in this case. Far back in the middle ages men
turned their attention to the "ferment" and to fermentation. Much was written, much nonsense and humbug published; almost no results were attained, but the beginning
was made. Men of the later time grasped the collected
material, regulated and systematized the inquiry and vied
with each other in its prosecution. Struggle and activity
were then so universal that there was a disposition to consider fermentation a special branch of chemistry, and
after treating of the fermentation of wine, beer, vinegar,
etc., it was suggested that the whole vital process might be
nothing more than a continual fermentation.

Notwithstanding all that has been said it seems best to
date the new epoch definitely from the beginning of the
sixteenth century, and this although we can reckon no
names or events of importance in the year 1501, and must
pass over a number of decades to reach Libarius the first
theorist of the second epoch. The reasons for such a division are various, partly to remove as far as possible all un-
certainty from the discussion, partly because at that memo-
rable time the general break with blind tradition and the
development of new intellectual and social conditions took
place in such a manner as to have a direct influence on the
history of beer and so connect the general revolution with
the province of zymotechnic inquiry. If we date from Laba-
rius we commit an anachronism, for he stands in the full
light of the new era. In short, beer and its history are
so intimately related to social life and its development that
we cannot consider the former alone and without regard to
the latter. The oldest book in this sort of literature at present
known, was published in 1530, under the title, "An Excellent

View of a Brewery connected with a convent in Bohemia (14th century), as described by Thaddeus Hagecius ab Hayck, 1585, in his book, written in Latin, under the title, *De cerevisia.*

Little Book of the Making of Wine and Beer so that they may
be Useful and Wholesome to Man. Printed at Erfurt by
Melchior Sachssen at Noah's Ark."* In 1551, a scholar
(Plocotamus) wrote *"De natura cerevisiarum et de mulso,"*
and somewhat later (1585) Thaddeus Hagecius ab Hayck
wrote in Latin a work with the title *"De cerevisia ejusque con-
ficiendi ratione, natura, viribus et facultatibus."* More important than any of these is a book written in German by Heinrich Knaust, its value consisting not so much in historical de-
ductions as in a review, grounded on the personal knowledge
of the author, of the facts regarding beer in his time. It is
chiefly through this volume that we are able to. form a clear
conception of the high development and actual power of beer
at the end of the sixteenth century. On the first page of the
book the master wrote in a style thoroughly characteristic
of the period with its swelling, stilted bombast and mag-
niloquence, the famous title, " Five Books of the Divine and
Noble Gift of the Philosophical, Precious and Admirable
Art of Beer Brewing. Also of the names of the most Admirable Beers in all Germany, and of their Natures, Tem-
peraments, Qualities, Individual Characters, Wholesomeness, and Unwholesomeness, whether wheat or barley, white
or red beer, spiced or not spiced. Newly revised and much
Fuller and More Perfect than the former edition. By Master Heinrich Knaust, Doctor of Law and of Medicine.
Published at Erfurt by George Baumann, 1575, in the
twelfth month."† As a matter of curiosity we reproduce

---

*Ein schoenes Buechlein von bereytung der wein und bier zu gesundheit und
nutzbarkeit der menschen gedruckt zu Erffurd durch Melchior Sachssen zu
der Archen Noe.

†Fuenf Buecher von der goettlichen und edeln Gabe der philosophischen

his view of the origin of beer.  According to this the men before the deluge ate herbs and vegetables and drank water, and he thinks it strange that they should ever have plucked up heart to become saucy on such a diet.  "After the deluge they received the gift of wine, and where no vines grew God taught them to make a drink of wheat and barley that was both healthful and agreeable and as well fitted to strengthen and support the human system as wine itself."

When a well known physician of Berlin, Dr. F.G. Zimmerman, felt himself compelled to declare beer a poison, it was Abraham A. Santa Clara of Vienna who, in his "History of the Discovery of Beer," entitled "Something for All," 1710, spoke as follows:  "Noah planted the first vineyard and the culture of the vine afterwards spread all over the world, but as some climates are too harsh for the grape and prevent its ripening, human ingenuity was forced to discover another drink which should not merely quench thirst, but like wine excite the brain.*  Among the Germans it is called beer, and its brewing requires a special experience, so that the men of this craft are not counted least among workmen."  So said also Ehinger, Fritsch, Germershausen,

---

hochteuren und wundersbaren Kunst Bier zu brauen.  Auch von Namen der vornempstere Biere in ganz Teutschland und von deren Naturen, Temperamenten, Qualitaten, Art und Eigenschaft, Gesundheit und Ungesundheit, sey ein Weitzen oder Gersten, Weisse oder Rotte Biere, Gewuertzet oder Ungewuertzet.  Aufs neue uebersehen und in viel wege ueber vorige edition gemehrt und gebessert   Durch Herrn Heinrich Knausten, beider Rechten Doctor.  Getr. zu Erfurt durch Georgium Baumann 1575 in 12.

*Der Noë hat zwar den ersten Weinstock gepflantzt welches Gewnechs nachmals durch die ganze Welt ausgebreitet worden ; weil aber etlicher Orten der rauhe Luft dem Weinstock zuwider und folgsam, solcher in dergleichen Orten nicht fruchtsam tuht, also hat der Menschen Witz ein anderes Trunk erfunden welches nicht allein den Durft loeschet sondern gleich dem Wein, auch den Tuermel in den Kopf bringt.

Gleditsch, Heuman, Hofman, Sensky, Solms and Trafen-
reuter. In all this scientific and learned emulation in the
matter of fermentation (zymologie) we learn plainly enough
that even the representatives of science did not confine their
attention to a purely theoretical consideration of the barley
juice, but hid the contents of many a can and mug behind
their wide stiff collars, the clergy taking their full share in
this part of the discussion. Luther's fondness for beer is
well known, and on the evening of that eventful day at
Worms, April 18, 1521, the Duke Erich von Braunschweig, sent him a pot of Eimbecker beer, to which he was
specially addicted. The students, whether of medicine or
theology, used every effort to follow faithfully the illustrious
example, whence perhaps it comes that the youth of the
high schools and universities, wedded to tradition, still de-
light to hang about the inviting, wide-yawning door of the
cool beer cellar. In the Renaissance, however, the last
trace of the *Biercomment* and *Bierspielen* was finally lost.

> *The common people would not sober stay,
> Could find to cup or mouth the nearest way;
> Enjoyed their life, and of the barley's blood
> Swilled day and night the brown and foamy flood.

Beer was retailed in beer-houses and vaults, and in warm
weather before the door, and places which had the hereditary right of brewing also sold beer occasionally in the living room of the house, and announced the fact by a mat-
weed stuck horizontally above the door. In this custom
we see plainly enough the origin of the later shop signs

---

*Des Volks gemeine Horte blieb nicht hinten,
Es wusste Kneip' und maul sehr wohl zu finden;
Im Hochgenuss des Seins, aus Schlauch und Fass
Soff's Tag und nacht das edle braune Nass.

In Oberpfalz (the Upper Palatinate), in the Schwarzwald
(Black Forest), and elsewhere, even now when a privileged
brewer wishes to give notice that he will sell on draught,
he hangs up a broom or a triangle of fir boughs. The pub-
licans of a later time simply exchange this primitive adver-
tisement for the more durable ones of tin and iron. Before
the windows of the pot houses were folding tables at which
the wagoners usually preferred to drink, and the wandering
bands, of whom there was then an immense number, were
accustomed to seat themselves at these same tables and pass
the time in riotous talk and games of dice until the " beer
bell " of the place broke up the assembly and drove them
to their homes and to the inn.*   When a fair was held the
women dealers in refreshments (Kretschenweiber) took
possession of the benches and sold their beer there in cups
of tin, stone or wood, while bread, meat, sausages, cheese,
etc., were brought from the neighboring stands of the
butchers and bakers, for even then people liked to do their
business where wine and beer were close at hand.   On any
occasion of public festivity beer booths were a prime necessity, bagpipes and fiddles were not  wanting and a lusty,
merry throng danced in the open space between the crowded
benches and tables.   The Netherlandish painters have left
us hundreds of cabinet pictures of these festivities and of
the manner and fashion in which they were carried on, and
their delightful and characteristic variations of the theme
enable us to form a vivid conception of what it must have
been.  Especially worthy of notice in this respect are
Teniers, (whose " Yearly Market "† in the Munich Pinak-

*See the Civil Law of Erfurt.

†The picture is eight feet high and twelve feet wide.

othek contains 1138 human figures, 45 horses, 67 asses, 37
dogs, etc., curiously crowded in a jovial throng,) P.
Brueghel, the Ostades, Brower, Jan Steen, who from a
fancy for this sort of life himself became a tavern keeper,
and Rubens, whose sketches in this sort are strikingly good.
During the "Thirty Years War," that is, at the very culminating point of the epoch, tobacco came into use and the
now inseparable pair, "beer and tobacco," played an important rôle together even then. Barley and "mixed corn" (rye
and wheat, barley and oats, oats and rye,) were chiefly
used for brewing purposes, but there were always those
who preferred plant beer. It is interesting to know that
pitch was supposed to give the product of fermentation a
better keeping quality.

We must not omit to mention that this beer worship was
not so well developed in South Germany where it is now
best marked, as in North Germany. Saxony, the Mark and
Pomerania were mentioned as "the great drinking countries." There was a swarm of names celebrated in beer,
and Knaust's book shows that it was held no small credit to
have drunk various noted kinds of beer where they were
made. There was a Lubeck Israel, an old Klaus (Brandenburg), a Goslauer Gose, a Hanover Braehan, a Soltzman at
Saltzwedel, a Rastrun at Leipsic, beer of Corvey, beer of
Harlem, Dantzic brew, Eimbecker brew, and many others.*
Of English beer, Hersford (Kamma) and the Yorkshire ale
were chiefly esteemed. Most celebrated of all, however,
was the Braunschweig *Mumme*, named for its discoverer,
Christian Mumme (1492). By the side of these brewing

*To these should be added the celebrated beers of Cottbus, and the Karthuser
of Frankfort on the Oder.—*Author.*

G

celebrities the old beer cities of the middle ages had retained their character into the time of the Renaissance, as for instance, Hamburg, with its wheat beer,* and others ; and many places made every effort to reach a similar position, partly by the adoption of new methods, and partly by the enlargement and increase of beer breweries.   In Nuremberg, for instance, the first white beer was brewed in 1541; in Vienna the brewery with a hundred towers was built in 1564 ; breweries were erected at Gumpendorf in 1689, and at St. Marx in 1706 ; and in 1633 there were established at Freiburg six malt-houses and twelve breweries.

The important beer privileges that had been so eagerly grasped by the monasteries and cities in the middle ages, were by hereditary right brought over into the new era. The landed estates of the nobles received back in 1517 the privileges which had been so long kept from them, and by this means all obstacles were removed from the beer traffic which had reached so hopeful a development during the middle ages, and it became possible for it to develop to an extent of which our own time need not be ashamed.   Now it is no great matter to transport beer from Vienna to Paris by rail and in iced compartments, but we can not but admire the successful enterprise that in those days and with such means of transportation as existed, could export Eimbecker beer to Lombardy as described by the Italian Arnoldus of Villanova in 1594, and even to Alexandria and Cairo.   Nuremberg was one of the great centers of the beer trade.   Rostock and Lubeck supplied all England and sent not less than 800,000 barrels yearly to that country until

---

*Wheat beer played an important rôle in the thirty years war.   Wallenstein himself was very much addicted to its use.

the business was checked by a marked increase in the quantity brewed by the English themselves. A number of the large English breweries were founded about this time.

In the households of the reigning princes, there was a strong tendency to supplement the native brew by imported products, and at such festivities as marriages, christenings, target-shooting and hunting, immense quantities of drink were swallowed. The cellar ordinance of Duke Ernst the Pious, in 1648, allowed for ladies of noble rank four *maas* of beer a day, and three *maas* for a " nightcap." How much ought in such circumstances to be the allowance for a man of similar rank, and of his hangers on is left to the imagination of the reader.

Noble families that had no brew-houses were obliged to supply themselves from the brewery of the prince. A beer tax also was levied on vassals who brewed their own beer. An excellent illustration of the condition of things is afforded by the celebrated Hofbrauhaus at Munich, in whose white-washed rooms every stranger still takes at least one *maas*. As early as the time of Louis the Severe, there existed a little court brewery at Munich near the *Burggasse*, but towards the end of the sixteenth century, the demand increasing and the facilities for production having long been inadequate, William V. proceeded to the building of the present brew-house, which was at first intended only for the making of white beer, the brown being still made in the old quarters. In 1708, however, brown beer also began to be made in the new establishment. This topic is treated in a stereotyped article which appears every year in the May number of the Munich Beer Gazette, under the title " Bock article," and gives the worshipful bock-drinking community

a solemn and moving account of the court brewery and its
products down to the minutest particulars.  As regards
bock itself, which is no longer an exclusive specialty of
Munich, as a drink under the same name is sold every year
in various cities, Graesse places its origin in the seventeenth century, and suggests that it was an imitation of the
Eimbecker beer,—the last rather in virtue of a general theory
and of a supposed play on words, Eimbeck, Aimbock Bock—
than as an actual fact.*  He says that " the Munich Aimbock or Bock was made before 1616, the same that is now
sold at the beginning of May on Corpus Christi day."  Now,
however, it has been shown that all through the second
half of the sixteenth century (1553–1574) Aimpecker and
Eimbecker beer was spoken of, and that there was an import of beer to Vienna from Eimbeck as late as 1771, while
no trace of any play of words on the name is discovered.
Moreover, that the " bock cellar "† (on the place of the
present Restaurant Bonner) was in full operation at the
beginning of the present century, is shown by Chr. Mueller
who wrote under Max Joseph, and described the manners of
the place very nearly as they were to be observed recently,
just before the disappearance of this historical locality, and
it is doubtless the fact that the larger half of the reputation
of Munich beer is due to this specialty.  Graesse, speaking
of the high reputation of Bavarian beer, in which he includes
as a matter of course that of Munich, is of the opinion that
the general preference for it does not reach back farther
than the early part of this century, and produces some important evidence to support this view of the case.  On the

*The Munich " Fremdenblatt " has lately expressed the same view.
†In a coach house of the old *residenz* in Munich, Bavaria.

other hand it is to be claimed in opposition that in such a
discussion a careful distinction is to be made between
Bavarian beer and Munich beer, since the renown of the
first is relatively new and hardly goes to the first twenty
years of the century, and its export did not begin in Munich,
and also because that city has not yet been able to attain to
the first rank as an exporter of beer.  The reputation of
Munich beer is older, for Mueller (1816) speaks of it as
celebrated, and complains that the excellence of the native
product is far surpassed by that of the Toelzer and Dachauer
beers, and that the latter prevail in the Munich beer shops.
This statement corresponds with the unfortunate situation
of the beer interest that was inherited from the previous
century, and that forces us to go back to the seventeenth
century for a time of unquestioned supremacy for beer.   In
connection with this subject should be mentioned the successful founding of the Munich Court Brewery by William
V. at the end of the sixteenth century, and these same old
rooms should be regarded as the center and starting point
where the fame of Munich beer was born and nourished,
and where even through all the epoch of perukes and cues,
after the fall of the monasteries that had contributed so
much to the reputation of Munich beer, it was preserved
from decay.

In the seventeenth century, in the time of Louis XIV.,
all Germany fell under the sway of French influence.
There were French conversation, prayers and oaths, French
amusements and French sins, French eating and drinking.
An effort to imitate all the French fashions that the cav-
aliers brought from Paris was a characteristic of the sad
season. that followed, a time sad for patriots, sad for

beer-brewers and for beer. Beer was *une boisson de commun.* The beautifully ornamented mugs and beakers were put away in the lumber-room (*rumpel kammer*) and champagne glasses from Paris took their place. At evening, where formerly the jovial barons and their chief followers had encamped round the carved-oak table and laid a strong grasp on the mug—there was now a service of cakes and tea, and where formerly milk and pepper or beer was used as a morning draught, the coffee breakfast constantly acquired more use and repute. The common people, however, stood fast for the old way, and were never better pleased than when the privileged beer came to honor. At this time, too, the change of rôles took place, and South Germany entered on its new and important course at the beginning of the present century. (The brewery at St. Marx was built in 1710, and in 1732 there were three brewhouses at Schwechat.)

It is as if the minds of men slumbered long, only to come at once into a never suspected activity. In the midst of the tumult we find Balling, Dreher, Sedlmayer, Kaiser, Otto and many others. Everything in brewing is changed. Laboratories spring out of the ground and discoveries and inventions come in countless numbers, brewing journals are started, schools opened, fairs and associations multiply, and all in the space of a single half century.

# CHAPTER IV.

From the account already given, it will be seen that beer not only took an early hold on the affections of the people, but kept its position wherever it was introduced. It is now well established in every civilized country and plays so important a part in the economy of nations that a review of the light in which it is regarded by different governments cannot fail to be both interesting and useful.

In Germany the state uses every possible means to provide good, wholesome beer for the people. It is the habitual beverage of most of the population, used by them at their meals and their places of amusement, cheering but not intoxicating, and rendering them temperate, industrious, healthy and contented, a people whose bravery is beyond question, and whose peaceable yet progressive qualities tend to make the nation powerful, and its government respected at home and abroad. And yet an advance by the government of half a cent a quart on the price of beer has in years not long passed caused a serious riot. Cheap, wholesome beer is considered a necessity of life, and the attempt to increase its cost an interference with the primary rights of the community.

In Austro-Hungary, too, for many years government supervision has secured the production of pure beer, which is sold at a very moderate price. Some of the breweries are very large and the product is by many held to be unsurpassed in quality. That of Vienna and Pilsen, in particular, is universally known and esteemed. Beer is thoroughly the national drink, and the beer gardens of Vienna are the resort of all classes, from the Emperor down to his private soldiers.

The most important men of the empire have extensive breweries, and among the great Austro-Hungarian brewers we find such names as Anton Dreher of Schwechat near Vienna, Count Arco Valley of Zell, Upper Austria, Count Arco Zinneburg of Kaltenhausen, Count Thurn Valsassina of Sorgendorf, and in Bohemia Count Thun Hohenstein of Alt Benatek, His Majesty the Emperor Franz Josef, Prince Carl Hohenzollern, Prince Trautmansdorf, Prince Josef Mansfeld, Prince J. A. Schwartzenberg, Prince Max Thurn Taxis, the Grand Duke of Tuscany, Rudolf Count von Schoteck and many others.

A correspondent says : " At Trieste the drinking of beer is universal ; from infancy to age light wine and beer are the common beverages." He states that on Saturday night a pretty large number of laboring people are "jolly drunk," but not savage drunk. The latter condition is unknown except among English and American sailors visiting the port. Among the better classes no instance is known of a merchant, lawyer, physician, shop-keeper, or master-mechanic becoming an inebriate and gradually losing position, prosperity and business, and sinking into a drunkard's grave. Sometimes an Englishman or American has ruined himself by the use of spirits—not of wine or beer.

Holland has brewed good beer for centuries, and though this country has been better known as a producer of gin, the national beverage is certainly beer. Professors Tilamus and Swingar of Amsterdam, and the Secretary of the

"Netherlands Society for the Abolition of Spirituous Drinks," say that gin drinking is no longer respectable, and they recommend beer as a daily beverage. The beer gardens of Amsterdam and Rotterdam are very widely known. Good bands are provided and people of all ranks congregate to sip beer, smoke, talk, or listen to the music. On his first visit to these places the writer made careful inquiries as to the consumption of gin and other spirits, and was agreeably surprised to learn that their use was practically confined to the lowest classes and that beer was the common beverage. To find a drunken man it was necessary to go to the docks and wharves, among the Irish and American sailors. Nine-tenths of the gin manufactured is exported to the United States, and most of its use at home is for medical purposes.

The little kingdom of Belgium ranks next Bavaria as a beer consuming country. There are three kinds of beer— Mars, a light beer and generally used by the laboring class, Lambic, strong and light, and the Faro, a mixture of Mars and Lambic. Brussels and Antwerp have some of the finest beer gardens in the world, which furnish music to their patrons equal to the best, and the general habits of the people are temperate. Drunkenness is hardly found even among the lower classes.

Spain even is becoming a beer drinking country. The beer formerly consumed there was imported from England, Germany and Austria, and in 1869 all the breweries in the country did not produce 500,000 liters, equal to 132,062 gallons, while the returns of the year 1878 show a production of over 4,750,000 liters, or 1,254,594 gallons—an astonishing increase in a wine producing country—and the beer

7

brewed at the Santa Barbara brewery at Madrid is taking
the lead of the imported article.

Sweden and Norway also recognize the necessity of pro-
viding a wholesome stimulant for the people, and for more
than a hundred and fifty years their respective governments
have given attention to the matter.  Not long ago patents
for the manufacture of ardent spirits, which had long been
held among the nobility, were revoked, and an attempt made
to secure temperance through the more common use of
malt liquors.  Mr. George Hayward, then proprietor of the
celebrated Lion Brewery at London, England,* was engaged by the government to superintend the introduction
of improved beer in Sweden, and the experiment proved a
thorough success.  As beer increased drunkenness diminished, and both government and people have recognized the
benefits of malt liquors.  According to figures lately furnished by Dr. Ellis Sodenbladh of the Swedish statistical
bureau, beer brewing has attained the position of a leading
industry in that country.  The annual product exceeds
twenty-six million gallons, and this result is largely due to
an increased tax on spirits and the remission of·all taxation
on beer, which may now be fairly considered the national
beverage.

Denmark formerly consumed great quantities of ardent
spirits, the amount used in proportion to the population
being even greater than in the prohibitory state of Maine.
The introduction of the excellent beer made by Jacobsen at
Carlsberg brought about an entire change.  Beer is now
the drink of the country and public feeling is strongly opposed to the use of whisky.  The people have become re-

---

*Mr. Hayward died a short time ago at Albany, N. Y.

markable for quiet and good order, and the police magistrates of the larger cities, as Copenhagen and Elsinore report that for a long time no cases of murder, homicide or theft brought before them have been traced to the influence of strong drink. Arrests for street disorder are very rare and chiefly confined among the foreign seamen. The consumption of beer is about twenty gallons annually to the individual, and this amount seems to produce only favorable effects, as the people are a strong, hardy race with an average longevity far above that of the United States. The advantages of all kinds that have followed the general introduction of beer are very remarkable.

In Russia, a commission was some time ago appointed to investigate the question of drunkenness in the empire. The use of strong ardent spirits had been almost universal. Drunkards were not to be reckoned by individuals or even families. Whole districts were plunged in habits of brutal intoxication and this national pest demoralized the armies, filled poor-houses and hospitals, the lunatic asylums and the prisons.

As a result of the labors of this commission, and in accordance with the unanimous report of its members, the Czar has recently conferred very valuable privileges on those who establish breweries in his dominions. The object being to secure for the people good beer at a low price, all taxes on beer and articles used in its manufacture have been abolished, while the use of ardent spirits is still further checked by the imposition of heavy duties on all introduced to the country, and severe taxes on its manufacture or sale ; and*

---

* Owing to a light crop the Russian government has prohibited the export of barley for the current year, 1879.

whenever the crop of barley turns out to be light, the government prohibits exporting the same.

In Greece, breweries are springing up about Athens and the Piræus, and all over the Levant and the neighboring islands, and the *ek krithon methu* (barley wine) of olden times is going to be the ordinary beverage of the people instead of the rather strong wines that the country produces.

In France during the reign of Napoleon III., it was discovered that the ardent spirits most in use were so adulterated as to produce serious injury to consumers apart from that which always attends the free use of these liquors. Spirits were used to a much greater extent than could be justified on any sound principle. The Emperor, whose practical judgment was excellent in matters not immediately affecting his own ambition, offered inducements to English and German brewers to establish themselves in the country and the consumption of beer was increased with very advantageous results. The change has already gone so far as to alarm the wine merchants, and according to the "British Mercantile Gazette" the consumption in Paris alone now reaches one hundred million *liter* bottles *per annum* or nearly half a pint a day to every Parisian, which is not bad for a beginning. The beer used, however, is still chiefly of foreign manufacture, the lager beer coming chiefly from Vienna and Bavaria, and the ale from Alsopp and Bass. Some American brewers of New York, Philadelphia and St. Louis received gold medals at Paris for the excellence of their beer, and are now shipping considerable quantities to that place.

Americans who have lately been in France must usually have been surprised to notice how *bogk* (lager beer) is already the common beverage in the fashionable *cafés* of the chief cities.

Some leading French savants trace a direct connection between the free use of beer and the national greatness and indomitable personal courage of their opponents in the late war, and hope by the development of the brewing interest to add to the traditional virtues of Frenchmen some of those displayed in the neighboring empire. The notion may be rather fine spun, but the actual benefit of the development of a home industry in beer will be none the less, and it cannot be doubted that their end will be at least partially attained, though perhaps not in so direct a fashion as they suppose. Monsieur Lunier has just brought before the French Academy of Medicine, some very interesting statistics on the use of fermented and other liquors. According to him, wine is still the national drink. The consumption of cider is diminishing, although still large, and brandy is much used to facilitate the digestion of cider. The more cider, the more brandy. The quantity of beer used, has considerably increased in most of the Departments, and he proves conclusively that most cases of accidental death in consequence of excess, occur in the departments where there is most drinking of spirits, that apprehensions for drunkenness are five times as numerous in these Departments as in those where wine is chiefly used, that drunkenness in the beer-drinking regions is hardly known, and that alcoholic insanity is almost everywhere in proportion to the consumption of ardent spirits. The only exceptions are La Vendée and Charente Inferieure where they drink only white wines, but use them in immoderate quantities.

French brewers are now engaged in forming an association and the first meeting has been announced to take place at Toulouse, in the late autumn of the present year (1879). The *Industriel de Lyon* speaks of the matter as follows:

" In consequence of their number, and as representing forty-two departments, the brewers who should support this association are most influential. They would, by means of combination, be able to properly protect their important industry, and struggle against errors of the past, such as excise regulations, octroi, etc. Besides the meetings of the Syndicate, whether held at Toulouse or Lyons, might take up general economical questions of interest to its members, and also deal with the fabrication of beer, malting, and the scientific phenomena, which are more numerous and complex than is imagined. Brewing, it is further asserted, is an industry of the future. Beer is a drink of progress on account of its refreshing and especially nutritive qualities. To produce beer cheap, appetizing to the eye, and agreeable to the stomach, is the program which the brewers of the South have in view, and which they must strive energetically to carry out if they wish to compete at all successfully with the German beers. The phylloxera is not an eternal enemy. Sooner or later science will neutralize its effects.

" In the South of France, therefore, the opinion is held that the greatest care should be given to the production of beer. Besides, people in the South do not drink the good wine which they produce; they export it. Money is more valuable to them than good wine. Inferior wine, however, remains, and is consumed to a great extent. We are of opinion that beer would offer to all considerable advantages; and therefore it is desirable that the brewing industry in the South of France should be developed in the fullest possible manner."

In England about the year 1833 the use of intoxicating liquors had increased to such a point that government applied itself to the discovery of some means of diminishing the consumption. The Duke of Wellington, whose long career as a soldier on the continent and elsewhere had taught him the beneficial influence of beer, and who saw clearly the amount of misery and degradation caused among his countrymen by the use of distilled liquors, introduced while Prime Minister, the well known "Beer Bill." Its passage was urged distinctly on the ground that a free consumption of beer would greatly diminish the use of spirits. The Duke himself strongly advocated the bill and instanced the continental beer-drinking countries as the happiest and most temperate on the globe.

On the other hand the so called temperance men appeared in large deputations to urge (against all reason) that whatever beer might be consumed would be in addition to the previous consumption of ardent spirits and not in place of it, or any part of it, that intoxication would be increased in a ratio correspondent to the amount of beer used, and in short that the proposed plan of reform was much like an attempt to quench fire by pouring on oil. The bill, however, was at last passed by a large majority and has proved very successful. The consumption of beer has largely increased, distilled liquors are less used, and, notwithstanding the assertions of some over-zealous partisans of total abstinence, we can prove by statistics carefully collected that the amount of drunkenness in the country began to decrease immediately after the passage of the bill. William E. Gladstone, the great English

statesman who, in the year 1868–9, carried through Parliament an act intended to promote the cause of temperance
by cheapening wine and beer and making their sale part of
the business of restaurants and confectioners' shops, wrote
a short time ago as follows: "I am opposed to coffee and
tea palaces as I believe they are more deteriorating than beer
shops. The stimulating properties of coffee or tea are greater
and more injurious than those of malt liquors."

The course advocated by the Duke of Wellington and Mr.
Gladstone has been fully justified by the results. Drunkenness has decreased and breweries have multiplied. The
measure of advantage is to be found in the increase of large
breweries whose product is distributed through many chan-
nels, for these furnish what is to take the place of the ardent
spirit formerly consumed when one was away from home or
wanted a change from the home-brewed ale to which he
was accustomed. They also attract the favor of the poorer
classes because they furnish so much more in bulk and nutritive power at the same or a less price.

There are, however, many small breweries, such as those
attached to country inns or to private houses. Some breweries also confine their business to supplying families with
pale and table ales, stout or porter, in small barrels of four
and a half, nine, and eighteen gallons. The number of
breweries in Great Britain—aside from those which are
strictly for private use—is, according to official returns,
twenty-six thousand, two hundred and fourteen, which it
will be seen is about nine times the number in the United
States. The cost of good ale is about one shilling sterling
a gallon.

It is worthy of notice that the brewers of England are

M.T. BASS, ESQ. M.P.
THE GREAT BURTON-ON-TRENT BREWER, ENGLAND.

distinguished for a wise generosity and public spirit, and
such men as Charington, Fox, Meux, Alsopp, Hanbury,
Buxton, Mann, Truman, Guinness, Walker and Bass, * will
be long remembered for the magnificent charities that en-
noble and perpetuate their names. To a greater or less degree the same characteristic comes to light in every country
where beer is established as the popular beverage. Jacobsen, a brewer of Copenhagen, before his death set aside
$280,000 to found a laboratory of scientific research. A
part of the money is to be spent in keeping up the laboratories attached to his brewery, in which chemical and physi-
ological researches are carried on with a view to establish
as completely as possible a scientific basis for brewing and
malting.

The generous juice of barley, seems to draw out the more
kindly and human feelings of all who have their dealings
in it. Can any such thing be said of distilled liquors?

The late Khedive of Egypt, who has done more for the
advancement of that country than any other ruler since the
time of the Pharaohs, perceived the advantages to be gained
by the introduction of beer, and granted very valuable privileges to a company of Swiss brewers, whose establishment
is now in full and successful operation at Cairo. The con-

---

*Michael Thomas Bass, the senior member of Parliament for Derby, is best
known as the largest brewer in the world. He is now over eighty years old,
and has been engaged in the brewery business founded by his grandfather for
about sixty-two years. He was educated at the Buxton Grammar School, and
has supplemented this early instruction by a course of reading that leaves him
not at all behind many University men in the matter of scholarly attainments.
He has always been noted for the efficient discharge of his public and private
duties, and has for more than thirty years represented the old town of Derby as
senior member of Parliament. His public and private gifts have been frequent and munificent, the last of importance being a free library for the town of
Derby.

sumption is chiefly in the cities which are largely inhabited by Europeans, generally disposed to drink beer if it is good and readily attainable, but sure to use stronger drinks if the beer is wanting, and perhaps, from the circumstance of residence at a distance from home, more apt to use any intoxicating liquor to excess.

Japan, a kingdom hardly known to us twenty-five years ago, and now recognized as one of the most highly civilized in the world, has thus far suffered very little from intoxicating drinks. Native stimulants have been used, and in some cases have proved as injurious as strong whisky, though perhaps more strictly harmful to the individual, and less so to his family and the community. The people are by nature and education gentle and polite, and their social manners are in many particulars a lesson to Europeans. They are usually temperate in all things, happy and contented. The Mikado, however, wisely considering that in the growing intercourse of Japan with foreign countries, a taste for ardent spirits can hardly fail to be developed, unless some counteracting influence be at work, has decided to foster the erection of beer breweries, and thus avert as far as possible an impending danger, while at the same time he gives his subjects an innocent and refreshing beverage. With this view, the representatives of Japan, now in Germany, have been directed to enter into arrangements with well-known brewers, for the erection of large breweries in Yokohama, Tokio, Saga, Nagasaki and Shidz-u-o-ka.

The Shah of Persia also, is so far convinced of the advantages of beer, as to have made arrangements during his last visit to Vienna, for parties there to undertake its introduction in his kingdom.

In Turkey, there are at Constantinople six breweries with an annual product of about one hundred and twenty thousand gallons. The hops are imported from Germany, but the other materials are supplied by the country. After the island of Cyprus passed from Turkish to English rule, it is worthy of notice that the first shipment by the *Thessalia* was fifty barrels of beer, a shipment well illustrating English national habits.

The condition of the beer trade in the United States being part of the general subject of this book, and especially illustrated in the chapter under the heading " The Condition and Prospects of the Beer Trade," and also in the list of breweries given in Appendix C, needs no remark here.

# CHAPTER V.

The production of beer, as of all other malt liquors, bears a striking similarity to the making of bread; the chief difference being in the quantity of grain employed, and the amount of water added. The one intended for a solid food is baked, the other for a liquid refreshment is boiled.

The process of making beer is as follows: A certain quantity of malted barley is taken and ground, it is then mashed with hot water, the sweet liquor or wort extracted, a portion of hops added, and the whole boiled until the preservative quality as well as the aroma of the hops is obtained. It is then allowed to cool, and afterwards fermented with yeast to produce the small quantity of alcohol it contains, and to give it life. According to analyses made by different chemists, lager beer contains 91.0 water, 5.4 malt extract, 3.5 alcohol, and the remainder—making in all 100 parts— carbonic acid. Ale and porter differ only in having a slight additional percentage of alcohol, and a large amount of solid extract.

The substantial and useful character of the chief ingredient of beer may be seen from the nature of an analysis of the malt which forms its basis. The result is from Dr. Lerner, whose researches in this direction have been of great value.

|  | DRY BARLEY. |  | DRY MALT. | DIFFERENCE. |
|---|---|---|---|---|
| Starch, . . . . . . . | 63.43 | minus | 48.86 | 14.57 |
| Proteic substances, . . | 16.25 | minus | 15.99 | 0.26 |

| | DRY BARLEY. | | DRY MALT. | DIFFERENCE. |
|---|---|---|---|---|
| Dextrine, . . . . . . | 6.63 | plus | 6.86 | 0.23 |
| Sugar, . . . . . . . | — | plus | 2.03 | 2.03 |
| Fatty matters, . . . . | 3.08 | minus | 2.50 | 0.58 |
| Cellulose, . . . . . . | 7.10 | plus | 7.31 | 0.21 |
| Other substances, . . . | 1.11 | plus | 3.16 | 2.05 |
| Ash, . . . . . . . | 2.40 | minus | 2.10 | 0.30 |
| | 100.00 | | 88.81 | |

In the ordinary process of bread fermentation, a portion of the sugar contained in the flour is decomposed and converted into alcohol. It has been supposed that the whole of this alcohol was expelled by heat during baking; but recent experiments indicate that a perceptible amount still remains in yeast-raised bread after baking. The result of six experiments, showed that one-third of one per cent. in weight of alcohol was obtained from fresh baked bread. From forty loaves of fresh bread, two pounds each, alcohol equal to one bottle of port wine may be extracted.

The celebrated Professor Balling of Prague, who has spent much time in the chemical analysis of different fermented beverages, arrives at the following result in reference to lager beer : " Lager beer manufactured of malt and hops according to the noble rules of brewing, properly fermented, stored for some time and perfectly clear, is a healthy and agreeable beverage,' which when partaken of quenches thirst and strengthens, and thus combines the qualities of water, wine and food. The water is the thirst-quenching element, the wine the enlivening, the malt extract (composed of sugar, gum, etc.) the nourishing, and the carbonic acid gas the refreshing, while the hop extract strengthens the stomach, helps digestion, acts on the bladder and is grateful to the human constitution. There is no doubt that lager beer brewed and stored strictly as before mentioned is hardly intoxicating."

An impression has gained ground in some quarters that as a matter of fact, beer is extensively and injuriously adulterated and certain persons claiming to be well informed have spread statements that potato starch, grape sugar, glycerine and molasses are added as substitutes for malt (barley), that Indian corn and rice are used instead of barley, that pine bark, quassia, walnut leaf, wormwood, bitter clover, aloes, picric acid, cocculus indicus and strychnine are substituted for hops, and that various chemicals are used to neutralize acidity or conceal dilution. A few of the first named would not be objectionable, unless in point of flavor, and as a matter of fact all of the substances named may at some time have been used by irresponsible brewers. A careful inquiry, however, has satisfied us that the adulteration of beer is rare, and one who reflects on the lively competition that exists in the trade must see how speedily and surely such a practice would be detected and exposed by business rivals. Touching the use of strychnine in particular, Dr. Ure says that

1st. "Strychnine is exceedingly costly.

2d. "It has a most unpleasant bitter, metallic taste.

3d. "It is a notorious poison whose use would ruin the reputation of any brewer.

4th. "It cannot be introduced into ordinary beer brewed with hops because it is entirely precipitated by the infusion of that wholesome, fragrant herb. * * * * Were the *nux-vomica* powder from which strychnia is extracted even stealthily thrown into the mash tun, its dangerous principle would be all infallibly thrown down with the grounds in the subsequent boiling with the hops."

When we remember the immense improvement in the quality of American beer within the past few years and learn how often expensive machinery and appliances have been abandoned after a short use in favor of something better, we can hardly believe that brewers who conduct their business after such a fashion, will at the same time try to make a petty profit by using poor material and so deteriorating the product on whose excellence the success of their business depends. The genuineness of beer from any established brewery may usually be taken for granted. In 1872 after an extensive examination of beers in Great Britain only six samples were found to be adulterated.*

An effort has been made by many so called temperance papers to disseminate an opposite view in this matter and the statements made can only be excused on the ground of ignorance—which in the circumstances is inexcusable. No doubt beer has been often adulterated, but to represent the practice as common or as prevailing in breweries that expect to live and that have a character to maintain is to speak in contradiction to the facts and to common sense. Lately at Newark, New Jersey, charges of this general nature were made by a total abstinence speaker and the matter was for once taken up by the brewers of the city, in whose behalf a well known member of the trade addressed the following letter to the orator of the day :

The Rev. W. F. Boole, Brooklyn :

Sir—In a lecture delivered by you at Park Hall, Newark, N. J., on Sunday afternoon, July 13, 1879, you are reported in the *Newark Morn-*

---

*Encyclopedia Britannica, Art. Brewing.

*ing Register* to have said: "The traffic is a traffic of compound poisons,
"and not even the finest imported liquors are free from them. Strych-
"nine and stramonium, two deadly poisons, are used in the manufac-
"ture of beer, and a little potash is added to prevent the taste. Bella-
"donna, one of the most virulent of poisons, is also used, and not less
"than 10,000 tons of the deadly cocculus are consumed. Cocculus is
"never given as a medicine, but it is drank daily by the masses in their
"beer and ale."

You, as a teacher of religion, should be a lover of truth. On behalf
of the brewers of the United States, I denounce this statement as a deliberate falsehood, and I challenge you to prove any part of it; and in
the event of your not doing so, or withdrawing your assertion, I shall
not only take steps to publish the fact that you are a willful perverter
of the truth, but also to prosecute you for slander.

Yours truly,

(Signed)   C. FEIGENSPAN.

Thereupon the lecturer made answer that the papers had
not reported him correctly. Here the matter might have
dropped, and there was in fact an end of this particular phase
of the question. The case, however, had made a stir and pres-
ently a representative of the teetotal party called at the office
of the United States Brewing Association to collect information which was given him as a matter of course. Then
came a proposition from the same party for a public discussion on the following extraordinary terms. Twelve propositions were to be advanced and supported by a practiced
speaker on the teetotal side. The representative of the
Newark Brewers was to have an opportunity to reply to
each, and the other speaker was then to sum up and con-
clude the discussion. The brewers' representative had only
three days notice and naturally declined any such arrangement in which all the advantage was evidently assumed by

the other side. The discussion also was to be confined to one evening, and a collection was to be taken up " to defray expenses." The Newark Brewers' Association, however, expressed their willingness to debate on fair terms and with one evening for each proposition, but this arrangement was declined. We have taken pains to procure the twelve propositions of the total abstinence club, and append them here chiefly in order to call attention to the fact that the greater part are especially treated in this book, while the others are touched incidentally or by direct inference. The propositions are as follows :

No. 1.—The use of malt liquors is a direct cause of intemperance.

No 2.—The use of malt liquors tends to the use of stronger liquors

No. 3 —Malt liquors, if habitually used to any considerable extent, tend to cause ill-health.

No. 4.—The claim that malt liquors are valuable as food is without foundation.

No. 5 —As a medicine, malt liquors are of use only to those who do not ordinarily use them, and are dangerous because of their tendency to create habit.

No. 6.—The theory that malt liquors can be substituted by consumers of alcoholic beverages for distilled liquors, to any important extent, is false.

No. 7 —Beer in this country is far more evil in its effects than in Germany ; but even there its bad effects, as used by the people, are obvious to every traveler who has no theory to maintain.

No 8.—The use of beer by the working classes has a direct relation to poverty.

No. 9.—The use of malt liquors by the masses has a relation

9

to crime, which, though differing in some respects from that of distilled liquors, is marked and alarming.

No. 10.—Beer saloons and gardens, as a whole, are demoralizing in their effects on individuals, families, and especially on children.

No. 11.—The great increase in the use of malt liquors and the increase in intemperance for the past fifteen years have been parallel, and are intimately connected.

No. 12.—That beer saloons should be subjected to the same restrictions under which ordinary grog-shops are placed.

Further comment would be superfluous, especially as this whole matter is, strictly speaking, a digression from the purpose of the chapter, although one that is so natural as to be almost inevitable.

There has also been much misrepresentation of the views of prominent men. For instance, the *Religious Herald* of Hartford, Conn., recently reprinted an article in which it is asserted that Professor Liebig " has proved to a certainty that as much flour as can lie on the point of a table knife is more nutritious than eight quarts of Bavarian beer, counted the best made. Also that the man who drinks two gallons of Bavarian beer a day for a year, gets only as much nutriment from his seven hundred and thirty gallons as he would from one five-pound loaf of bread or three pounds of flesh!" The article has been extensively copied all over the country and is calculated to do much harm by throwing the influence of an important name on a side where it was never intended to go.

Now it is barely possible that Professor Liebig made such a statement as to nutriment of a special form, though we are not aware of any passage that can give the least color to the assertion. On the other hand his real view appears in such passages as the following: "Pure lager beer, when taken with lean flesh and little bread yields a diet approaching to milk; with fat meat, approaching to rice or potatoes." And again, " In beer-drinking countries it is the universal medicine for the healthy as well as for the sick, and it is milk to the aged." These views are shared by almost all the eminent men who have made a scientific study of beer, and the opinions and results reached by a large number of chemists of high authority will be found in a subsequent chapter. We have anticipated thus much here because in describing beer as it is, it seemed necessary to indicate to some degree what it is not, at least so far as to explain that it is not generally adulterated, and is not wholly useless, as a large party constantly asserts it to be.

# CHAPTER VI.

## THE DEVELOPMENT OF ALE, PORTER AND LAGER BEER.

It has been already mentioned that the earliest beers were made without hops. After the use of this plant was discovered beer brewing as an art made rapid progress, and not only did every country make its own special sort of beer, but many varieties existed side by side in most of the German states and in England. Experiments were made with all sorts of grain, with potatoes and with plants and herbs, the object being in every case to produce a wort whose beer should have special advantages in point of flavor or cost or both. Gradually, however, most of the materials were quietly dropped, although potatoes are still used for the Strasbourg beer, and wheat forms an important element of the famous white beer of northern Germany. Barley is the grain that has universally been found best adapted to the purpose of making a brown beer of an agreeable flavor and of moderate price. With the question of material thus practically settled, it might be supposed that the difference between various brews of beer would disappear. On the contrary the number of varieties is to-day greater than ever before. Every step in the manufacture, from the selection of the grain and hops on to the final delivery of the product to the consumer, has something to do with the characteristics of the beer, and the difficulty does not lie in producing something new, but in reproducing accurately what has once been successfully tested.

Whatever the distinguishing features of the product, it is

still beer, and any one specimen of the genus has the general properties of all the others. All beer has a notably small percentage of alcohol, the strongest ales and porters showing less than many specimens of cider ; all contain an appreciable amount of solid nutriment which in some heavy-bodied beers is quite considerable ; all are palatable and wholesome, and all are adapted to take the place of ardent spirits and thus reduce intemperance and drunkenness to a *minimum.* It is hardly necessary to explain that in this book the word beer is used in its wide sense. When special varieties are meant they are spoken of by name unless the context is such as to remove all doubt.

After the time of experiment and the disuse of most of the grains, etc., that had been tried, there still remained two well-marked varieties differing essentially in the mode of fermentation, and our modern ale and lager beer may be taken as types of the two kinds. The former is fermented rapidly at a high temperature and the fermentation checked while a considerable portion of sugar still remains unchanged, while the latter is fermented slowly and thoroughly at a low temperature. The first process is the one originally employed everywhere and has held almost undisputed ground in England, where, as might in such circumstances be expected, ale-brewing has reached its most thorough development. At the beginning of the eighteenth century there were in that country three recognized sorts, ale, beer and two-penny, differing chiefly in the quantity of malt used for each kind. These were often mixed to suit customers and in 1730, to avoid the trouble of constant mixing, a new drink was brewed, called "entire," and meant to resemble the triple compound. This was afterwards known as porter, and at present the general distinction is between porter and ale, though we still hear of small beer. The variety of ales, however, is very great. They are made of all colors and all degrees of strength, very bitter like the pale ale, and sweetish like the Scotch ale, so long-lived that they can be exported to hot climates and kept for years, and so short-lived that they must be used within three or four weeks. Some are perfectly clear and bright, and resemble nothing so much as Rhine wine, of whose flavor also they have an indescribable suggestion, while others are dark with solid extract and possess a characteristic delicate flavor that resembles nothing else. In this respect America is yet far in the rear. There is plenty of good ale but there has been no demand sufficient to cause so varied a supply or to develop so well-marked special flavors. When, however, we remember for how long a time cider was the common drink of the people to the exclusion of beer, and see how, in spite of such an obstacle at the start, the business gradually gained ground, and when we remember that outside the larger cities, even twenty years ago, ale was almost sure to be dull and muddy and very apt to be sour, we must admit that American ale-brewers have accomplished much. They have succeeded so far as to secure a large sale for their brew, and so far that now almost anywhere one is certain of a tolerable glass of beer—unless the existence of a prohibitory law excludes everything but whisky. Their success appears the more striking because of the recent great increase in the use of lager beer, for enormous as is the consumption of the latter it has hardly produced any effect on the sales of the ale-brewers. There is a large number who prefer the flavor of ale, others drink it from habit and will always do so, others drink it because they ape English fashions, others because the comparatively secluded and unsocial character imported from England to our ale-houses suits them better than the more social and gregarious customs of the lager beer garden, some even because it is usually the more costly of the two beverages. Some doubtless prefer it because it usually contains a little more alcohol than lager beer, and very many use either beer indifferently according to circumstances and convenience.

As to porter there is little that need be said. Its origin has been already mentioned, and when we add that the color is due to browned malt and its flavor to seeds or the like we have stated all that would interest the general reader. It is essentially a heavy-bodied ale, however great the superficial unlikeness.

The difference in the manner of fermentation of ale and lager beer has been previously indicated, but the following passage from Professor Liebig will be found of interest: "In that country (Bavaria) the malt wort is set to ferment in open backs with an extensive surface, and placed in cool cellars having an atmospheric temperature not exceeding 8° or 10° C (46½ or 50 F.). The operation lasts from three to four weeks; the carbonic acid is disengaged, not in large bubbles that burst on the surface of the liquid, but in very small vesicles like those of a mineral water or of a liquor saturated with carbonic acid when the pressure is removed. The surface of the fermenting wort is always in contact with the oxygen of the atmosphere as it is hardly covered with froth and as all the yeast is deposited at the bottom of the back under the form of a very viscid sediment, called in German *unterhefe*."

The process thus described results in the production of a beer which will not sour even if kept exposed to the air for a long time. Barrels only half full have remained uninjured for months. It is to be noticed, however, that both ale and lager beer can be prepared under many modifications of the main plan, and both are often made for immediate use without regard to keeping qualities and pass by the names of present use ale and Schenck beer.

As lager beer usually contains a little less alcohol than ale, it has been most commonly spoken of by those who are striving to eradicate intemperance by introducing beer in the place of ardent spirits. The difference in alcoholic strength is not, however, so great as many persons suppose, the percentage in ales ranging from 8.88 to 5.36, while that of lager beer varies from 6.50 to 3.06. The kind of beer to be preferred for the work in any country is that best suited to the tastes and traditions of the people. On the continent of Europe and in America lager beer has thus far played the more prominent part, while in England the responsibility of all that has been accomplished belongs to ale.

It is not improbable that the English brewing business has already reached its culminating point. A large part of the annual product has long been exported to the colonies, and now these are beginning to brew beer for themselves and will soon have a supply of their own make, sufficient in quality and quantity to make them independent of the mother country. With us the case is different. The consumption is increasing rapidly, and brewers show a wise liberality in securing new processes and appurtenances, and spare no effort to improve the quality of their product.

Those who make the best beer secure the most custom, and the fraternity are fully aware of the fact. All this rivalry cannot fail to benefit the consumer. Every year sees better ale and lager beer sent over the country, and every year something is contributed to the solution of the problem in brewing—to produce a mild beer that with more extract than is now found shall contain even less alcohol, and remain bright and refreshing. Whether full success in such an attempt is to be sooner reached by the ale or lager beer brewers remains to be seen, or it may well be that some new malt beverage may be discovered, unlike either of the others and superior to both. Such a result would be no more striking than other steps in progress already made, and brewers of large experience are to be found who believe that some such discovery is impending. In the meantime we have the satisfaction of knowing that America already produces malt liquors made from native materials that are wholesome and agreeable and at least up to the average of similar liquors made in countries where brewing has been carefully studied and extensively practiced for centuries, while with us it is chiefly a recent growth. The degree of success that is possible when we take into account the natural resources of the country and the enterprising character of the brewers is hardly to be realized.

10

# CHAPTER VII.

## THE CONDITIONS AND PROSPECTS OF THE BEER TRADE.

I believe that Germans are destined to be really the greatest benefactors of this country by bringing to us—if we choose to accept the boon—their beer. Lager beer contains less alcohol than any of the native grape wines. This fact, with the other fact, that the Germans have not the pernicious habits of our people, would, if we choose to adopt their custom, tend to diminish intemperance in this country.

DR. HENRY J. BOWDITCH,
*Chairman of the State Board of Health of Massachusetts.*

Geniesst im edlen Gerstensaft
Des Weines Geist, des Brodes Kraft.

The strength of bread, the fire of wine
O noble barley juice are thine.
TIVOLI.

The brewing of ale has been so long an established industry in this country and advances so regularly from year to year as to offer no striking facts for comment. With lager beer the case is different, and the rapidity of the increase in its use is something remarkable. Fifty years ago it was hardly known as a beverage in the United States. Now and then some good old German would import a keg from his native home in the old country, to be drunk on the occasion of some great family festival, and call up in his adopted home thoughts of the merry days of youth and friendly faces, last seen perhaps in some deep valley of the Tyrol or in the shadows of a city that was old when the Pilgrims landed at Plymouth Rock. But in the case of so good a creature as lager beer such occasional and almost poetical use could not always remain the only one, and at last a German of Philadelphia conceived the idea of erecting a

FREDERICK LAUER'S PARK BREWERY. READING, PA.

lager beer brewery.    According to the Hon. Frederick Lauer
of Reading, Pa., (and we have all reason to put implicit
faith in his version) it was introduced by one Wagner, a
practical brewer who came from Germany to the United
States in a sailing vessel in the year 1842, and shortly after
landing he brewed the first lager in a miserable shanty on
the outskirts of Philadelphia, and thus became the Gambrinus of America.    (We would here refer the reader to the
biographical sketch of Frederick Lauer, Esq., in Appendix A.)

His success induced another German to try the same
experiment on a small scale in the city of New York, and
from this insignificant beginning the business has increased
to its present immense proportions, so that there are now
according to the latest return of the Internal Revenue Department at Washington, no less than two thousand eight
hundred and thirty ale and lager beer breweries in active
operation.    The number is in fact considerably larger than
that given by the Department, owing to the method of re-
turning only those in actual business at the beginning of
the year and to other causes.    The annual product according to the Department figures, is over three hundred million
gallons.    More exactly the figures are, 303,147,552 gallons,
or 9,473,361 barrels.    In addition to this there are numerous
private breweries where beer is made for home consumption
but not for sale, and these do not fall under the Internal
Revenue regulations and are consequently not reported.

Figures as given below in reference to the capital invested
in the brewing, malting and hop business, and taken after
careful investigation from the best sources attainable, will
give the reader a faint idea of its vast extent.

## CAPITAL.

| | | |
|---|---:|---:|
| Capital invested in 2,830 breweries in operation at the end of the last fiscal year, (taking the low estimate of $10.00 upon every barrel of malt beverage produced, viz. : 9,473,361 barrels at $10.00, | | $94,733,610 00 |
| Capital invested in 485 malt-houses of all dimensions having altogether a malting capacity of 35,227,984 bushels : | | |
| Real estate, | $16,567,562 00 | |
| Capital invested in the production, | 18,620,950 00 | |
| | | $35,188,512 00 |
| Capital invested in 1,614,654 acres of land under cultivation for barley, | | $72,659,430 00 |
| Capital invested in 67,216 acres of land under cultivation for hops, | | 2,689,232 00 |
| Capital invested in gathering ice needed for brewers, | | 15,000,000 00 |
| Capital invested in fodder of all kinds, | | 5,000,000 00 |

## LABOR.

| | |
|---|---:|
| Men employed in breweries now in operation; men 22,640; annual wages, | $13,584,000 00 |
| Men employed in malt-houses; men 3,045; annual wages, | 1,324,575 00 |
| Men employed in the culture of barley, 10 men to every 100 acres; men 16,446; annual wages, | 4,844,000 00 |
| Help employed in the culture of hops, 1 person to every 10 acres; persons 6,721; annual wages, | 2,016,630 00 |
| All other adjuncts necessary as capital invested by architects, builders, wagon and harness-makers, coppersmith, coopers, machinists, etc , will amount to not less than, | 60,000,000 00 |
| Total, | $307,039,989 00 |

A glance at the figures just quoted is enough to show that this branch of industry has become very important. Such a production implies the contribution of a large amount of capital, and after careful investigation of the most trustworthy *data* we find that there are more than three

hundred million dollars invested in breweries, malt-houses
and other adjuncts of the manufacture of beer in the United
States. The direct investment however, is not the only
thing to be considered. A business of this magnitude furnishes occupation not merely to vast numbers of laborers,
but also to thousands of men who follow some profession or
trade, such as architects, civil engineers, masons, carpenters,
coopers, coppersmiths, wagon and harness-makers, and the
like.

The following table exhibits the production of the various
states and territories for the last year, together with the increase or decrease as compared with the previous year, and
also the amount of brewers' manufacturing tax collected :

| NAME. | BBLS. | INCREASE. | DECREASE. | BREWERS' MFG. TAX COLLECTED. |
|---|---|---|---|---|
| North Carolina, | 4 | 4 | ...... | $100 |
| Maine, | 7 | ...... | 7,024 | ...... |
| Alabama, | 74 | ...... | 110 | ...... |
| Arkansas, | 104 | ...... | 6 | 100 |
| Vermont, | 173 | ...... | 112 | 115 |
| South Carolina, | 586 | ...... | 246 | 100 |
| New Mexico, | 847 | ...... | 164 | 245 |
| Arizona, | 1,030 | 299 | ...... | 100 |
| Idaho, | 1,207 | 457 | ...... | 100 |
| Wyoming, | 4,227 | ...... | 132 | 260 |
| Dakota, | 4,548 | 1,213 | ...... | 640 |
| Montana, | 4,596 | 1,005 | ...... | 580 |
| Georgia, | 5,690 | ...... | 1,319 | 620 |
| Delaware, | 7,387 | 215 | ...... | 250 |
| Washington, | 7,473 | 544 | ...... | 480 |
| Utah, | 7,909 | 25 | ...... | 205 |
| Texas, | 9,585 | ...... | 4,859 | 2,362.49 |
| Tennessee, | 10,278 | 9,572 | ...... | 320.84 |
| Nevada, | 12,002 | ...... | 387 | 1,640 |

| NAME. | BBLS. | INCREASE. | DECREASE. | BREWERS' MFG. TAX COLLECTED. |
|---|---|---|---|---|
| Oregon, | 13,028 | 2,776 | ...... | $1,480.50 |
| Virginia, | 14,302 | ...... | 1,195 | 316.67 |
| Colorado, | 21,185 | 1,242 | ...... | 360.50 |
| W. Virginia, | 22,157 | Same Amount. | ...... | 858.83 |
| Kansas, | 24,102 | 1,801 | ...... | 1,890.67 |
| Nebraska, | 28,403 | 4,455 | ...... | 2,460.75 |
| Rhode Island, | 32,510 | 4,514 | ...... | 2,640.50 |
| Louisiana, | 38,275 | 375 | ...... | 2,210.30 |
| Connecticut, | 51,235 | ...... | 8,239 | 2,008.34 |
| Minnesota, | 103,020 | 12,329 | ...... | 9,435.82 |
| New Hampshire, | 113,740 | ...... | 4,954 | 8,760.40 |
| Kentucky, | 116,493 | 15,810 | ...... | 3,570.88 |
| Indiana, | 170,573 | 7,881 | ...... | 6,937.49 |
| Iowa, | 171,951 | 14,271 | ...... | 11,449.99 |
| Michigan, | 185,606 | ...... | 2,592 | 11,266.67 |
| Maryland, | 218,642 | 9,496 | ...... | 6,583.35 |
| California, | 346,369 | ...... | 5,628 | 15,327.91 |
| Wisconsin, | 463,409 | 20,345 | ...... | 17,954.17 |
| New Jersey, | 478,782 | ...... | 11,979 | 5,608.34 |
| Missouri, | 507,963 | 46,793 | ...... | 5,762.50 |
| Illinois, | 550,976 | 29,270 | ...... | 11,470.82 |
| Massachusetts, | 572,098 | 77,639 | ...... | 3,904.22 |
| Ohio, | 908,254 | 89,468 | ...... | 17,066.70 |
| Pennsylvania, | 957,060 | ...... | 20,848 | 17,358.05 |
| New York. | 3,285,498 | 125,646 | ...... | 32,601.01 |

The percentage yielded by the several leading states to the total government income from malt beverages during the last fiscal year is shown in the following table :

| New York | having | 405 | Breweries, | contributed | 34.31 | per cent. |
|---|---|---|---|---|---|---|
| Pennsylvania | " | 383 | " | " | 10.07 | " |
| Ohio | " | 207 | " | " | 9.41 | " |
| Massachusetts | " | 35 | " | " | 5.94 | " |
| Illinois | " | 154 | " | " | 5.75 | " |

| Missouri | having | 65 | Breweries, | contributed | 5.21 | per cent. |
|---|---|---|---|---|---|---|
| New Jersey | " | 69 | " | " | 5.00 | " |
| Wisconsin | " | 248 | " | " | 4.89 | " |
| California | " | 213 | " | " | 3.69 | " |
| Maryland | " | 82 | " | " | 2.31 | " |
| Michigan | " | 141 | " | " | 2.13 | " |
| Iowa | " | 150 | " | " | 1.94 | " |
| Indiana | " | 101 | " | " | 1.82 | " |
| Kentucky | " | 34 | " | " | 1.24 | " |
| New Hampshire | " | 4 | " | " | 1.20 | " |
| Minnesota | " | 140 | " | " | 1.17 | " |
| All other States and Territories | " | 399 | " | " | 3.92 | " |
| | | 2,830 Breweries. | | | 100.00 | |

It thus appears that 96.08 per cent. of the revenue was derived from the sixteen states just mentioned. They contain 2431 breweries as against 399 in the remaining states and territories. The stamps issued to brewers during the year indicate a sale of 9,473,361 barrels, put up as follows :

| In hogsheads, | 1,140,361 barrels. |
|---|---|
| In barrels, | 1,220,000 " |
| In half-barrels, | 1,325,000 " |
| In quarter " | 4,650,000 " |
| In third " | 71,000 " |
| In sixth " | 277,000 " |
| In eighth " | 790,000 " |
| | 9,473,361 |

Enormous as the above figures may seem we are to remember that a great majority of the breweries in the country have been erected within the last fifteen years, and it is certain that no other branch of industry can show equal

progress during the same time.  The following tables, showing the imports and exports of beer for the past few years,
demonstrate the strong position American beer is taking at
home and abroad.  The imports decrease.  The exports increase, and this is the best proof that our brewers produce
an article which is equal if not superior to the foreign, and
we have no doubt that with the help of wise laws they will
soon be enabled to compete with those of any nation and
thus not only enrich the coffers of the United States Treasury but add in other ways to the welfare of our great
country.

### IMPORTATION OF FOREIGN BEER INTO THE UNITED STATES.

|       | Gallons.  | Value in Dollars. |
|-------|-----------|-------------------|
| 1872, | 1,989,713 | $1,485,781 00     |
| 1873, | 2,289,053 | 1,827,763 00      |
| 1874, | 2,088,858 | 1,752,559 00      |
| 1875, | 2,167,251 | 1,742,120 00      |
| 1876, | 1,490,150 | 1,161,467 00      |
| 1877, |   974,277 |   758,850 00      |
| 1878, |   767,709 |   592,707 00      |

### EXPORT OF BEER OF DOMESTIC PRODUCE.

|       | IN BOTTLES. | | IN CASKS. | |
|-------|---------|------------------|----------|------------------|
|       | DOZENS. | VALUE IN DOLLARS. | GALLONS. | VALUE IN DOLLARS. |
| 1870, | 1,076   | $2,250  | 66,467  | $23,759 00 |
| 1871, | 1,570   | 4,077   | 105,213 | 34,301 00  |
| 1872, | 2,205   | 5,340   | 77,639  | 27,829 00  |
| 1873, | 3,443   | 7,712   | 103,009 | 36,743 00  |
| 1874, | 2,897   | 6,245   | 99,135  | 33,357 00  |
| 1875, | 3,633   | 7,600   | 61,661  | 16,604 00  |
| 1876, | 7,045   | 13,007  | 99,310  | 29,657 00  |
| 1877, | 37,876  | 51,077  | 144,244 | 40,138 00  |
| 1878, | 76,475  | 108,279 | 119,579 | 38,918 00  |

It will be seen from this table that whilst the export of beer in casks has not considerably increased, the increase in the export of bottled beer has been very large. In 1870 we exported 1,076 dozens, and in 1878, 76,475 dozen! This trade has especially been encouraged by the Philadelphia Centennial Exhibition, as it enabled us to show to the world the quality of our production.

The gigantic establishments that, in many cases cover entire blocks, are monuments of very lucrative enterprise and ought to be the pride of the American people. The truth is, that, notwithstanding a yearly sale of more than 300,000,000 gallons, the consumption of beer is yet in its infancy. With an increasing number of persons it ceases to be a luxury and takes rank with the other articles of daily food. The demand for it in all parts of the United States is increasing so rapidly that existing breweries are enlarged and improved, and new ones are springing up in every direction. In Appendices D, E and B will be found a list of breweries in the United States with the names of the proprietors and the product of each, together with the total product by States, as also the production *per capita* in the various countries of Europe, the total production in the same countries, and the number of breweries in each, and we trust that these tables will not only be of service to the trade and to students of this question, but also serve to give some prominence to the men who have done much for the advance of genuine temperance and who deserve a more substantial recognition than any it is in our power to give.

All this progress is a natural result of the actual benefits beer has bestowed on mankind, and these again follow logically and as might be expected from its constitution, con-

11

taining as it does a large portion of water from which all
organic impurities are eliminated, a certain quantity of nutritive malt extract and a very small percentage of pure
alcohol, obtained by fermentation and entirely free from the
injurious properties it acquires in distillation, together with
some of the carbonic acid gas so thoroughly approved by
consumers of soda water.    It offers to the public a beverage
at once healthy, nutritious, and mildly stimulating, and as
refreshing and exhilarating as tea, coffee or cocoa.

Those who travel know very well the injurious effect of a
change of water.    In no two districts are the waters alike,
and we could point to many instances where removal from
East to West or from North to South and the consequent
change of water has resulted in disastrous effects upon individuals.    Any inconvenience of this sort would be diminished or altogether avoided by means of a free use of beer.
Another similar advantage of beer is mentioned by Joseph
Coppinger in his work on brewing, called "The American
Practical Brewer, etc.," published in New York in 1815.
After recommending new ale as a preventive and yeast as
an antidote to malarial fever, he continues: "Brewing, in
every country, whose soil and climate are congenial to the
production of the raw materials, should be ranked among
the first objects of its domestic and political economy.    But
a still more important consideration is the health and morals
of our population, which appears to be essentially connected
with the progress of the brewing trade.    In proof of this
assertion, I will beg leave to state a well-known fact; which
is, that in proportion as the consumption of malt liquors
have increased in towns, in that proportion has the health of
our fellow-citizens improved, and epidemics and intermit-

JOSEPH SCHLITZ BREWING COMPANY

HENRY UHLEIN,
President.

ALFRED UHLEIN, Sup.t

AUG. UHLEI
Secretary.

MILWAUKEE

FOR HISTORICAL SKETCH, SEE APPENDIX C, PAGE 180.

tents become less frequent. In the country it is well known that those families who make frequent use of good beer during the summer, are in general healthy, and preserve their color ; whilst their less fortunate neighbors, who do not use beer at all, are devoured by fevers and intermittents. These facts will be less doubted when it is known that yeast, properly administered, has been found singularly successful in the cure of fevers." The views thus expressed more than sixty years ago have recently received much attention and are now advocated by many eminent authorities who hold that they are confirmed by both fact and theory.

The sum of the whole is that the beer brewing business has within a short time increased immensely—and strictly on the more general recognition of the merits of the product —and that there is every reason to anticipate at least an equal increase in the near future. Beer is already taking the place of ardent spirits and mixed drinks, and not long ago there appeared in the New York *Sun* the complaint of a bar-keeper who said in substance that the occupation of a skilled compounder of fancy drinks was gone, for anybody could draw beer and beer was what everybody wanted. Large gatherings now are more orderly than a few years ago and the reason is to be found in the general use of beer instead of whisky. At Coney Island the proprietors speak of the change as wonderful, and say that but for beer they could not get on, while now a disorderly occurrence is rare, no matter how great the throng. The same thing may be seen at the various races and in all such great assemblages of people who gather for enjoyment, and under the old regime were sure to become riotous.

# CHAPTER VIII.

## COMPARATIVE ADVANTAGES OF BEER OVER DISTILLED OR SPIRITUOUS LIQUORS.

The peculiar advantages of beer as a wholesome and re-freshing beverage, as compared with either ardent spirits or water have never been so clearly displayed as in the late war between France and Germany—and it may with truth be asserted, that it has triumphantly withstood the trial, and fully maintained its reputation.

The German military surgeons, in their official report to the Imperial medical board, bear witness to the superiority of beer over wine. They not only state that the refreshing quality of the carbonic acid gas contained in beer makes it especially grateful to men fatigued by a long march, or ex-hausted by a day's fighting, but lay still greater stress on its usefulness in the hospital and ambulance, and say that when it could be obtained it was administered with great success as a cordial, both to the wounded, and to convales-cent soldiers placed for the time under their care. They add the interesting fact, that throughout that campaign the wounded invariably evinced a great longing for beer and that when brought into hospital with shattered limbs or se-vere cuts or gun-shot wounds, their first request was usu-ally for a glass of beer. The same was true after severe operations, and the drink was found to compose and fortify their unstrung nerves. The natural inclination to beer as a restorative was very conspicuous among the soldiers who were on exposed outpost duty during the cold weather at the time of the blockade and siege of Paris. The supply was scanty, and common soldiers did not hesitate to pay army followers a large price for a glass containing only a few mouthfuls of beer. The report of the Director General of the medical staff of the Imperial army is in the same tone, and concludes with a strong recommendation not only to supply the soldiers with rations of beer instead of spirits when employed on active duty, but also to introduce it as the usual beverage of the army in time of peace and when on home service.

Professor Moleschott, the distinguished physiologist, in his work on the chemistry of food, treats of beer and makes the following statements: " The weak alcoholic solution called beer contains nearly the same proportion of albumen as is found in fruits, some sugar and gum, and another constituent which is composed of carbon, hydrogen and oxygen, is soluble in water and is called the bitter principle of hops. * * * Fermented liquors, particularly lager beer taken in moderation, increase the secretion of the digestive juices and promote the solution of the food, and further, a good lager beer partakes of all the advantages of the alcoholic beverages and at the same time quenches thirst by the large amount of water it contains. Hence lager beer is particularly adapted to satisfy the frequent thirst caused by physical exercise, and it is a laudable custom to refresh artisans who have to work hard, with a glass of this beverage. Its albumen, equal to that of fruit, even supplies a direct substitute for food."

To this we may add that a laborer who has repeatedly experienced its invigorating property will by no means admit the truth of the assertion that a half-pound loaf of

bread and a pint of water are more supporting than a pint
of beer. A glass of good beer may often be better than food
or physic. We do not always want food and we seldom
need physic, but a glass of beer is often a useful refreshment when the stomach is not prepared for the one and the
system has no need of the other. Excessive physical labor,
long endurance of hunger, or anything else which has a de-
bilitating influence, affects the appetite for solid food and
unfits the stomach for its reception. At such times beer
has an excellent effect, both in affording some present refreshment and in preparing the system for more substantial
food—and no such advantage can be found in the use of
water, and nothing like an equivalent in that of ardent
spirits. Richmond Sheen, an eminent authority, says:
" That beer is nutritive and salubrious cannot be doubted.
It proves a refreshing drink and an agreeable and valuable
stimulus and support to those who have to undergo much
bodily fatigue."

In cases of mental depression too, a glass of beer has
often the same good effect as food after physical exhaustion.
On this point Professor T. K. Chambers of New York very
justly says : " It is certain that the habitual use of some stimulant, particularly beer, bestows on a large class the nervous energy necessary to digest food enough to exist upon
and get through other vital functions. By this stimulus
they are enabled to be useful members of society instead of
the mere drones they must become during the rest of their
existence under a total abstinence regime."

The records of disease and the bills of mortality in beer-
drinking countries show longer lives and a less percentage
of sickness than prevail where malt liquors are replaced by

other beverages.*  Not only is this true but the social condition of the people is better in countries where beer is recognized and encouraged by government, and a very striking illustration of this truth may be found through a comparison of the state of Maine and the kingdom of Bavaria. Bavaria is the most noted beer-drinking country on the globe and Maine is distinctively known as the prohibitory state. The forms of government are radically different and an American naturally holds that the republican is superior to the monarchical, i. e., tends to promote the greater happiness of the individual. Let us see what can be learned about the matter, and first as to the terms of the comparison.

The advantages and disadvantages in the struggle for existence are about equal in amount though naturally different in character.  In Bavaria, society is old, habits strong, the fetters of trade not easily broken, untilled land scarce and the population dense.  In Maine there is abundance of new land, much timber yet unconsumed, no limits on a choice of occupation, a new society and a sparse population.  The state has a climate that stimulates to industry and the men pride themselves on their strength and energy.  In Bavaria few receive aid from the state or the municipality; while in Maine, the records in this respect are frightful.  Maine has in addition all the advantages that can be obtained by means of the most stringent prohibitory law ever devised, a law that, according to its advocates, must tend to secure peace, prosperity and happiness. Which of these countries should have most paupers, men

*The Germans are the healthiest class of New Yorkers. Statistics show that the mortality among them is nearly 38 per cent. less than that of other citizens, while their increase by births is larger, and the same is found to be generally true of Germans all over this continent.

who are unable to find their own living and are supported
at the cost of the state? As a matter of fact the number
in Bavaria is very small while the record of Maine is bad
not merely in comparison with the old monarchy but as set
against that of the United States at large. The last census
shows one pauper to every 171.65 of the population of
Maine, while the pauper rate of the whole country was
only one in 502.47.

Again, the condition of Bavaria is such as favors emigration to a large extent, yet her population, in spite of it, increased 4.5 per cent. during the last census decade while
that of Maine decreased .02 *per cent.* during the same time,
and *Maine was the only state in the Union where a decrease
occurred.* We have seen that in the original comparison
the *pros* and *cons* were pretty equally balanced. The difference is that Bavaria encourages the use of beer and
Maine prohibits it. It must not, however, be supposed that
the prohibitory law suppresses the sale of spirituous drinks.
On this point abundant evidence will be shortly presented,
and we need only say here that we know on the best authority that " no one need go without his whisky in Maine,
though a glass of beer is not to be had for love or money."
The reason is obvious, beer is bulky and difficult of con-
cealment while spirits can be easily hidden. In this connection notice that in the United States between 1860 and
1870 the production of beer rose from something more than
a million barrels to over eight million and that during the
same time the pauper rate decreased from one in 379.09 to
one in 502 47, a striking and very significant fact which
may well be commended to the attention of our legislators
and others interested in the connection between the pro-

verbial thrift of the German emigrant here and his indulgence in beer. The intellectual advance of the beer-drinking countries is so notorious as to need no special comment here.

At present a recapitulation of some characteristic national habits in the matter of drinking, things well known to every one who has given the subject attention, will serve both as a further illustration of the superiority of beer over other beverages and as a comment on what has been previously said of the modern history of beer-drinking in the more important civilized countries of the world.

The Scotchman drinks his "mountain dew," a strong whisky containing over 54 per cent. of alcohol,—and Scotland has long been noted for intemperance. The Russian grows sullen and sluggish over his vadka or kwass, containing 52.68 *per cent.* of alcohol, and drunkenness and crime follow as natural results. The volatile Italians and Spaniards drink their mild wines as freely as their mothers' milk and do not disgrace themselves or become a nuisance to others by beastly intoxication. Frenchmen were formerly to be placed in the same category but recent debates in the French Academy of medicine have developed the fact that in parts of France and in some Swiss cantons the powerful and seductive influence of brandy, absinthe and schnapps has diminished the consumption of wine and gone far to undermine the health and morals of the people. The excitable Irishman drinks eagerly and rapidly his strong whisky which contains more than 57 per cent. of pure alcohol and rouses all his combative qualities so that merry-making is almost sure to end in a fight, and trials of strength or skill which begin in good feeling end with broken heads and general tumult. The more sedate German drinks slowly, with much smoke and animated conversation, a beer which has only about four *per cent.* of alcohol. He imbibes great quantities and may become merry or dull according to the length of his potations, but he rarely if ever fights. The Englishman drinks much in a solid matter-of-fact way, but is learning to substitute beer for a great part of the stronger liquor he formerly consumed and becoming temperate in the same ratio. The American Republic, though chiefly British in its origin and therefore inheriting a taste for strong liquors, has become by immigration truly cosmopolitan, and is on the high road to temperance secured by a general use of fermented drinks. One great obstacle in the way is the wonderful variety of " fancy drinks," whose names catch the ear as surely as their ingredients tickle the palate. They entice young and old, seduce by their novelty or piquancy and carry many thousands on the straight road to drunkenness and its accompanying moral and physical wreck. The practice of " treating " is also very common and very injurious. It leads to a hasty and immoderate consumption that has little or no regard to the requirements of the individual and has by some been considered the real foundation stone of a habit of intemperance. The Rev. Henry Ward Beecher, in a recent address before the Business Men's Society of Brooklyn, favored " moderation in drinking and total abstinence from treating." He said he never drank beer until he was sixty years old, after which time he became fond of it, and evidently believed that its use is a means to temperance for the people. There are many who might say nearly the same thing. We are learning to appreciate malt drinks and the tendency is unmistakable, although it must be admitted that, on the whole, the disposition of the people is, as yet, more nearly like that of the Celt than the Tenton.

Mr. W. A. Lawrence of Waterville, N. Y., in a paper chiefly devoted to facts respecting the growth of hops, thus speaks of the general question—beer *versus* whisky: "The fact is that the quality of beer, as a light and refreshing drink, has been wonderfully improved within the past few years. A bottle of beer to-day has but about half the strength of the beer of twenty years ago, and half the strength of ordinary wine and cider. The beer of to-day is just what the American people want—a cool, mildly refreshing, stimulating and palatable drink. Wine is too expensive for a common drink. Cider is too sour and strong. Whisky is not a drink at all but a drug, and you have to take water after it as you do after taking other drugs, and it ought to be kept in a drug-store for sale and nowhere else. But beer is not only agreeable and refreshing and cheap, but it is mild, and generally peaceful and good-humored in its effects. It is true a man can get drunk on it, but a man won't. A hog may, but most beer-drinkers are not hogs, but hard-working men who know what they want and what fills the bill, and if they wanted to get drunk they would drink whisky and get a good deal bigger drunk at less expense and in half the time.

"The great majority of the beer-drinkers in America are these same hard-working men and women, who also drink beer with their food as we all do our tea and coffee. But in addition to these, who are mostly our German citizens, there are thousands of men, old Americans, who have learned to love beer, who will drink it as long as they live and will live the longer for drinking it. It is among the native Americans that the demand for beer and hops is increasing. The Germans always did drink for fifteen generations back, as much as they could hold, and in spite of all the theories of our anti-beer, total abstinence friends, the Germans in Germany and in this country seem to be still above ground; and so far as this country is concerned, as myself, an American citizen, and the son of American ancestry for five generations back, I wish to God we could trade off about two millions of native American whisky-drinkers now in the "solid South," for two millions of hard-working Germans who would do their own work, and drink their own beer, and keep clear of fights and strikes and riots and greenback conventions, as they keep clear of them here in the North to-day.

"Now everybody knows that whisky is full of the devil and that beer is full of humor and good fellowship; and it can hardly fail to rejoice the heart of every good hop-grower to find that in raising hops for beer he is incidentally engaged in the great "temperance movement" of leading men away from bad whisky to good beer. I know this is not what the professional temperance lecturers say, but what do I care what they say? A temperance lecturer is generally a retired whisky drinker and can see snakes in everything, including beer. Or he is a clergyman and has acquired the habit of talking with no one to contradict him and hence is careless of his facts. Or he is a paid professional, and knows that if war is made on whisky alone, whisky would soon be driven to the drug-store and no more temperance lecturers needed or paid for. I do not hesitate to affirm that I know more about beer by experience and contact and study than the whole crowd of temperance lecturers put together. They 'mean well' to be sure; and so do I. The difference between us lies in the fact that they don't know what they are talking about, and I do, because I am personally familiar with something like a thousand breweries in the United States and have peculiar advantages for information.

"And I am sick and tired of sitting in churches built by hops, whose clergymen's salaries are paid by hops, whose congregations live by hops, and that is by beer at first or second hand, and there listening to wholesale denunciations of beer, and even to cold-blooded, cold-water propositions to pass a general United States law making it illegal to manufacture beer anywhere in the country. One hop-grower who paid out over two thousand dollars to the poor women and children of one village last fall for picking hops, got up and left a church where some of this anti-beer nonsense was being aired, but as a general thing a man can talk against beer in a hop church with as little restraint as a missionary to Greenland feels in preaching hell-fire to his shivering congregation. The brewer is far away, and the connection between hops and beer is kept carefully out of sight. But to a carnal mind like mine it does seem a mean trick for a hop-grower to send out a hop-dealer with a flag of truce to the brewers and sell him hops in a friendly way, and meanwhile the hop-grower is lying in ambush behind a stack of hop-poles, ready as soon as his hops are sold to blaze away at the brewer with a prohibition bullet or ballot. I believe there are very few hop-growers who are capable of such meanness as this, but I do believe there are a great many who do not realize the close

connection between hops and beer, and to these I say respectfully, as I did two years ago in a prominent hop
paper, 'If you believe beer is a bad thing, plow up your
hop-yards and put in corn and potatoes. It is true that
somebody may turn the corn and potatoes into whisky, but
that is not your fault. Corn and potatoes must be had for
food. But there is no such excuse as this in the case of
hops. The hops are raised on purpose for beer. Not one
bale in a hundred is used for yeast or medicine. Therefore
you are the "outside man" of the brewery, and if beer is a
fraud you are a party to a fraud, and you are not an honest
man. We believe that the making of beer is an honest and
praiseworthy occupation, no better and no worse than any
other branch of manufacturing goods that are wanted
either for use or pleasure.'

"When I say we, I mean the men who believe in a radi-
cal distinction between fermented liquors and distilled.
Such men as Rev. Dr. Howard Crosby, and Dr. William A.
Hammond, formerly medical director of the United States
army, and Dr. Willard Parker, the leading practicing physician of New York, and a most earnest Christian man. Dr.
Parker says in the *Christian Union:* 'Fermented liquor is
the work of God; distilled liquor is the work of man or the
devil or both.' 'It is the still that does the harm. It is
the still that takes the alcohol out of its proper place in a
liquid where it is not ordinarily found in a larger proportion than six or seven per cent., and where it rarely intoxi-
cates, and never if taken in moderate quantities, and con-
centrates it in a substance that is a deadly poison. Take
away the still and we should have peace and plenty on
earth. We could then leave the vinous liquors alone. I

would compromise with all my heart on that ground, and I would go to work and preach just as old Solomon did: Don't use too much.' If with such men as Crosby and Hammond and Parker you believe beer should be distinguished from whisky, then go and raise your hops; pick them clean and get clean money. Take your glass of beer like an honest man when you feel it will do you good. Let it alone like an honest man when you think it will do you harm, just as you would a cup of coffee when you were bilious. Sign no pledges, nor encourage your children to sign them, except those against distilled liquors. Encourage no temperance movement that does not move in the right direction—against whisky and in favor of beer as a temperance drink; a drink that is killing out whisky faster than whisky killed Ireland, a drink that will build up the American constitution as it has built up the German."

We append tables showing the percentage of alcohol in a great variety of wines, spirits, malt and fermented liquors, according to analyses made by Brande, Gerhardt, Liebig, Prof. A. B. Prescott, Dr. Andrew Ure, William Ripley Nichols, professor at the Technological Institute of Massachusetts, and other chemists of well known reputation.

PORTUGUESE WINES.

| Port | contains 14.27 to 25,83 per cent. of alcohol. |
| Bucella | "       18.49            "    "    "    " |

SPANISH WINES.

| Sherry | contains 13.98 to 23.86 per cent. of alcohol. |
| Malaga | "       17.26 to 18.94 "    "    "    " |

MADEIRA AND CANARY ISLANDS.

| Madeira | contains 14 9   to 24.42 per cent. of alcohol. |
| Malmsey | "       12.86 to 16.40 "    "    "    " |

### FRENCH WINES.

| | | | |
|---|---|---|---|
| Claret | contains 12.91 to 17.11 | per cent. of alcohol. |
| Claret Chateau Latour | " 7.78 | " " " " |
| Claret Vin Ordinaire | " 8.99 | " " " " |
| Champagne | " 11.30 to 13.80 | " " " " |
| Burgundy | " 12.16 to 16.60 | " " " " |
| Hermitage | " 12.32 to 17.43 | " " " " |
| Sauterne | " 14.22 | " " " " |
| Frontignac | " 12.79 | " " " " |

### ITALIAN WINES.

| | | |
|---|---|---|
| Marsala | contains 18.20 to 26.03 | per cent. of alcohol. |
| Lacryma Christi | " 19.70 | " " " " |
| Falernian | " 18.99 | " " " " |

### CAPE WINES.

| | | |
|---|---|---|
| Cape Madeira | contains 18.11 to 22.94 | per cent. of alcohol. |
| Constantia | " 14.50 to 19.75 | " " " " |
| Muscat | " 18.25 | " " " " |

### PERSIAN WINE.

| | |
|---|---|
| Sheraaz | contains 12.95 to 19.80 per cent. of alcohol. |

### BRITISH WINES, CIDER, ETC.

| | | |
|---|---|---|
| Grape | contains 18.11 | per cent. of alcohol. |
| Raisin | " 23 30 to 26.40 | " " " " |
| Currant | " 20.55 | " " " " |
| Gooseberry | " 11.84 | " " " " |
| Orange | " 11.26 | " " " " |
| Elder | " 8.79 | " " " " |
| Mead | " 7.32 | " " " " |
| Cider | " 5.21 to 9.87 | " " " " |
| Perry | " 7.26 | " " " " |

### HUNGARIAN WINES.

| | | |
|---|---|---|
| Tokay | contains 9.88 | per cent. of alcohol. |
| Red Wine | " 13.20 to 19.04 | " " " " |
| White Wine | " 12.10 to 12.16 | " " " " |

### GERMAN WINES.

| | | | |
|---|---|---|---|
| Hochheimer | contains | 8.88 to 14.37 | per cent. of alcohol. |
| Johannisberger | " | 8.71 | " " " " |
| Rüdesheimer | " | 6.90 to 12.22 | " " " " |
| Rhenish Wine | " | 7.00 to 7.58 | " " " " |

### OHIO WINES,

According to analyses received from Messrs. Parisette Bro's, N. Y., and made five times within

six months,        contain   6.11 to 11.30 per cent. of alcohol.

### CALIFORNIA WINES.

| | | | |
|---|---|---|---|
| White and Red, dry, | contains | 8.40 to 12.90 | per cent of alcohol. |
| Sweet Wines | " | 6.20 to 13.80 | " " " " |

### SPIRITUOUS LIQUORS.

| | | | |
|---|---|---|---|
| Irish Whisky | contains | 53.90 | per cent. of alcohol. |
| Scotch Whisky | " | 54.52 | " " " " |
| Holland Gin | " | 53.80 | " " " " |
| French Brandy | " | 53.40 | " " " " |
| St. Croix Rum | " | 53.68 | " " " " |
| Batavian Arrack | " | 53.70 | " " " " |
| Russian Vadka or Kwass | " | 52.68 | " " " " |
| Ordinary American Whisky contains | | 52.60 | " " " " |
| Bourbon Whisky contains | | 51.00 | " " " " |
| Whisky with much foreign matter contains | | 44.50 | " " " " |

### ENGLISH MALT LIQUORS.

| | | | |
|---|---|---|---|
| Ale—Burton | contains | 8.88 | per cent. of alcohol. |
| " Edinburgh | " | 6.22 | " " " " |
| " London | " | 6.20 | " " " " |
| Brown Stout | " | 6.80 | " " " " |
| London Porter | " | 4.80 | " " " " |
| London Small Beer | " | 2.56 | " " " " |
| Edinburgh Beer | " | 5.36 to 7.35 | " " " " |

13

### GERMAN BEER.

| | | | |
|---|---|---|---|
| Bavarian Augustiner | contains | 3.40 to 6.80 | per cent. of alcohol. |
| Salvator | " | 4.02 to 4.20 | " " " " |
| Vienna | " | 4.20 to 5.60 | " " " " |
| Berlin Tivoli | " | 4.60 | " " " " |
| Berlin Tivoli Export | " | 5.40 | " " " " |
| Copenhagen | " | 5.04 | " " " " |

### AMERICAN MALT LIQUORS AND CIDER.

| | | | |
|---|---|---|---|
| New York Porter | contains | 6.20 to 8.40 | per cent. of alcohol. |
| New York Ale | " | 5.40 to 6.90 | " " " " |
| Albany Ale | " | 5.40 to 6.20 | " " " " |
| Lager Beer | " | 3.06 to 6.50 | " " " " |
| American Cider | " | 5.80 to 11.60 | " " " " |

Two analyses of beer brewed in the celebrated Brauerei Koenigstadt, of Berlin, were found to give the following results:

| | |
|---|---|
| Alcohol | 4.501 per cent. by weight. |
| Saccharine | 1.893 " " " " |
| Dextrine | 0.861 " " " " |
| Albuminoids | 0.630 " " " " |
| Hop-bitter, extractive and saline matter | 2.296 " " " " |
| Acid | 0 005 " " " " |

Unfermented extract 5.680 per cent.

The second analysis was of dark colored beer, and was as follows:

| | |
|---|---|
| Alcohol | 4.250 per cent. by weight. |
| Saccharine | 1.950 " " " " |
| Dextrine | 1.053 " " " " |
| Albuminoids | 0.621 " " " " |
| Hop-bitter, extractive and saline matter | 3.386 " " " " |
| Acids | 0.005 " " " " |

Unfermented extract 7.010 per cent.

Good lager beer properly brewed and fermented, and stored for some time, should contain in one hundred parts, 90 water, 5.6 malt extract, 3.50 alcohol, and the remainder carbonic acid.

The following analyses show more particularly the percentage of extract and of alcohol contained in the best known varieties of lager beer of this country:

| | EXTRACT. | ALCOHOL. |
|---|---|---|
| New York, | 3.6 per cent. | 4.8 per cent. |
| "    " | 3.7 "    " | 4 4 "    " |
| "    " | 4.2 "    " | 5.3 "    " |
| Staten Island, | 3.2 "    " | 5.9 "    " |
| Milwaukee, | 4.3 "    " | 5.6 "    " |
| Newark, | 4.2 "    " | 5.6 "    " |
| Philadelphia, | 4.2 "    " | 6.0 "    " |
| Chicago, | 3.9 "    " | 5.2 "    " |
| Cincinnati. | 3.4 "    " | 5.5 "    " |
| Boston, | 3.6 "    " | 5.6 to 6.0 "    " |
| Hartford, | 3.6 "    " | 4.9 "    " |

A similar table made after results obtained by C. F. Chandler and embracing several kinds of ales and lager beers reads as follows:

| | PERCENTAGE. | | CONTENTS PER IMPERIAL PINT. | |
|---|---|---|---|---|
| | ALCOHOL. | EXTRACT. | OUNCES OF ALCOHOL. | OUNCES OF EXTRACT. |
| Allsop's Burton Ale | 8.25 | 13.32 | 2.16 | 2.77 |
| Bass's Ale | 8.41 | 11.75 | 2.18 | 2.42 |
| Edinburgh Ale | 4.41 | 3 58 | 1 12 | .72 |
| Guinness Stout | 6.81 | 6.17 | 1.74 | 1.25 |
| Munich Lager Beer | 4.70 | 6.10 | 1.19 | 1.22 |
| Munich Schenck Beer | 3.90 | 5.07 | 1.00 | 1.16 |
| Munich Bock Beer | 4.60 | 9.02 | 1.17 | 1.90 |
| New York Lager Beer | 5.86 | 4.32 | 1.48 | .88 |

In this table the term extract includes all the substances left when the alcohol and water are removed by evaporation.

In view of the figures above given and of the fact that the lighter beers form the bulk of the malt liquor consumed in the country, we are safe in assuming an average alcoholic strength of not more than 5½ per cent. for the total product. This product we have already seen to be 9,473,-361 barrels, which, on the basis just assumed, yields 521,-034 barrels or 16,673,088 gallons of alcohol. Now according to statistics from the department at Washington the consumption of native spirits was in 1878 over 70,000,000 gallons containing about 37,000,000 gallons of alcohol. The cost of the native and foreign ardent spirits, wines and liquors used in one year reaches $500,000,000, and it is among the drinkers of spirits that we find most of the pauperism and crime of the country. Those who drink beer use something that as far as alcohol is concerned is more expensive than distilled liquors and yet spend less than $120,000,000, as against the $500,000,000 above mentioned. It should be noticed that while rum, gin, brandy, whisky, etc., contain over 50 per cent. of alcohol, ales never reach nine per cent., and lager beer seldom reaches six per cent. and is often below four.

An examination of these tables taken in connection with the other facts mentioned should be sufficient to give a general idea of the nature and extent of the claims to be made in favor of beer as a common beverage. Others will come to light in the course of our discussion, and particularly in the chapter entitled, "What Authorities Say," in which are embodied the conclusions of some of the most noted scientific investigators of our time.

# CHAPTER IX.

## BEER BREWING A BENEFIT TO FARMERS.

Thus far we have been chiefly occupied with the sanitary and social advantages that attend the general use of beer in a community, but there is another phase of the question that is worth careful attention. Barley and hops are the foundation of beer and we propose to show in this chapter some of the benefits that attend their cultivation for brewing purposes and which are by no means confined to the cash price received from the brewer. They can be raised to good advantage when there is no such home consumption, but the real possibilities of these crops are only attained when there are breweries near at hand. How this is true will be understood after an examination of the following statistics.

The cultivation of hops is in itself a more important industry than is generally supposed, but for the purpose of this chapter it is of so much less consequence than that of barley that it may be dismissed in very few words. A few years ago our own production was not sufficient to supply the brewers, and in 1872 we paid in round numbers $785,525.00 to foreign growers. The next year the import was $1,310,627.00 and in 1874 reached $1,303,686.00. Since that time the tide has turned and each of the past four years has shown an export to a considerable amount, the figures taken in the order of the years being as follows : 1875, $1,286,500.00; 1876, $1,348,521.00; 1877, $2,305,-355.00; 1878, $2,152,873.00. The yearly consumption in this country is about 30,000,000 pounds, which after having served their purpose in the brewery, furnish an excellent manure, especially for potatoes.

According to the last report of the United States Commissioner of Agriculture, there were in 1877, no less than 1,614,654 acres under cultivation with barley, and the product was 34,441,400 bushels at an average value of 70 cents a bushel, making a total value of $24,028,644.00 for the crop. The average yield to the acre was 21.3 bushels, and the average value to the acre $14.91, as against $10.72 for hay, $9.54 for corn, $9.25 for oats, $8.87 for rye and $15.08 for wheat. Only three crops, potatoes, tobacco and wheat yielded a higher value to the acre, and only six, wheat, corn, potatoes, oats, hay and cotton had a greater total value. Again, the northern latitudes produce the best barley and accordingly we find that in the six Eastern States, the average value to the bushel was a little over 78 cents. In these states the number of acres under cultivation was only 51,065, the product 986,900 bushels, the average value to the acre $15.11, being more than that of any other crop except potatoes. Notwithstanding all this, we do not even now raise enough for home consumption. The import of barley in 1877 was no less than 10,285,957 bushels at a value of $7,887,886.00 on which a duty of 20 cents per bushel was paid by the consumer, in addition to charges for freight and commission, all of which could and should have been saved to our people. Nearly eight million dollars is too large a sum to neglect when it lies at our very hand.

We have said that high latitudes are favorable to barley. It is chiefly grown in the northern tier of states and in

ISRAEL PUTNAM,

*The great American General, Brewer and Tavern Keeper
at Brooklyn, Conn.  (1718–1790.)*
*See Page 27.*

Canada, and a state like Maine for instance would find immense advantage in an enlarged production of this crop
even under existing conditions.  But suppose the restriction on brewing were removed, that instead of being
crushed out by local law it were encouraged and fostered.
It is not easy to compute the material assistance such a
course would be to the farming community and the state
at large, and yet the direct gain would be small in comparison with the incidental advantages.  For the proper illustration of this point we must ask the reader to follow and
keep in mind two separate series of facts which we are
about to present.  The first statistical and relating to the
" refuse " of brewing establishments, and the second
general.

The breweries of the United States use annually about
30,000,000 bushels of malt, which yields, according to A.
Schwarz of New York, 2½ per cent. or 750,000 bushels of
" sprouts."  Now in estimating the comparative value of
different kinds of fodder according to the albumen contained it is usual to take hay as the basis of comparison.
Air-dried meadow hay contains 7 per cent. of albumen.
" Sprouts " contain from 24 to 30 per cent., so that a hundred bushels of sprouts, weighing 1,200 pounds, are equal
in value to 4,628 pounds of hay, and the annual product of
sprouts as above stated to 34,710,000 pounds of hay.  This
same 30,000,000 bushels of malt yields at least 35,000,000
bushels of " grains," having a weight of 1,520,000,000
pounds, and from 4 to 5 per cent. of albumen.  Taking 4½
per cent. as the average, 100 pounds of grains have the
same nutritive value as 64 pounds of hay and the value of
the product reaches that of 973,241,000 pounds of hay.  It

is a proved fact that cattle fed on grains give better milk than when any other fodder is used and this fact is specially appreciated in New York and New Jersey, where the grains and sprouts are largely used with most excellent results. These products must by no means be confounded with the "slops" from distilleries, which is utterly different in character—*as indeed every product of the still seems to be tainted with some portion of the curse that has always clung to spirituous liquors.*

The second and general consideration is this: The past agricultural history of New England shows a succession of specialties, each running its course until the advent of another which existing circumstances made more profitable. The first was grain (except barley), then came wool, and then potatoes, while the last and most promising is dairy farming. It is yet in its infancy but it is already important. One thing is sure, that farming on the old-fashioned plan has seen its day in New England. The natural advantages of the West enable it to raise and deliver many crops cheaper than they can be grown in the older part of the country, and under the influence of this competition Eastern farmers have grown poorer and poorer unless they have taken up a specialty or possessed some unusual natural advantages. We submit that the combination of dairy farming with the growth of barley will, even under the existing laws, prove very remunerative. The facts already adduced point directly to this conclusion. The figures show that barley is a profitable crop and that northern New England is well adapted to its growth. Moreover it thrives on a comparatively poor soil while most of the other natural products that rank high in value involve a large expense for manure, and in many cases a great deal of hand labor. Dairy farms are known to pay well. What then will be the result of combining the two industries as above indicated on terms favorable to both? But this can only be successfully done by the establishment of breweries, and sooner or later the people will understand all these facts and act accordingly. *Remove the laws that now make brewing impossible, and a new industry will spring up as if by magic*—we might well say three new industries—for barley culture and dairies will grow to keep pace with the demands and the grants of brewing. For it must be remembered that brewing is not like some other forms of manufacture. What it takes with one hand it gives with the other. It receives the farmer's grain and pays him a good price ; it gives him valuable fodder and manure for a sum that is small in proportion to the benefit conferred. It helps put in motion the wheels of another separate business, the manufacture of cheese and butter, and it is again the agricultural community who profit by the development.

*Living in an age of progress we must recognize the fact and adapt ourselves to it or we shall inevitably fall behind, and we do not believe that the men of New England will long close their eyes to the advantages offered by such a course as has been indicated. The change must come, and sooner or later, a part of the change must be the resolute and successful demand for a repeal of the laws that choke industry. Maine men in especial have everything to gain. Their business is stagnant, their population decreasing, poverty staring them in the face and enforced idleness eating like a canker into their very nature. They have it in their power to change all*

14

*this, to become rich, revive trade, make the state famous for progressive energy, and banish the intemperance that now accompanies and aggravates all their other ills and is accompanied by the other corrupting evils that, as experience shows, always spring up in the shadow of a prohibitory law.* The matter well deserves more space than we can give, but we have presented the leading facts and must leave them for the examination and mature reflection of all who are interested. Great things have been expected of beet-root culture in Maine and other states, and we cannot close this chapter without a word in reference to this topic. The Commissioner of Agriculture, in the prefatory remarks to his last Report, says : " The effort to produce a sugar beet, and the belief and expectation of many that the beet would be made to yield in this country as in Germany and France, of good quality, in sufficient abundance, and at a sufficiently low cost, to make it pay has not been realized —although no pains and money have been spared to insure success." The difficulty is that the sugar beet will not thrive on poor or exhausted soil, unless it is heavily manured. Such has been the constant experience in those places where the experiment has received most attention, *viz.*, Chatsworth, Ill., Sauk county, Wis., and some parts of the state of Maine.* New England is unfit for beet-root culture, partly by nature and partly by the exhaustion of the soil, while on the other hand it is as we have said eminently adapted to barley. Even had the expectations of the more reasonable part of the beet-growers of Maine been

---

*The state of Maine is assisting the experiment with beet-root by granting a premium of one cent a pound on all beet-root sugar produced in the state, but even with this help the industry has failed to establish itself to any considerable extent.

realized, the material advantages to the people would not have compared with those to be attained by the encouragement of breweries, the growth of barley and hops and the establishment of dairies.   All these things go together and stimulate other branches of industry.   There will be more demand for other crops, particularly hay and oats, and for lumber for vats, barrels, tubs and building purposes.   A busy temperate people must thrive *and we have shown what will make them busy and temperate.*

# CHAPTER X.

We have now reached a point at which we may properly recur to a topic already suggested and inquire a little more carefully into the actual working of the prohibitory laws. On this head we shall confine ourselves chiefly to the testimony of men who have made the matter a thorough study, and that not at a distance, but in the very midst of the operation of such laws, and as Maine is the state which led the way in the prohibitory movement and has since followed that course with most persistency, it is proper that it should occupy most of our attention during the inquiry.

Not long ago a number of the most prominent men of the state, men of different political parties, wholly above reproach, and especially fitted by official position or private observation to form a just opinion in the premises, became so well convinced of the evils of the present system, and its detrimental effect on the people, as to unite in an effort for its amendment. Their movement took form in the presentation by Mr. Fox of Portland, a lawyer of high reputation and a member of the Legislature, of the following proposed Act:

"*State of Maine*, 1879.

"An Act in relation to Cider, Native Wines, Ale, Porter, Lager Beer and Malt Liquors.

"Be it enacted by the Senate and House of Representatives in Legislature assembled, as follows:

" Cider, Native Wine, Ale, Porter, Lager Beer and other Malt
Liquors, when pure and unadulterated, shall not be considered
intoxicating liquors within the meaning of the laws of this
State."

The bill was referred to the Committee on Temperance
and able arguments in its favor were made by Gen. Gorham, L. Boynton, Hon. Nathan Webb and C. G. Yeaton,
all men highly respected by the people of the state, of the
strictest integrity, and with no inducement to make other
than an impartial statement.    Three gentlemen who have
successively held the office of county attorney of Cumberland county for about fifteen years past and who are all
Republicans, have unanimously testified against the present prohibition law.    They are Gen. Chas. T. Matlock, C.
F. Libby, Esq., and Nathan Webb.    Similar views are
held by such men as Gen. W. S. Tilton of Logan Springs,
Judge Goddard, postmaster of Portland, M. P. Frank of
Portland, Speaker of the House, Dr. Edw. Dana and many
other influential citizens.    No party, however, was willing
to go to the people on this issue and the bill failed to pass,
although there is good reason to hope that when the next
attempt is made some who have previously upheld the
present law will have learned to take a different view.
Much new light is constantly thrown on the influence of
the present statute, and can hardly fail to produce an ade-
quate effect.    A minority report of the committee was presented and contains so much of interest and importance
that we cannot do better than to reproduce it in these
pages.    Its statements are those of men who understand
the subject of which they treat and are worth a careful
reading.

REPORT OF THE COMMITTEE ON TEMPERANCE, OF THE
FIFTY-EIGHTH LEGISLATURE OF MAINE, 1879.

" The Committee on Temperance have listened to the
able and exhaustive arguments presented on both sides of
the matter in hearing, and the minority of said committee
respectfully present their views in dissent from the report
of the majority.    The law regulating the sale of intoxicating
liquors, commonly known as the prohibitory liquor law has
had a trial of more than a quarter of a century.    Its severity
has no parallel in the laws of any other civilized country.
Although enforced with all the power of the state, court
records show that the number of prosecutions and convictions is increasing, at great expense to the tax payers.
Country towns pay their share for the enforcement of this
law in cities without corresponding benefit to themselves.
The cost of its execution is a burden on an over-taxed
people.    A detailed statement which is hereto annexed
shows the cost for officers to enforce the law."

The details are here omitted but " the total reaches the
enormous amount of $220,000.    The records of the Insane
Hospital show a gradual increase of patients caused by excessive use of intoxicating liquors.    At the present time
that institution has nearly double the number of inmates
from that cause alone, which it had when the present prohibitory law was enacted.    While the law, with singular
inconsistency, does not recognize pure and beneficial kinds
of intoxicating liquors as property when intended for sale
by other than city or town agencies, and makes no distinction between the sale of adulterated liquors and pure
liquors, it authorizes their indiscriminate sale in numerous
city and town agencies.    Liquor-drinking is not done

openly to so great an extent but the consumption is as
large. It is notorious that quantities of strong liquors have
for years been transported into the state from the Provinces, and especially from Massachusetts, which has
drained us of millions of dollars which might have been
kept at home under liberal laws. Liquor runners from
New York and Boston penetrate every nook and corner of
our state to rob our people and eat out their substance.
Liquors are also imported in bond, and under the protection
of the Federal Government they cannot be seized in bulk.
They are consumed in families and in club-rooms which have
been organized in large towns and cities, under that most
dangerous guise of social drinking. The liquor agencies
authorized by law have vended in some years more than a
hundred thousand dollars worth of liquors for medicinal,
mechanical and manufacturing purposes only, as is supposed. We consider these liquor agencies as leeches upon
the people. The question is whether a law, the severity of
which is without example, having failed to accomplish the
ends for which it was designed, according to experience
and the testimony of officials serving under it, who with
singular unanimity give their verdict against it, ought to be
so amended that cider, native wines, ale, porter and particularly lager beer, shall not be considered within the
meaning of the statute.

"History shows that every nation has its peculiar stimulants in stronger or milder forms. Men crave stimulant.
It is an undeniable fact, both in the light of history and experience, that in countries like Germany, France, etc.,
whose climate is not unlike ours, drunkenness is known
scarcely more than the strong liquors which cause it.

Cheap light wines and nutritious malt beverages supersede strong drink. Everybody uses them at his meals and as a common beverage. The people of those countries are among the healthiest, happiest, most prosperous and temperate on the face of the globe. We appeal to the wisdom of this Legislature and the consideration of the people whether it would not promote the cause of temperance and the material welfare of our state to give the amendment proposed a fair trial. It would tend to promote harmony by removing an irritating and festering sore from our politics. Good citizens without distinctions of party view with alarm the inroads that this law in its operation is working upon our social and material interest, driving away business, depreciating real estate, shackling enterprise, cheating labor, increasing taxes, educating intolerance and hypocrisy, influencing elections and encouraging bribery and perjury and the clandestine compounding, sale and use of poisonous liquors."

Darius H. Ingraham of Portland.
Gorham L. Boynton of Bangor.
F. B. Farrel of Van Buren.
Arthur Moore of Machiasport.

    This is the statement of men whose characters stand so high as to give great weight to their opinion and leave nothing to be objected to their statement of fact.

    Again, Governor Garcelon is not a man to make hasty or unfounded statements in an important matter and he has been for many years an eminent physician of large practice and a close observer of the habits of the people. But read this summary of an address delivered by him be-

fore the Maine temperance convention : " He called attention to various kinds of intemperance, which have generally escaped the notice of reformers in that state.   He
spoke of the use of tobacco as an increasing evil, especially
among the young, and said that in addition to chewing and
smoking, snuff-dipping was becoming prevalent, a fact of
which many are ignorant and which excites surprise.   The
use of opiates, Governor Garcelon remarked, had increased
to an alarming extent.   Many a man, he said, had appeared upon the stand advocating temperance, who had in
his pocket a bottle of laudanum or black drops, which pave
the way to an early grave.   The ladies carry chloroform
and ether to moisten the handkerchief with which to allay
nervous excitement.   As a practicing physician and ob-
server of human nature, he placed all these forms of intemperance in the same category with the intemperate use of
spirituous liquors, all of which demand correction.   Is the
change from the intoxicating liquors to opium an improvement ?   Governor Garcelon has, undoubtedly, done the
people a timely service by directing attention to this and
other evils, and if followed up it will be found that the
' Maine Law ' has not been the grand instrument of reform which it is claimed to be."

At a convention held at Bangor, Me., July 1, 1879, a
resolution in favor of local option was presented by Mr.
Charles F. Swett, a considerable part of whose speech is
here reproduced, as it deals in facts of great importance to
the present discussion :

"In supporting this measure, I wish to distinctly define
my position.   I am a practical temperance man ; a total
abstainer.   I have belonged, and do now belong, to every

15

temperance organization in the state of Maine, except the Reform Club. I have had much experience in endeavoring to 'reclaim the fallen and save others from falling,' and I therefore claim to be as conversant with the practical workings of our prohibitory law as any man in this hall, and I declare, from my experience, that that law, so far as it contributes to lessening the evils of intemperance, is a complete failure, and a costly one to the people of this state. * * * In Cumberland county there are four deputy sheriffs, whose business it is to enforce the liquor law. These men get from $7,000 to $9,000 per year for their services. Of course they never reform a drunkard, but they can afford to contribute $3,000 a year towards the campaign fund—and they do—and the people furnish the money. Every liquor-seller thrown into jail for sixty days pays the high sheriff a profit of $1.50 per week. When there is an average of say fifty of these cases his profits will be $4,000 per year, from this source alone. The people furnish the money, and the sheriff 'comes down handsomely' for the campaign fund. True, there are no men reformed, but the party gets the 'sinews of war.' And so it is all over the state.

"The cost of the execution of the prohibitory law is a burden upon our over-taxed people. The report of the temperance committee of our last Legislature showed that although the 'law was enforced with all the power of the state,' court records prove that the number of prosecutions is annually increasing, at great expense to the tax-payers. From June 1, 1877, to June 1, 1878, the cost of enforcing the prohibitory law, in Cumberland county alone, reached $28,000. In the same ratio, applied to the population of the whole state, the cost reaches the enormous sum of $220,000, annually. But we would not complain of the expenditure even of this vast sum if the results were, in any degree satisfactory. But they are not. The advocates of the Maine law make bold claims, but their claims are not substantiated by the facts. Outside of Maine, and even in the back towns of this state, remote from the cities, people are given to understand that liquor is not sold in Maine, and therefore there is less crime here than formerly. Neal Dow says, 'We have little crime here because we have banished its cause.' Let us look at the facts. In 1851, there were 87 convicts in the state prison. We had then a population of 584,000, while to-day it is probably 625,000. Last year's state prison report shows the number of convicts to be 206, while 69 more were serving in jail work-shops. So the number of convicts has increased, *under the prohibitory law*, over threefold, while our population has remained comparatively the same. Does that speak well for prohibition? Now, take the city of Portland. In 1856, there were 650 arrests for drunkenness, in a population of 27,000. In 1876, twenty years later, with a population of about 30,000, there were 1800 arrests for drunkenness, and in no year of the last eight has the list fallen below 1,200. And this under a vigorous enforcement of the prohibitory law. Does that speak well for prohibition? During last week, over 200 barrels of liquor were brought into Portland, by the various railroads and steamboats, *for home consumption*. Does that speak well for prohibition?

The secret drinking in club-rooms in Portland is three-fold that which formerly took place at open bars, while the

traffic outside has been driven into worse and worse hands
every year, until it has, with a few exceptions, been taken
away from respectable men, whose interest it would be to
conduct it with some show of decency, and given into the
undivided management and control of the low and criminal,
so that while 'the law is enforced with all the power of
the state,' the upper classes get drunk at the club-rooms,
and the lower classes get drunk at the shops in the slums.
Does that speak well for prohibition?  The vilest liquors
possible to make are manufactured for the market in this
state, and even our state liquor agent could not, or did not,
*keep pure* liquors even for medicinal purposes.

"Private club-rooms have multiplied in Portland, under
the operation of the prohibitory law, (there being over 80
in that city at the present time,) and our young men just
starting out in life are exposed to all the dangers of the
drunkard's life, and no law can stop them.  In these club-
rooms, boys who would never go to saloons to get drunk,
who would never learn to gamble were it not for their
club-room temptations, who would, in short, grow up honest and respected citizens, are being ruined every day.
This evil ought to be remedied by prompt and decisive
action.  Fathers who love their sons; mothers who pray
for their boys; sisters who mourn over their disgraced
brothers; wives who weep over the wreck of what
were once good men and true husbands; citizens who
care for the good name and prosperity of their commu-
nities, ought to labor to shut these accursed gates of hell!
Let us commence the good work by striving to repeal
the prohibitory law, which is a positive detriment to the
cause of temperance, an incubus upon the mercantile

interests of Maine, and a curse to the young men of our cities."

In Massachusetts we have very important testimony to the same effect, a part of which is very ably and carefully summarized in an article which we insert here, retaining for convenience a portion at the beginning which might equally well be placed under a different heading:

"The state Board of Health of Massachusetts, in the Tenth Annual Report, published in January, 1879, say, under the head of 'Intemperance': 'A more severe public judgment of drunkenness, in recent times, has undoubtedly tended to very much decrease its prevalence; and it is generally believed that light German beer is used more and more each year, at least in our state, to the exclusion of stronger liquors - *a change which it is of course desirable to hasten by legislation, so far as that can be done, either by removal of restrictions on the sale of mild liquors, and heavily taxing the stronger spirits, or by any other just and proper means.*' This is the reiterated public expression of men to whom the state of Massachusetts has committed the general care for the health of her people. For the former public utterance of this opinion the chairman of the Board, for years past, has been most bitterly assailed by prohibitionists; but, undaunted by these intemperate and abusive attacks, the state Board of Health confirm the statement of their honest conviction by repeating the same, and embodying it in an important public document.

"In harmony with this public expression of opinion by the state Board of Health, appears the action of the Committee on License of the Board of Aldermen of the city of Boston. In their report of September, 1878, to the City

Council, this committee say : 'It may be objected that the committee have been too liberal in their recommendations of the issue of licenses, but their experience has convinced them that the "lunch rooms," established chiefly for the sale of lager beer and edible refreshments, ought to be regarded as victualing saloons, even if facilities are not maintained for regular meals, and no cooking is done on the premises. The committee feel satisfied that the consumption of lager beer, now so general, tends, in fact, to exclude from sale and use more ardent spirits, and thereby diminishes crime and pauperism. It is well known that in the old countries, where beer and light wines are accessible, without restraint, at a small expense, and are freely used by all classes of people, cases of intoxication are very rare. The committee are confident that drunkenness, and consequently pauperism and crime, will be diminished in this state, if no restrictions were placed on the sale of lager beer, for it then could be provided at such a low price as to effectually supersede the use of strong liquors. They therefore submit for the consideration of the City Council the following order :

"' *Ordered*, That his Honor the Mayor be requested to petition the next Legislature for such amendment of chaptar 99 of the statutes of 1875 as will allow the sale of cider and lager beer without any license being required therefor.'

"It must be admitted, that in the state of Massachusetts, the liquor question has been as fully discussed, and the various legal expedients connected therewith have had as fair and full a trial as in any other state in the Union. It may therefore be claimed, without presumption, that to the results there attained, and the opinions there formed, when coming from official and authentic sources, the careful consideration of other state governments should be given. Acting from this view, we draw the attention of the reader to a very instructive report of the results of an investigation relative to drunkenness and liquor-selling under prohibition and license legislation contained in the Tenth Annual Report of the Massachusetts Bureau of Statistics of Labor, issued as a public document in January, 1879. This investigation was undertaken at the special request of Governor Rice, whose object was to place on record a statement, as a basis for an intelligent consideration of the question, of as reliable a character as could be secured by impartial statistics. These statistics are drawn from official sources, and, as far as the figures are concerned, are thoroughly reliable.

" The years 1874 and 1877 were selected for comparison, because 1874 represented the last full year under the operation of the prohibitory law, and 1877 the last full year under the license law. The advantages resulting from this selection of years, if any, are on the side of the prohibitory law, because that law, in 1874, had been in operation for a number of years, while the license law, in 1877, had only been in force a year and a half.

" Four circulars were prepared and addressed by the chief of the state Bureau of Statistics and Labor to town clerks, city clerks, chiefs of police, to standing justices, clerks of district, municipal and police courts, and trial justices. These circulars solicited information regarding the sales of liquor, prosecutions therefor, and arrests and convictions for drunkenness for the prohibitory year 1874 and the license year 1877. The completeness of the investigation may be seen from the following statement:

" Circular ' A ' was sent to 325 Town Clerks ; 322 answered.

" Circular ' B ' was sent to 19 City Clerks; 19 answered.

" Circular ' C ' was sent to 19 Chiefs of Police; 19 answered.

" Circular ' D ' was sent to 132 Court and Trial Justices; 130 answered.

" This is a total of 490 returns of 495 circulars of inquiry sent out. There can be no question that the investigation was exhaustive, for the few towns which did not answer are unimportant places. From the information thus obtained and tabulated in detail in the Report, the following totals are derived :

### ARRESTS FOR DRUNKENNESS.

| | |
|---|---|
| Under the prohibitory law, 1874, | 28,044 |
| Under the license law, 1877, | 20,657 |

### CONVICTIONS FOR DRUNKENNESS.

| | |
|---|---|
| Under the prohibitory law, 1874, | 23,981 |
| Under the license law, 1877, | 17,862 |

### NUMBER OF PLACES WHERE LIQUOR WAS ILLEGALLY SOLD.

| | |
|---|---|
| Under the prohibitory law, 1874, | 5,609 |

### NUMBER OF PLACES LICENSED TO SELL LIQUOR.

| | |
|---|---|
| Under the license law, 1877, | 5,273 |

### JUDGMENTS ON COMPLAINTS FOR ILLEGAL SALES.

| | |
|---|---|
| Under the prohibitory law, 1874, | 3,644 |
| Under the license law, 1877, | 1,693 |

" It will thus be seen that the number of arrests for drunkenness under the operation of the license law, during the year 1877, as compared to the prohibitory year 1874, shows a decrease of fully twenty-five per cent. In the number of convictions for drunkenness the difference in favor of the license year is at the same rate. The number of places where liquor was *illegally* sold under the prohibitory law of 1874, was larger by 336 than the number of places *licensed* in 1877. It is evident from these returns that the prohibitory law has failed to prohibit, or even to regulate, the sale of liquor, while it is equally apparent that the license law, as a legislative measure, not only regulates the sale of liquor, but decreases drunkenness.

" A law, to be effective, must have the support of the people ; the prohibitory law will never be thus supported, as common sense will teach that it is neither just nor judicious, to make somebody else than the drunkard himself responsible for his failing; and is not just this the questionable theory upon which prohibition is based ?

" The prohibitionists condemn the use of alcoholic beverages of every kind, as the prolific source of sin and vice. Nothing less than total abstinence finds favor with them. To them, the terms use and abuse have no distinctive meaning, and their curse falls upon brewery and distillery alike. It must be admitted that as long as alcoholic stimulants are used, intemperance will exist, and that the evil of drunkenness will only disappear with their total suppression. In view of the actual state of social habits, and the position which alcoholic beverages hold in civilized life, as now constituted, no sane person will believe such a total suppression possible. There are no means by which a

16

habit, transmitted from generation to generation, and forming so important an element in the development of the civilization of the human race, can be uprooted.  Alcoholic
stimulants once invented are never again abandoned, and
seem to be destined to co-exist with man.  The deplora-
ble vice of drunkenness has always accompanied their use,
and all attempts of rulers and philanthropists, the severest
penalties and the sincerest compassion, have alike failed to
suppress the evil.  But it does not follow that, because the
temptation of excessive use is too strong for some to be re-
sisted, the great mass of people, who can and do use these
beverages in moderation, should be made responsible for
the weakness of the few.  Nor does it follow that the in-
tensity of the temptation is to be regarded as an excuse for
the drunkard.  Excess in the gratification of a desire, however natural, to the injury of others, is to be condemned
morally and legally.  Many actions of man, which the
moral and legal code of society brands as a crime, and pun-
ishes as such, are the result of an inordinate gratification of
instinctive desires implanted by nature, upon the proper
indulgence of which the very propagation and the happiness of the human race depends, as for example, the instinct of self-preservation, of procreation and of acquisition.
The more civilization advances, the more moral and intellectual discernment governs natural impulse, the less excess in the use of alcoholic stimulants the world will see.
The vice of intemperance prevails to a far greater extent
among the ignorant and uneducated than among the cul-
tured classes of society.  The spread of culture and education will do far more for temperance than the indiscriminate prohibition of the sale of alcoholic stimulants and the

signing of pledges; it will divest the indulgence of the social cup of vulgarity, and will punish immoderation by social ostracism; by giving to the pleasure of exhilaration an ideal character, it will make the vine and the hop the emblems of harmless enjoyment. A clearer perception thus establishes a standard of ethics, which recognizes a proper gratification of the innate craving for enjoyment and exhilaration, as an essential to human happiness, but draws the line between what is permissible and what is not, between the becoming and the unbecoming. The craving for improvement of condition and for enjoyment is strongly developed in man—happily for him, for it is the very spur that urges him on to the physical improvement which is the necessary concomitant of mental advance. The love for exhilarating stimulants is but one phase of this craving As such it is entitled to and has found recognition in our social laws, and the temperate use of alcoholic beverages is sanctioned by a practice as wide-spread as civilization itself, and by all classes, whatever their station or condition in life. Contravening legal statutes will always be found either wholly inoperative, or to fall far short of the intended effect. Whenever and wherever the temporary enforcement of a law prohibiting the manufacture and sale of such beverages has taken place, the cure, as far as the suppression of stimulants is concerned, has generally proved worse than the disease."

The following particulars, taken from the report under the title of "Nativity of Prisoners," given by the Chief of the Police of Boston, become very interesting when considered in reference to the usual drink of the classes mentioned. The table shows first the number in Boston of

Irish and Germans, the number of prisoners of each nation
and the percentage of prisoners to the whole population :

|  | POPULATION. | No. OF PRISONERS. | PERCENTAGE OF PRISONERS TO THE POPULATION. |
|---|---|---|---|
| Irish | 56,900 | 14,673 | 25.78 |
| German | 5,606 | 364 | 6.49 |

Similar general results are found more or less marked
wherever such laws are in force.  Druggists tell us that as
a rule the consumption of opium in various forms from par-
egoric to laudanum has increased, bitters are more extensively used and in some places Scotch snuff for " dipping"
has come into demand.  The amount of opium annually
imported is greater than that received by China a hundred
years ago, and there is reason to suppose that many who
are called reformed drunkards have adopted opium in some
form and thus given themselves to a new bondage no whit
better than the old.  Notice that the increase in the sale of
opium keeps pace in a very fair measure with the enforcement of prohibitory laws.  One dealer in drugs in Hartford, Conn., recently advertised for sale five thousand
pounds of opium, certainly a good dose for the land of
steady habits.  In the state just mentioned both prohibition and " local option " laws have been tried and neither
can be considered a success.  Under the present " local option " many towns wholly forbid the sale of spirituous and
malt liquors, and this fact has given great prominence to
suits arising out of the sale of what is called Schenck beer,
which is substantially lager beer.  The courts at last
decided that this article is not intoxicating within the

meaning of the act, and though the decision as to intoxicating quality is just, the fact that this beer is allowed while lager beer under its own name is forbidden shows how great a part prejudice instead of reason has played in the contest. "Peripatetic gin mills" are increasing in about the same ratio as "temperance societies" and "temperance detectives." Those who pass by the name of temperance reformers seem in many cases to lose the sense of human charity and brotherly kindness, and little else can be expected when we remember how often they are the slaves of this single idea and how in all ages of the world bigotry has been attended by cruelty. Before giving one striking instance of cruelty which it is to be hoped has since been sincerely regretted by all concerned, we must reiterate that any law which every one knows to be constantly violated brings law into disrespect and demoralizes the community so far forth. The case to which reference was just made was mentioned in the New York *World*, and although other matters are added the whole is of sufficient interest to bear reproduction. The article is as follows:

" Some time last September an old lady by the name of Stack who kept a farm at Northfield, Vt., sold two glasses of cider to a man by the name of Timothy Hogan, who informed against her and secured her conviction and a fine of $20 and expenses. In consideration of her age, sickness and poverty, she was allowed a short time to pay her fine, but not being prepared with the cash in January, she was arrested by Deputy Sheriff Avery, and, notwithstanding the severity of the weather, hauled off to prison in an open sleigh to Montpelier insufficiently clad. While in confinement sickness and poor treatment combined caused a rapid

decline, until her niece, a domestic in a hotel, borrowed
sufficient money to pay her fine and effect her release.
Her death followed shortly afterward, caused, no doubt, by
the treatment she had received.  This at the hand and in
the cause of philanthropic reformers is bad enough, but
worse remains.  Here is a temperance man's description of
the system by which these reformers are guided, and which
one of our conscientious judges in Connecticut not long
since truly denounced as infamous.  The state referred to
is the state of the 'Green Mountain Boys,' and noble
Ethan   Allen—Vermont.   The   manner   of   prosecuting
liquor cases is by what is known as the 'spy system.'
Every informer who can secure the conviction of any
person receives a portion of the fine imposed.  A respectable justice of the municipal court in one of the most important towns in the state is authority for the statement that
there are certain justices of the peace who make a special
arrangement with these informers and come in for a share
of the profits, so that outside of the merits of the case conviction is a foregone conclusion every time.  The prohibitory law in force in this state makes it a crime for a man to
sell even a glass of cider.  In the past few weeks the
*World* correspondent has visited Rutland, Burlington, St.
Albans, Montpelier and other towns in the state, and found
in every place that at the hotels and elsewhere liquor was
sold and no questions asked.  In this, as in every other
state, where a similar law has been in force, people with
money and influence can freely engage in the traffic with
none to molest or make them afraid.  The class of spies or
informers who engage in the work of prosecuting liquor
cases are the lowest people in the community.  They are

despised by everybody except fanatical temperance reformers, who employ and encourage them. A prominent citizen, who has held high office in the state and is one of the substantial business men, said the other day: 'The result of the prohibitory law has been to honey-comb the social community with hypocrisy and immorality. I have closely investigated the course of events since this " temperance wave " has swept the state, and while drunkenness is not on the decrease other forms of immorality are certainly on the increase. I would not permit my daughter, or any respectable young lady over whom I might have any influence, to even attend the evening meetings of these temperance societies, as I think it has been conclusively proved that they promote immorality.' Such a statement coming from an influential and respected citizen, who himself practices and inculcates temperance principles, shows the tendency of the prohibitory movement in this state."

It would be an easy matter to collect volumes of evidence on this question of the real effect of prohibitory laws, all going to show that they do not prevent intemperance, that they do lead to the use of other stimulants, that they undermine the character of the community, and that, from whatever point of view regarded, they must be considered harmful to the individual and to the state. Enough, however, for our present purpose and for the space at command has been already said. Those best informed will be most ready to say that the presentation above given does not overstate, but rather falls short of displaying the corruption that creeps in where a prohibitory law is in force.

# CHAPTER XI.

What shall we do to prevent the evils of a too free use of intoxicating drinks, and to make our people truly temperate?

This question was ably discussed in the State Board of Health of Massachusetts some years ago, and Dr. Bowditch, the chairman of the board, expressed himself at that time as follows: "I am confident that our people could be gradually led to a higher temperance by appeals to common sense while deprecating the evils of intemperance, by observing that the use of some liquors is deleterious, while the temperate use of others does little or no harm. I deem a love of stimulants as much a human instinct as any other of the so-called human instincts. And the proposition of total abstinence from stimulants because intoxication prevails widely in the community, seems to me as preposterous as it would be to advise universal celibacy because of the existence of gross evils in connection with those instincts that lead to the divine institution of marriage. By classifying all liquors as equally injurious, and by endeavoring to further that idea in the community, are we not doing a real injury to the country by preventing a free use of lager beer instead of ardent spirits to which our people are so addicted? In the sincere belief, gentlemen, that this analysis of our correspondence will, eventually at least, tend to help onward the most excellent cause of temperance everywhere, and in the hope that none will be offended at the expression at times, of my own individual opinion, which in the course of the discussion I have deemed it my right and duty to give, I remain

Your colleague and friend,

HENRY J. BOWDITCH,

*Chairman of the State Board of Health of Massachusetts."*

In his annual report to the State Board of Health, Dr. Bowditch said, speaking of the question of temperance in connection with the use of light wines and beer, " I fully agree with all that has been said of the value of light wines as an aid to temperance, but I sincerely believe that Germans are destined to be really the greatest benefactors of this country by bringing to us—if we choose to accept the boon—their beer. Lager beer contains less alcohol than any of the native or foreign grape wines. This fact with the other fact that the Germans have not the pernicious habits of our people, would if we chose to adopt their customs tend to diminish intemperance in this country. From the study I have made, lager beer can be used freely without any apparent injury to the individual, or without intoxication, and would be really a promoter of the temperance cause, and if we could so manage as to furnish the people with lager beer and dispense with distilled or alcoholic liquors entirely, the community would be immensely benefited." And on page 301 in the same report, the Doctor properly said, "Whisky-drinkers are seen staggering through the streets or lying insensible in some corner, wherever this beverage is used. But among the light wine tipplers and beer-drinkers, even when drinking freely, drunkards are very seldom seen."

17

We have previously shown that in many cases the introduction of beer has added to the welfare of society, and
that its use is perfectly consistent with habits of sobriety
and temperance.  From this we drew the inference that the
production should be encouraged and its increase hailed as
a sure pledge of improvement in the matters of drunkenness, disorder and crime.  The same conclusion was reached
by Dr. Bowditch as the result of correspondence conducted
with a view to ascertaining fully the actual state of the
case at home and abroad.  He caused a series of inquiries
to be carefully prepared and forwarded to thirty-three resident American ambassadors and to one hundred and thirty-
two consuls, also to many other men in private or official
positions, whose statements and opinions would be entitled
to respect.  When the answers were received the unanimity of the opinions expressed was almost startling.  *All* are
in favor of beer as a light, wholesome beverage, superior
even to the light wines.  Following are given a few extracts from the great mass of answers received:

A physician in Massachusetts writes, " I should make a
distinction between the use of intoxicating liquors and the
lighter drinks.  What a blessing it would be for the community if we could furnish the people with the best of
lager beer and dispense with distilled liquors entirely."

Another physician, also resident in Massachusetts, says,
" I have had a very large practice among the Germans for
twenty years, and my observation has been that they are
remarkably free from consumption and chronic diseases.  I
have attributed it to their free use of lager beer, and do
conscientiously believe that the moderate use of this beverage is beneficial."

A letter from the consulate general of the United States at Frankfort-on-the-Main, reads thus: "Twenty years ago the state of affairs in reference to temperance was different. By the improvement in making beer and the selling of it to the people at large, at low prices, things have changed wonderfully. Drunkards have disappeared. A great deal less of cider and wine is consumed. Everybody now generally drinks beer. Intoxication has decreased. It cannot be said that the general health of the people suffers in this part of Germany. In the city of Frankfort, with a population of over one hundred thousand, and an average annual mortality of fifteen hundred, hardly five persons on an average have died of delirium tremens, which all the eminent physicians here attribute to the free use of lager beer."

Mr. John Jay of the United States Legation at Vienna says: "I am advised by those in whose judgment I have full confidence, that the chief drinks in Austria are wine but particularly beer, the latter of which is drunk by all classes of society at home and at places of amusement, and that but comparatively a small amount of spirituous liquors is consumed except in Galicia. Touching the relative amount of intoxication in the country where I am residing, and that seen all over the United States, I do say that I have seen more intoxicated persons in the streets of New York in one day than I have chanced to see in Vienna during the past year."

Baron Liebig, the eminent chemist, makes the following statements: "Beer unites in its composition a number of constituents whose action is such as to more or less completely neutralize the alcohol whose tendency is to exalt the function of the brain and nervous system."

"Fermented juices, in general, differ from spirits in containing alkalies, organic acids and certain other substances."

"Pure lager beer when taken with lean flesh and little bread yields a diet approaching to milk, and with fat meat, approaching to rice or potatoes." And in another place, "In beer-drinking countries, it is the universal medicine for the healthy as well as for the sick, and it is milk to the aged."

Dr. Schlaeger of Vienna, also a distinguished chemist, says:

"It is my opinion, based on numerous cases that have come under my professional observation, that delirium tremens and other maladies to which inebriates are subject are caused chiefly by the use of *distilled liquors*. Therefore the manufacture and sale of beer should be encouraged. It should be free from taxation in order that it may be placed within the reach of all at a low price and thoroughly take the place of ardent spirits."

The editor of the Chicago *Tribune*, writing from Germany, says: "Drunkenness is so rare and infrequent that it may be said not to exist. I have traveled thousands of miles through Germany, in various directions, visiting nearly all the chief cities, and have made diligent inquiry of American consuls and other well-informed persons, and received but one answer everywhere, *viz.*, no drunkenness among the Germans; public sentiment would not tolerate it; the habits of the country are all against it. And what is the reason of this freedom from inebriation? It is the total absence of whisky and the substitution of lager beer."

Mr. Y. G. Hurd wrote to Mr. Bowditch in reference to

the beer question and after referring to the records of the
Essex police court and alluding to intemperance caused by
ardent spirits, continued as follows : "Of all our commit-
ments 60 per cent. are directly traceable to drunkenness.
Is the enforcement of a prohibitory or any other law alone
to rid us of the monster ? Were there only the pecuniary
interest of the liquor traffi; to meet, powerful as it is, the
result would not be doubtful. But there are climatic influ-
ences, the universal desire for stimulants, the education of
our civilization for some centuries, social customs and
hereditary tendencies, all tending in a greater or less degree
to perpetuate the evil. * * * * * A visit to Chicago
and my observation there of the habits of the German
population, first brought to my mind doubts that total abstinence will ever be an accomplished fact. I visited the
beer gardens on Sunday to see how the Germans spend
the day. There was a band of music, a dance floor, rude
seats and tables like our New England picnics, in a beauti-
ful grove, and lager in such quantities as I had never conceived. Everybody, old and young, drank and seemed to
continue to drink during the afternoon. But lager was the
only beverage. No liquors, no drunkenness and no fights
or disorderly conduct. The young men and maidens were
merry and danced, the elder drank and talked with the
gravity and dignity becoming to respectable German citizens; the children sipped their glass of lager and gamboled
on the grass, and all went home apparently sober, to resume
without doubt, their usual avocations on the morrow.
There were probably two thousand persons taking their
weekly recreation, and this was only one of half a dozen
similar places about the suburbs of the city. Now if this

had been an American or Irish congregation, and the beverage the usual vile concoctions called whisky, gin and brandy, would not the closing scenes of the afternoon have been very different? Broken heads, bloody noses, and the wayside strewn with the wrecks of humanity in beastly intoxication. I thought if we could be rid of the grosser liquors—banish them, put them in the pale of dangerous drugs to be only dispensed by the physician like other poisons, and substitute the lager of the Germans and the light wines of France and *our own country*—should we not be doing our best to exterminate the curse of drunkenness? I expect we shall yet come to this conclusion. The difficulty is that with the tastes of our people, lager and wines will be, indeed, now are, a cover for the sale of the grosser liquors, and worse than all, these liquors are without exception, adulterated or poisonous. I have written at your request this somewhat candid statement of my present views as briefly as possible."

A physician who has under his professional charge, a large institution for the maintenance of aged persons, informs us that the demand for stimulus in the form of tea is a matter of constant observation, and he moreover gives it as his opinion that from twenty to twenty-five per cent. of the whole number are *tea sots*, drinking tea regularly from four to six times a day and as much oftener as they can procure it. They show the effect of this over-stimulation by increased mental irritability, muscular tremors and a greater or less degree of sleeplessness. Another fact to the same purport has been communicated to us by a friend. A domestic in the family sometimes appeared intoxicated and as it was certain she could not get at any of the liquors generally considered intoxicating, the circumstance excited no little surprise and curiosity. At last the problem was solved by the discovery that she drank large quantities of the strongest tea. This it will be seen is in exact conformity with the opinion of Mr. Gladstone as previously quoted, and more or less marked cases of the same nature have doubtless been observed by many of our readers.

A. Schwarz, Esq., of New York, the editor of "Der Americanische Bier-Brauer," a man known in both hemispheres, as an able writer and chemical student, who by his life-long study in fermented beverages has won for himself the thanks of every brewer, writes thus: "Among all drinks, as well those which nature furnishes in abundance as those which are produced by human skill, lager beer especially commends itself by its properties as an excellent beverage.

"Milk contains nutritious substances (protein) and various salts.

"Wine contains alcohol and small quantities of salts.

"Mineral waters, which render such valuable service to the diseased human organism, contain carbonic acid and salt.

"Coffee and tea contain volatile aromatic oils and alkaloids.

"Strong spirituous liquors, as whisky, brandy, rum, arrack and gin, contain only more or less alcohol, with some etherial oils.

"The various popular so-called temperance drinks are distinguished only by their watery contents, which are flavored with sugar and extracts of plants and herbs to make them taste less insipid.

"Beer contains protein, alcohol, salts and carbonic acid gas, and hence possesses nutritious, stimulating and refreshing properties.

"It is not our intention to write a eulogy of beer. We will only state in its favor what cannot be denied by any man, be he a physician or a mechanic, a philosopher or a manufacturer, a chemist or an engineer, a wine-drinker or a temperance man.

"We denote as extracts of beer those solid substances which are not, through the fermentation of the wort, transformed into volatile bodies, and therefore remain as a sediment after the evaporation of the beer. This extract consists of malt sugar obtained by the mashing process, of albumen contained in the malt and now dissolved, and of certain salts, especially phosphoric salt, which were originally contained in the barley, and have not been lost during the process of brewing.

"The amount of the extract of beer mainly depends on the original concentration of the wort and on that state of fermentation in which the beer is consumed; it varies from three to eight per cent.

"By virtue of its protein and its salts, it has a very nutritious effect upon the human organism, and though it does so in a less degree than meat or bread, yet on account of the form of solution in which it appears in the beer, it is easier assimilated, i. e., it easily enters the organism and plays a prominent part in the formation of milk, muscle, flesh and bones,—and the quantity of alcohol contained in beer is so small and so much diluted with water, that it can produce intoxication only if consumed in a very great quantity, i. e., by an immoderate use."

An international congress has just been held in Paris on "Alcoholism," and the Belgian delegate, Dr. Barella, constituted himself the champion of beer. He contended that the consumption of spirits should be discountenanced, because these beverages are harmful, and that the consumption of beer should be encouraged, because it is a sound, wholesome and harmless drink. He pointed out that in countries where the wines are good, and the beers agreeable and nutritive, much less spirits are consumed, and *vice versa*.

Following is a summary of the points made in the report of Dr. Bowditch previously quoted. They will be found useful and interesting, and the whole document deserves the highest praise for thoroughness of investigation, caution of statement and fairness of spirit.

1st. Stimulants are used everywhere, and at times abused, by savage and by civilized men. Consequently intoxication occurs all over the globe.

2nd. This love of stimulants is one of the strongest instincts. It cannot be annihilated, but may be regulated by reason, by conscience, by education, or by law when it encroaches on the rights of others.

3rd. Climatic law governs it, the tendency to indulge to intoxication being not only greater as we go from the heat of the equator towards the north, but the character of that intoxication becoming more violent.

4th. Owing to this cosmic law intemperance is very rare near the equator. It is there a social crime and a disgrace of the deepest dye. Licentiousness and gambling are small offenses compared with it. To call a man a drunkard is the highest of insults. On the contrary at the north

18

of 50° it is very frequent, is less of a disgrace and is by no means a social crime.

5th. Intemperance causes little or no crime toward the equator. It is an almost constant cause of crime either directly or indirectly at the north above 50°.

6th. Intemperance is modified by race as shown in the different tendencies to intoxication of different people.

7th. Races are modified physically and morally by the kind of liquor they use as proved by examination of the returns from Austria and Switzerland.

8th. Beer, native light grape wines and ardent spirits should not be classed together, for they produce very different effects on the individual and upon the race.

9th. German beer and ale can be used even freely without any very apparent injury to the individual, or without causing intoxication. They contain very small percentages of alcohol (4 or 4.5 to 6.50 per cent.). Light grape wines, unfortified by an extra amount of alcohol, can be drunk less freely but without apparent injury to the race, and with exhilaration rather than drunkenness. Some writers think they do no harm but a real good if used moderately. They never produce the violent crazy drunkenness, so noticeable from the use of the ardent spirits of the north. Ardent spirits, on the contrary, unless used very moderately, and with great temperance, and with the determination to omit them as soon as the occasion has passed for their use, are almost always injurious, if continued even moderately for any length of time, for they gradually encroach on the vital powers. If used immoderately they cause a beastly narcotism which makes the victim regardless of all the amenities and even the decencies of life, or perhaps they render him furiously crazy, so that he may murder his best friend.

10th.  Races may be educated to evil by bad laws, or by the introduction of bad habits.  France and a small part of Switzerland are beginning to suffer from the introduction of absinthe and other spirituous liquors.  Especially is this noticeable since the late Franco-German war.

11th.  A race, when it emigrates, carries its habits with it.  For a time at least, those habits may override all climatic law.

12th.  England has thus overshadowed our whole country with its love of strong drinks, and with its habits of intoxication, as it has more recently covered Ceylon, parts of the East and Australia.

13th.  This influence on our own country is greater now than it would have been if our forefathers, the early settlers, had cultivated the vine, which would have been practicable, as seen by the examples of Ohio and California, and from the fact that the whole of the United States lies in the region of the earth's surface suited to the grape culture.

14th.  If these early settlers had done this our nation would probably have been more temperate, and a vast industry like that of France, of Spain and of Italy and Germany, in light native wines, would long ago have sprung up.

15th.  The example set by California and Ohio* should be followed by the whole country, where the vine can be grown.  As a temperance measure it behooves every good

---

*Ohio has already made very great progress in this direction, and its wines are lighter than those of California.  [Author.

citizen to promote that most desirable object. We should also allow the light, unfortified wines of Europe to be introduced free of duty instead of the large one now imposed. Instead of refusing the German lager beer, we should seek to have it introduced into the present "grog shops" and thus substitute a comparatively innoxious article for those potent liquors, which now bring disaster and death into so many families.

16th. The moral sense of the community should be aroused to the enormity of the evils flowing from keeping an open bar for the sale of ardent spirits, while those for the sale of light wines and of lager beer or ale should not be opposed, except for the sale to habitual drunkards after due notice from friends. Sellers violating such law might be compelled to support for a time the family of their victim.

17th. The horrid nature of drunkenness should be impressed by every means in our power upon the moral sense of the people. The habitual drunkard should be punished, or if he be a *dipsomaniac*, he should be placed in an inebriate asylum for medical and moral treatment, until he has gained sufficient self-respect to enable him to overcome his love of drink.

We give next an extract from an article written by Dr. Willard Parker, which article was printed March 20th, 1879, in the *Religious Herald*, a temperance paper published at Hartford, Conn. Dr. Parker says : " We have never had a single case of an inebriate in the asylum at Binghamton, (N. Y.,) who came here from using fermented beverages, he may have begun with them and gone on to other and stronger liquors, but the mere fermented beverages did not make an inebriate of him ; * * * and while men use simply fermented liquors with no more alcohol than comes from their fermentation, drunkenness is but little known." He says also that fermentation is a process of nature which will continue to exist as long as there is sugar and starch. Fermentation is the work of omnipotence, not the work of man, it grows out of the very constitution of things and is as truly a divine process as growth itself.

Professor Mulder of Amsterdam remarks in the preface to his "Chemistry of Beer," page IV., " I dare say without exaggeration that we find united in beer all the wholesome substances that are met separately in the various carbonic acid mineral waters, in wine and in bread," and in reference to the alcoholic property of beer he says, page 461: "Many people are prejudicially influenced by the frequent misuse of alcoholic beverages and kept from reasoning honestly and truly as to their salubrious effects in a diluted form such as we find in beer. If we consider the beneficial effects of good beer on the system we cannot help attributing a share in the result to the alcoholic element, even if it be held that alcohol has in itself no nutritive power." The same opinion is held by Prof. Pittenkofer, the renowned and well-deserving chemist and hygienist, on the strength of numerous observations and results of minute examination.

Professor Stahlschmied formerly at Berlin and at present at the royal polytechnic school at Aix la Chapelle, says in his work " Chemistry in reference to Fermentation," page 255: " Up to the present time, experiments on the nourishing properties of beer have not been sufficiently numerous to furnish definite conclusions. It is not so much the small amount of organic extract that is to be considered as the ashes and phosphates which are here provided in a form easy of assimilation. In this respect beer is next to milk and furnishes an aliment that is directly bone producing." It is well known that beer is very commonly taken by nursing women on account of its nourishing and milk-producing qualities and the fact furnishes evidence from experience to the same purport as the technical statement just quoted.

The report of the Department of Agriculture at Washington as far back as the year 1866 speaks as follows: "The intemperate use of beer is like the intemperate use of anything detrimental to health, but a moderate use of pure beer will aid digestion, quicken the powers of life, and give elasticity to the body and mind and will not produce any of the terrible results named by fanatics and ignorant people. In certain forms of dyspepsia it is a valuable assistant to other remedies and in some cases of debility requiring a mild tonic and gentle stimulant beer has been found of the greatest benefit.

Touching the nutritious properties of beer as compared with the grain from which it is made Professor Mulder says: "The food value of beer as compared with grain is as one to fourteen, no account being made of the food value of the alcohol contained in beer. The albumen value of beer as compared with grain is as one to six, the fat as one to seventy and the chemical salts as one to twenty-five. On the whole, the latest and most trustworthy results of scientific investigation go to show that a well brewed beer, properly compounded with hops and well matured, is to be considered a beverage which has a

most beneficial influence on the transmutation of substances in the human body; if moderately taken."

Sir Henry Labouchere, editor of "Truth" and formerly
member of Parliament for Windsor and Middlesex, an
accomplished linguist, and fitted both as an original think-
er and by experience in the diplomatic *corps* at most of the
capitals of Europe, to form a just opinion, says that experience shows that beer is a most wholesome beverage, that
when pure it is not intoxicating and can be drunk freely,
that its use adds to the health and strength of man, that
intoxication hardly exists where it is the national beverage
and that its introduction in all parts of the world would be
a blessing to mankind.

Professors Ure and Huxley, Dr. Harvey, Dr. Abercrom-
bie and Bayard Taylor, the celebrated traveler and recent
ambassador at the court at Berlin, as also our great statesman and historian George Bancroft, all came, after careful
study and personal observation, to the same conclusion,
that beer is not only healthy, refreshing and enlivening as
a beverage, but also an excellent means of rooting out the
love of strong drink and securing genuine temperance.

Dr. A. Baer, member of the Royal Sanitary Council,
and chief physician at the prisons of Berlin and Ploetzen-
see near Berlin has, within a few months, published a valuable work on alcoholism.   He says, "Beer is of all drinks
best adapted for a stimulating beverage of general consumption.   It combines with the refreshing, animating and
thirst-quenching elements, distinct nutritive qualities,
mainly due to the abundant presence of certain salts, and
thus becomes one of the very best substitutes for extract of
meat.   The greater number of characteristic principles of

the one are found in the other, but the decided nervous
animation experienced after drinking beer is cheifly due to
the large portion of phosphate of potassa, which *Mitcher-
lich* says forms 20 parts in 100 of beer ashes, and which,
according to Ranke, constitutes the principal active ingredient in meat broth. To the presence of this salt, beer
owes its strengthening influence during convalescence and
in cases of general debility, and its marked tendency to
produce corpulency, as shown in beer drinkers. In addition to this the bitter principle of the hops has a tonic
power of marked value in assisting digestion while the
modicum of alcohol has a stimulating and animating effect
on the brain. On the whole, beer as a beverage cannot
be excelled, as it possesses a number of qualities which
jointly have a most salutary effect upon the human
organism."

In a report presented a short time ago to the Industrial
Society of Mulhouse the well-known Dr. Schoellamer thus
speaks of beer:

"Beer is one of the best drinks that we can recommend,
its consumption being most wholesome. Good beer ought
to be regarded as an excellent drink, capable in itself of re-
placing all other fermented drinks. Thus its moderate
consumption must be strongly recommended. If its price
is high a great obstacle is placed in the way of a natural
consumption.

"Beer contains from two to eight per cent. of alcohol, a
dose of carbonic acid equal to three or four times its volume; when it is exposed to the air it loses all its gas. It
contains besides azote and phosphates; for example, a liter
of good beer, made exclusively with hops and barley, con-

tains 0.80 gr. of azote, which corresponds to 5.26 grains of albuminoid matters. There are again from 0.60 gr. to 0.80 gr. of phosphoric acid, that is as much as in 530 grammes of meat or 220 grammes of bread. The solid extract of beer contains salts favorable to nutrition, etc. It is on these accounts that beer may be considered a beverage of the first order.

"It slacks thirst admirably, and as it contains a great deal of water it is perhaps the best of all for that purpose. As an alcoholic drink it is superior to all spirituous liquors. It is the most tonic, the most operative, and the most nourishing. Complete drunkenness is almost impossible with ordinary beer, whatever quantity may be consumed; what is known as "alcoholism" is not produced by it. In fact beer exercises on the human economy a tonic, nutritive, diuretic, and slightly stupefying action, the last effect being due to the essential oil contained in the hops, but large quantities must be absorbed before this effect can be produced."

Professor W. Nasse, president of the Society of Medical Officers of Insane Asylums in Germany, presented for consideration at their annual meeting held at Hamburg, Sept. 17, 1876, the following question: "How can we specially assist in preventing the injury which results from the use of alcoholic liquors?" It was decided that the only means was in promoting the use of good mild beer. The same opinion has been expressed by Dr. Selman in an address delivered at Dusseldorf, and also by Dr. Roller of Illenau, a meritorious specialist in mental diseases, and by Professors Griesinger of Zurich and Schreiber-Berzelius of Sweden. All the authorities just quoted hold a high rank

10

in their profession, and contributions from their pens frequently appear in the *Quarterly Journal of Inebriety*, published at Hartford, Conn.

The Contemporary Review has lately published a series of papers on the same topic, written in a popular style by several London physicians of celebrity, including Dr. Walter Moxon, Sir James Paget and others, and all opposing the doctrine of total abstinence and declaring themselves in favor of beer as a promotive of the real temperance cause. Dr. Albert T. Bernays, too, has considered with great minuteness the cause of intemperance and his conclusion is that beer is the safest kind of alcohol and should be adopted as a common beverage by all classes of people.

In the Minnesota Legislature when the prohibitory law was under consideration, Dr. Riley, a representative from Houston county, spoke as follows : " In the district where I reside there is a large number of Germans who have come from the old country and planted grapes, and now there are magnificent vineyards stretching along the hillsides where formerly there was not grass enough to feed a sheep. They raise large quantities of very fine grapes which they ship all over the country. They also make very fine wine. The proposed law will destroy these vineyards of my constituents. * * * Perhaps it will be necessary to pass a law to protect those miserable drunkards who cannot protect themselves but it is not necessary to restrain others of their liberty to drink when they want or need it.

" Why, I have seen ladies at a tea-party, perhaps not drunk, but certainly very jolly from drinking tea, and yet they come to this Legislature with petitions signed by all whom they could influence or bulldoze into signing, men, women or children to the number of ten thousand. There are eight hundred thousand people in Minnesota, and we are proposing to let these ten thousand override the other seven hundred and ninety thousand. They claim as prohibitionists that drinking tends to impoverish the people. Do you believe that? Look at the Germans! Many of them take a piece of land that would scarcely support a hog and make a fortune of it. They all drink beer. They take their wives and their children to the beer garden and sit down and drink their beer every day, and even the babe in arms will stretch to get a taste of it. These people are not impoverished by it. These people are so healthy in my neighborhood that I have actually not been able to make a living out of my German constituents.

" They say it tends to the degeneration of the human race. How does it happen that in New England where prohibitory laws are in force the race has so degenerated that they do not seem to be able to raise any children? Look at the Germans who drink beer all the time. You will find a large family of healthy children in almost every German house. Are they degenerated?

" The children of total abstinence people are constantly dying. From the vital statistics of Minnesota I learn that over two thousand children died last year under two years of age. They would not have died if they had been fed on good wholesome beer. I would advise mothers—and I have advised them in my practice—to give their sickly children plenty of beer, and I know I have saved many an infant's life. Beer is the best cure for dyspepsia in the world. I have cured women of this terrible disease by advising them to drink three glasses of beer every day, and I say again to you mothers that if you will drink beer and feed your children on beer you will raise more and healthier children.

"Referring to the vital statistics of the state, I find that but six men died of intemperance during last year—two of delirium tremens and four of something else, which they could n't tell anything about, and so called it intemperance. And yet you want to stop drinking. Eleven were killed by horses during the same time. Why don't you abolish horses—never use them or go near them? Thirty-five committed suicide. Why don't you prohibit the use of firearms and knives, and drain all your lakes and rivers for fear some poor fool will drown himself? Some 152 died of heart disease. I don't want any heart in mine. Twenty ladies were scalded to death. You ought to prohibit the use of hot water for fear that more ladies will get into it and perish.

"England away across the sea has brewed beer for many hundred years and will continue to brew for thousands of years more, and to the fact that the English people have drunk beer all that time I do conscientiously attribute her present greatness. Beer-drinkers are slow but sure. Look at Germany, that great nation. We could not pay her for the money we have borrowed of her. Her great army, the best in the world, her great statesmen, her philosophers, were all raised on beer."

The Hon. Frederick Lauer in a speech before the Brewers' Convention at St. Louis, June 4, 1879, thus presents a phase of the beer question which is certainly of importance: "What we now want to ensure the future happiness and

HONORARY PRESIDENT UNITED STATES BREWERS' ASSOCIATION.

prosperity of the country is the enactment of liberal laws to induce the industrious classes of overcrowded Europe to flock to our shores.  We want immigration for the purpose of building up our towns and cities, developing our manufacturing enterprises, and cultivating the millions of fertile acres in this country now lying idle.  The thrifty German is accustomed to his daily ration of beer.  In the land of his nativity he has his parks and public gardens, where family unions and social gatherings take place amid the ecstatic influence of the foaming lager.  The English, Irish, Scotch, and people of other European countries are noted patrons of malt liquors.  The greatest liberality should, therefore, be shown them in the indulgence in their customary beverages in the land of their adoption.  With the more general use of malt liquors the hundreds of quack medicines now in the market will disappear, as it has been proved by experience in countries where malt beverages are the popular drink, that health and longevity are marked features, and dyspepsia and chronic complaints are rare. The tide of emigration is again swelling to this country. According to the *New York Herald* of the first of May last, the total number of immigrants landed at New York for the first three months of 1879 was 11,288, more than two-thirds of whom came from Germany, England and Ireland.  The emigration of aliens to the United States from 1789 to 1877 is set down in round numbers at 10,000,000, who, with their descendants have built up this great nation.  Since May 5, 1847, the emigration to this country has reached 5,732,183 souls.  In view of these facts nothing should be done to interfere with the happiness of those who seek our shores, but by means of wise laws they should be protected in the enjoyment of their rights and privileges.　To be successful as a government we should invite immigration, and develop our great natural resources, and then by promoting health and temperate habits by the adoption of beer as the national beverage, we will increase as a nation, and be in truth and in fact the greatest country on the face of the earth."

# CHAPTER XII.

In the foregoing pages it has been impossible to give a hundredth part of the evidence that lies ready at hand in this matter of the use and effects of beer, but we have endeavored, by careful selection, to present such as must have weight with all readers. Nothing has been stated as a fact which cannot be amply corroborated, and no inference drawn that did not seem to be fully warranted by the premises. It has been shown that beer is wholesome, and so mildly alcoholic as to make drunkenness from its use very uncommon. A man who drinks in order to become intoxicated, can, no doubt, accomplish his purpose with beer; but such men are almost unknown where beer is the common beverage. This abnormal impulse usually comes only in consequence of a course of ardent spirits.

The evidence as to the cure of intemperance by the introduction of a free use of beer is especially important, and one of the most striking instances of such success is to be found in the case of Denmark, to which we desire again to call special attention. This is the central point of the whole question. Heartily desiring the progress of genuine temperance, and fully believing that all efforts in the direction of prohibition are false in theory and injurious in practice, that they do not prevent intemperance and do produce many other evils, we hold that the safe and only course is to popularize the use of beer, and cannot doubt that government would do well to foster its manufacture in

every practicable way, and that taxation on the product
should be abolished, or at least made very light. Such a
course would not merely secure the very end which has
been unsuccessfully attempted by prohibitory laws, but it
would do much more. It would diminish the poor rates,
save the money spent in prosecutions, which, after all, do no
real good, and incidentally improve the whole business condition. Some refreshing, stimulating drink the people will
have, and legislators should seek to guide the instinct, not
eradicate it. Men of the highest scientific authority have
again and again pronounced beer to be not merely harmless,
but beneficial. Experience in the countries where it is
most used develops the same result, and the readiness with
which it is adopted in place of ardent spirits, whenever it is
of good quality and low price, shows how easily the experiment of temperance on this basis can be tried. Even advocates of total abstinence must admit that beer is better
than whisky. The fact that it adds greatly to the enjoyment of a people must not be ignored. Here in America
we are apt to forget all but the work-a-day part of life, but
the demand for recreation exists and must be gratified in
some way, and almost always recreation is social, and is
made more enjoyable and cheerful by some mild stimulant.
It refreshes and enlivens, and so contributes directly to the
social happiness that is the object sought.

It is to be hoped that legislators in general will soon
learn to take broader views than seem generally to have
prevailed in the past. Statesmanship is not bounded by
the views of one or the other party and is affected by no
popular clamor. It does not enact a law because it is
loudly demanded by a certain set of persons, especially if

these persons have a hobby to ride, no matter how earn-
estly they may believe in it. A statesman will see for instance in this temperance question, that the stay of drunkenness must be through a social change. Legal prohibition can do little while all the other conditions of the
problem remain unchanged. Something must be given for
what is forbidden. If beer is encouraged ardent spirits can
be driven out, and when this idea is once thoroughly understood and put in practice we shall have the temperance
era, so long expected and so ardently desired.

There is another subject which we approach with some
reluctance, knowing that however carefully our words may
be weighed, there is a large number of estimable individuals throughout the country and particularly in the Eastern states, to whom they will probably give offense. We
allude to what is called the Sunday question, and the topic
is treated here because in this country beer drinking is, in
the common mind, intimately associated with the German
Americans and their custom of spending part of Sunday in
recreation in a beer garden. The fact that they do so has
been more than once used as an argument against them
and against the use of beer, as if there were any real connection between the character of the drink and such a custom on the part of its greatest consumers even supposing
the custom to be actually harmful or immoral. As such a
feeling exists, however, it seems worth while to call attention to the fact that what is known as the New England
Sunday is not an essential part of Christianity as so many
honestly suppose, but something that in comparison with
Christianity is new and local. We need hardly say that in
the early days of the church it was distinctly taught that

20

the time of the Jewish sabbath was past and for several hundred years this view was generally held. Notice the following passages from the New Testament:

"The law and the prophets were until John. * * Old things are passed away; behold all things are become new. * * Brethren ye have been called unto liberty; only use not that liberty for an occasion to the flesh, but by love serve one another. For all the law is fulfilled in one word, even in this: Thou shalt love thy neighbor as thyself. * * Love worketh no ill to his neighbor.

"If we love one another, God dwelleth in us, and his love is perfected in us. * * For love is of God; and every one that loveth is born of God and knoweth God. He that loveth not, knoweth not God; for God is love. * * But he that hateth his brother is in darkness, and walketh in darkness, and knoweth not whither he goeth, because that darkness hath blinded his eyes.

"A new commandment I give unto you, that ye love one another. * * Love is the fulfilling of the law."

Jesus himself taught the disregard of the sabbath as a day of ceasing from labor or recreation and are we to suppose that both his teaching and practice had no meaning?

Paul says, "One man esteemeth one day above another: another esteemeth every day alike. Let every man be fully persuaded in his own mind. Let no man therefore judge you in respect of a holy day or of the new moon or of the sabbath days."

The first legal enactment requiring an observance of Sunday as a Sabbath, was foisted upon the Christian world A. D. 321, by Constantine the Great—a heartless tyrant who had caused seven members of his family to be put to death in cold blood, that he might attain political and religious supremacy!  He embraced Christianity because the Pagan priests and pontiffs could not grant him absolution, and would not fraternize with such a murderous monster! Hence he became the father of the so-called Sunday laws. Even Constantine's decree did not interdict recreation nor the tillage of the soil.  In general, through the Christian world, the day was a holiday, such as it now is on the continent of Europe.  There the hours of service in the churches fall, usually, in the morning, and are strictly observed while the rest of the day is universally given to enjoyment.  Let those, however, who are accustomed to cry out at the notion of a continental Sunday, remember that they are themselves the innovators, and let them, too, examine the following passages from the writings of men whose names must command respect, and not one of whom would speak in such a matter without mature consideration :

" It will be plainly seen that Jesus did decidedly and avowedly VIOLATE THE SABBATH.  The dogma of the assembly of divines at Westminster, that the observance of the Sabbath is a part of the moral law, is to me utterly unintelligible."—Archbishop Whately.

" As for the seventh day, that has gone to its grave with the signs and shadows of the Old Testament.  Its imposition by law leads to blood and stoning to death those who do but gather sticks thereon ; a thing which no way becomes the gospel."—Bunyan.

" The law of the Sabbath being thus repealed, that no particular day of worship has been appointed in its place is evident."— Milton.

" They who think that by the authority of the Church, the observance of the Lord's day was appointed instead of the Sabbath, as if necessary, are greatly deceived.—Melancthon.

\* \* "And truly we see what such a doctrine has profited; for those who adopt it far exceed the Jews in a gross, carnal and superstitious observance of the Sabbath."—John Calvin.

"As regards the Sabbath or Sunday, there is no necessity for keeping it; but if we do it ought not to be on account of Moses's commandment, but because nature teaches us from time to time to take a day of rest. \* \* If anywhere the day is made holy for the mere day's sake, then I order you to work on it, to ride on it, to dance on it, to do anything that will reprove this encroachment on Christian spirit and liberty."—Martin Luther.

"These things refute those who suppose that the first day of the week (that is, the Lord's day), was substituted in place of the Sabbath, for no mention is made of such a thing by Christ or his Apostles."—Grotius.

Tyndale the martyr, Erasmus, Paley, McNight and a host of other Christian authorities, were and are of the same opinion regarding Sabbath observance. England and America stand practically alone in retaining so much of the Jewish Sabbath. Here is a letter from Benjamin Franklin to Jared Ingersoll of New Haven, Conn., which bears directly on the subject and may be read with both interest and profit by those who concern themselves in Sunday laws.\*

PHILADELPHIA, December 11, 1762.

"I should be glad to know what it is that distinguishes Connecticut Religion from common Religion :—communicate, if you please, some of these particulars that you think will amuse me as

---

\*The original is in the possession of the New Haven Colony Historical Society.

WILLIAM PENN,

The Quaker Brewer, and Founder of Pennsylvania, 1644—1718. (See page 26.)

a virtuoso. When I traveled in Flanders I thought of your excessively strict observation of Sunday; and that a man could hardly travel on that day among you upon this lawful occasion, without Hazard of Punishment, while where I was every one traveled, if he pleased, or diverted himself in any other way; and in the afternoon both high and low went to the Play or the Opera, where there was plenty of Singing, Fiddling and Dancing. I looked around for God's Judgments, but saw no signs of them. The Cities were well built and full of Inhabitants, the Markets filled with Plenty, the People well favored and well clothed; the Fields well tilled; the Cattle fat and strong; the Fences, Houses and Windows all in Repair; and no *Old Tenor* anywhere in the Country;—which would almost make one suspect that the Deity is not so angry at that offense as a New England Justice."

B. FRANKLIN.

A correspondent of the New York *Staats-Zeitung** writes as follows: "The Emperor of Germany has made a contribution to the discussion of the Sunday question, that is very much to the point. It is an address to the Prussian Synod, which had recently objected to the holding of a review on Sunday, and reads thus: ' He who instituted the Sabbath has declared that the Sabbath was made for man, and not man for the Sabbath. The puritanic and Calvinistic conception of the Sabbath as a day of penance and repentance, has always been foreign to the feeling and taste of the German people.'"

These words of the Emperor will receive the hearty assent of every German-American, and preachers and pietists may as well understand that Germans in America will struggle as long for their free Sunday as Germans in their

---

*New York *Staats-Zeitung*, Nov. 1, 1879.

old home have for a free German Rhine. They have con-
quered back the "sacred stream" and something more into
the bargain, and we here shall have no less success in securing a free, cheerful Sunday, if we remain united and true
to our principles.

England formerly held the same views that then and
since have prevailed on the continent, but gradually the
liberty of the day was restricted and its character wholly
changed. We have lately met with an excellent summary
of the course of legislation that produced this result. It
marks clearly the various stages of the restrictive process
and we cannot do better than reproduce it here for the
benefit of readers to whom it may prove novel.

" Prior to the statute of 1676, any act done on Sunday,
except in proceedings of courts, was of the same binding
force as if performed on any other day. Parliament sat on
that day, for in the reign of Edward I., in 1278 and 1305,
three statutes were made on Sunday. Nor did the first
restraining laws make any distinction between Sundays and
other holy days. Thus the statute of 28 Edward III., Cap.
14, in 1357, says : " Shewing of wools (*i. e.*, by merchants)
shall be made at the staple every day in the week except
the Sunday and solemn feasts of the year." No further
enactment was made touching the matter in question for
nearly 100 years ; but in 1448 was passed the act of 27
Henry VI., Cap. 5, entitled, " Certain days wherein fairs
and markets ought not to be kept," which sets forth that
" The King hath ordained that all manner of fairs and
markets in said principal feasts (of Ascension, Corpus
Christi, Assumption, and All Saints) and Sundays and
Good Friday shall clearly cease from all shewing of any

goods or merchandises (necessary victuals only except) ;" but in recognition of the fact that there had previously been no such restriction, it is provided that " Nevertheless, of his special grace (the King) granted to them power which of old time had no day to hold their fair or market, but only upon the festival days aforesaid, to hold the same authority and strength of his old grant within three days next before said feasts or next after."

The act of 4, Edward IV., Cap. 7, in 1464, seems to have been occasioned by some special irritation from the dishonesty of leather-dressers and shoemakers; for, after sundry stringent provisions applying to them generally, it is provided that " No person, cordwainer or cobbler, within the City of London * * * upon any Sunday in the year, or in the feasts of the Nativity or Ascension of our Lord, or in the feast of Corpus Christi, shall sell, or command, or do to be sold, any shoes, huseaus, or galoches, or upon the Sunday, or any of said feasts, shall set or put upon the feet or legs of any person, any shoes, huseaus, or galoches." This statute was repealed in 1522, but re-enacted, in part, in 1604.

In 1552 was passed " An act for keeping holy days and feasting days" (5 and 6 Edw. IV., Cap. 2), the preamble of which is an instructive example of the pains taken by all Christians, Catholic and Protestant, prior to the seventeenth century, to deny that Sunday or any other holy or feast day, possessed of itself any sacredness or any higher claim to observance than that of convenience for the purpose of uniformity in worship. It ran thus: " For as much as at all times men be not so mindful to laud and praise God * * * as their bounden duty doth require; therefore, to call men to remembrance of their duty and help their infirmity, it hath been wholesomely provided that there shall be some certain times and days appointed wherein the Christian should cease from all kinds of labors; ·* * * neither is it to be thought that there is any certain time or definite number of days prescribed in Holy Scripture, but that the appointment, both of time · and also of the number of the days, is left by the authority of God's word to the liberty of Christ's Church to be determined and assigned orderly in every country by the discretion of the rulers and ministers thereof, as they shall judge most expedient for the true setting forth of God's glory and the edification of their people ; be it therefore enacted, that all the days hereafter mentioned (to wit: Sundays, the Feast of the Circumcision, and twenty-two other feast days that are named, and Mondays and Tuesdays in Easter Week and Whitsun Week) shall be kept and commanded to be kept holy days, and none other." It was further provided, " That it shall be lawful to every husbandman, laborer, fisherman,   *   *   *   upon the holy days aforesaid, in harvest, or at any other time of the year when necessity shall require, to labor, ride, fish, or work any kind of work at their free wills and pleasure."   This Protestant law was repealed the next year by the Catholic government of Mary, and restored in 1604, in the first year of James I.   It is strikingly similiar to the decree of Constantine the Great, made in the year 321 : " Let all Judges and people of the town rest, and all the various trades be suspended, on the venerable day of the sun.   Those who live in the country, however, may freely and without fault attend to the cultivation of their fields   *   *   *   lest, with the loss of favorable opportunity, the commodities offered by Divine Providence should be destroyed."

In 1558 (1 Eliz., Cap. 2, Sec. 14,) was passed the first law requiring attendance upon public worship " upon every Sunday, and other days ordained and used to be kept as holy days," upon pain of church censure and a fine of twelvepence.

The English Puritans of the time of James I., were the first to impose the name and character of the Jewish Sabbath upon the first day of the week, and those who came to America brought the name and the idea with them. To that seventeenth-century influence, and not to any scriptural or ecclesiastical teaching of any earlier time, are we indebted for sermons on Sunday observance. The doctrine held on that subject by most evangelical Christians is not yet three hundred years old.

In 1625 was passed a law (1 Car. I., Cap. 1,) that " There should be no meeting, assemblies, or concourse of people out of their own parishes on the Lord's day, for any sports or pastimes whatsoever; nor any bear-baiting, bull-baiting, interludes, common plays, or other unlawful exercises or pastimes used by any persons within their own parishes." " *This statute*," says Blackstone, " *does not prohibit, but rather impliedly allows any innocent recreation or amusement within their respective parishes, even on the Lord's day, after Divine service is over;* " and, *in point of fact, both Charles I. and his father before him issued proclamations encouraging such amusements after Divine service.*

In 1676 was enacted the well known "Lord's Day act," of 29 Car. II., Cap. 7, which prohibits generally all work, labor, and business on Sunday, except works of necessity

21

and charity, and which, with more or less modification, forms the basis of all Sunday laws now extant in the United States. Exceptions to this law in favor of hackney coachmen, fishwomen, and chairmen, were enacted in 1694, 1699, and 1710, and a clause prohibiting bird hunting was subsequently added, but it remained in substance until alterations and repeals of English laws ceased to have any force in this country."

As an historical matter the question is not very abstruse and the truth is well enough known to scholars everywhere; should there not then be charity for honest convictions?

In many cases the practice for years has been tolerably liberal while all the time the old and stringent puritanical Sunday laws of 1702 were retained on the statute books liable to be enforced whenever a minority should choose to demand their revival.

Such cases have recently been seen in many places in this and other states, but particularly so in Newark, N. J., where the enforcement of such an old act forbidding the sale of beer and other beverages on Sunday caused a reaction of unexpected violence, and very characteristic of the profound change that has already taken place in the popular conception of the day. The circumstances in brief were as follows: A considerable number of prohibitionists had organized under the name of the Law and Order Association for the purpose of enforcing the Sunday law and preventing the licensing of bar rooms. Numerous prosecutions were made and carried through to conviction under the old state law after having failed in the city police courts. Thereupon the Citizens' Protective Association

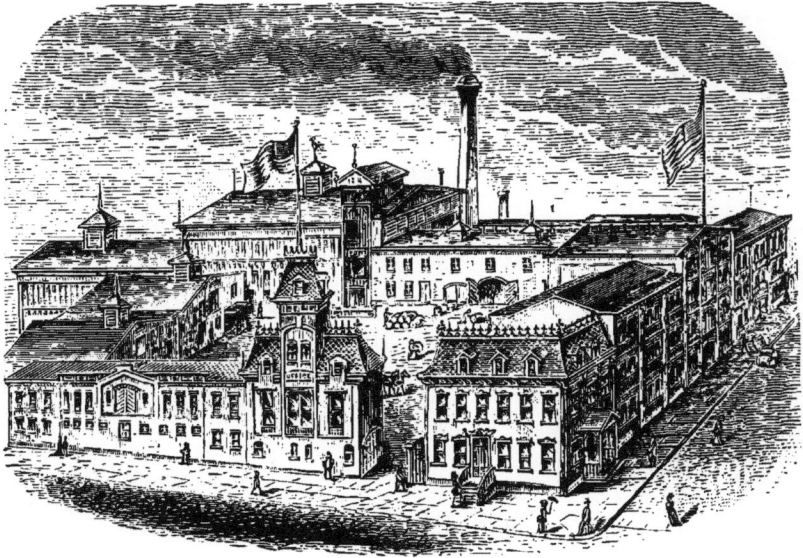

# Belmont Avenue Brewery,

NEWARK, N. J.,

## GOTTFRIED KRUEGER, PROPRIETOR.

*For historical sketch, see Appendix C, page 183.*

was formed and in September, 1879, a demonstration was
made by a great procession, and the adoption of resolutions
calling for a repeal of the law which, after lying idle so
long, had suddenly been revived to the great injury of an
established business, and with manifest injustice to a large
number of peaceable citizens who conceived their rights to
be interfered with, inasmuch as a law long inoperative must
practically be regarded as a dead letter and ignored by those
who, if they had supposed it to possess vital power, would
have removed from its jurisdiction or taken pains never to
come within it. The procession numbered ten or twelve
thousand and great enthusiasm was displayed, not only in
the ranks, but by residents all along the line of march. The
matter was evidently one which took a deep hold on the
feelings of the community and none the less because of a
common feeling that they had been unfairly treated by the
appeal to a law not in harmony with the spirit of the times
or of abstract justice. A crowd is very apt to be wrong
and it is easy to stir up the people, but here the crowd had
more reason on its side than it was itself aware of, reason
founded on history, and making the law that had been enforced an unwarrantable attack on personal liberty. They
felt that it was so, though few probably would have been able
to give a clear explanation of the feeling or trace its justi-
fication by the facts. As for enthusiasm, we are told that
it needed no stimulus and can easily believe it to have been
so, for aside from the more abstract and philosophical justice of their complaint, there was the immediate smart felt
by men who lose the day of recreation to which they have
looked forward all the week, or find that they are to suffer
a pecuniary loss and that their occupation is not only

checked but stigmatized. The matter made a great excitement and called out many bitter paragraphs on both sides, but chiefly among the more narrow-minded and pharisaical of so-called religious press. We have no space or disposition to go into the details of their criticism, even for the sake of illustrating how far misrepresentation and innuendo may be made to stand in place of careful statement and sound argument. The case has been spoken of because it is in some sense typical, because it represents the course of public thought and feeling, and the change which even within two or three generations has come over the rigid enactments of puritan early settlers. These puritans did much good but it was all tempered and shadowed by an austere severity that has no merit in itself and that crushes out much the better part of life and obscures many a truth that in itself is clear as noonday. The mind of the people has changed. It is time that the law should be changed also. The *Christian Union* has said, " The sooner the issue is made in Chicago between a whole sabbath and none at all, the sooner the Christian element in the community will win the victory it will deserve. Half a sabbath is hardly worth fighting for." We say that the best rule for observing the day is that which gives the greatest amount of harmless freedom and enjoyment to the greatest number, each according to his own judgment and conscience. Our foreign element is very large and has its own beliefs and traditions, as dear and as implicitly held as those of any one whose training and practice have been after the strictest sabbatarian pattern.

We have attempted here no argument, but simply given some cardinal facts, and now leave the matter in the hope that those who dissent will at least respect honest utterance and not allow their objections on this one point to prejudice them against our discussion of the value of malt beverages as aids to genuine temperance and useful friends to man.

We close as we began, with the words which seem to us to indicate the only practical road to real temperance, and record again our motto

BEER AGAINST WHISKY.

# APPENDIX A.

The tables here given have been prepared with great
care after a thorough examination and comparison of authorities. The discrepancies and errors discovered in various published statements of a similar nature have made the
task a difficult one, but it is believed that the present results
will be found substantially accurate. Table A gives a list
of the chief beer producing countries, with the population
of each, its annual product in hectoliters and gallons, the
number of its breweries and the production per head of
population. The countries are arranged in the order of
product *per capita*. Table B gives the same countries arranged in the order of total production, and for convenience
of reference repeats the product *per capita*.

## TABLE A.

| | Population. | Production in Hec- toliters.* | Production in gal lons. | Number of Brewer- ies. | Production per head of population. |
|---|---|---|---|---|---|
| Bavaria, | 5,022,390 | 12,422,272 | 329,110,208 | 6,240 | 65.5 |
| Wurtemberg, | 1,881,505 | 3,480,795 | 92,241,067 | 2,604 | 49.0 |
| Belgium, | 5,336,185 | 7,942,000 | 210,463,000 | 2,500 | 39.4 |
| Great Britain and Ireland, | 31,628,338 | 47,000,000 | 1,245,500,000 | 26,214 | 39.0 |
| Baden, | 1,507,177 | 1,297,893 | 34,394,164 | | 22.8 |
| Denmark, | 1,940,000 | | 38,800,000 | | 20.0 |

*Hectoliter—26⅖ gallons wine measure.

| Population, | Production in Hectoliters.* | Production in Gallons. | Number of Breweries. | Production per head of population. |
|---|---|---|---|---|
| Saxony, | 2,760,586 | | 52,520,480 | | 19.0 |
| Holland, | 3,865,456 | 2,078,000 | 55,067,000 | 5E0 | 14.2 |
| Prussia *proper*, | 25,742,404 | | 257,630,403 | 10,480 | 10.0 |
| United States, | 38,558,371 | 10,848,446† | 336,301,826 | 2,830 | 8.7 |
| Switzerland, | 2,759,854 | 890,000 | 23,585,000 | 400 | 8.5 |
| Austro Hungary, | 36,373,000 | 11,323,444 | 300,071,266 | 2,353 | 8.3 |
| Norway, | 1,806,900 | 420,000 | 11,130,000 | 34 | 6.1 |
| Sweden, | 4,484,542 | 1,000,000 | 26,500,000 | 94 | 5.9 |
| France, | 36,905,788 | 7,370,000 | 195,305,000 | 3,110 | 4.4 |
| Trieste and Dalmatia, | 522,800 | 52,575 | 1,393,237 | 3 | 2.6 |
| Russia *proper*, | 65,504,659 | 3,040,000 | 80,560,000 | 520 | 1.2 |
| German Principalities, not above enumerated, | 5,813,296 | | 119,670,460 | 940 | 20.5 |

## TABLE B.

| | PRODUCTION. | GAL. PER HEAD. |
|---|---|---|
| Great Britain and Ireland, | 1,245,500,000 | 39.0 |
| United States, | 336,301,826 | 8.7 |
| Bavaria, | 329,190,208 | 65.5 |
| Austro Hungary, | 300,017,266 | 8.3 |
| Prussia *proper*, | 257,630,403 | 10.0 |
| Belgium, | 210,463,000 | 39.4 |
| France, | 195,305,000 | 4.4 |
| Wurtemberg, | 92,241,067 | 49.0 |
| Russia *proper*, | 80,560,000 | 1.2 |
| Holland, | 55,067,000 | 14.2 |
| Saxony, | 52,520,480 | 19.0 |
| Denmark, | 38,800,000 | 20.0 |
| Baden, | 34,394,164 | 22 8 |
| Sweden, | 26,500,000 | 5.9 |
| Switzerland, | 23,585,000 | 8.5 |
| Norway, | 11,130,000 | 6.1 |
| Trieste and Dalmatia, | 1,393,237 | 2.6 |
| German Principalities not above enumerated, | 119,670,460 | 20.5 |

*Hectoliter— 26¼ gallons wine measure.
†Barrels.

It will be seen from the above table that Germany, exclusive of German Austria, brews the enormous quantity
of 885,646,782 gallons of beer, or about 20.7 to each individual in a population of 42,727,360.   Most of this is consumed at home, and great quantities are imported from
Christiana, Norway, and Copenhagen, Denmark, while ale
and porter are largely brought from England.

It is worthy of notice that Bavaria, which has been
known for centuries as the cradle of men of arts and sci-
ences, stands at the head of the list of beer producing countries.   With a population of only about five millions, it
brews three hundred and twenty-nine million gallons. or
65.5 gallons to every individual; and next in rank is the
little kingdom of Wurtemberg, the native state of the great
Schiller.   Munich, the capital of Bavaria is especially celebrated for the long array of men of arts, letters and science
who have either been born there or adopted it as a residence.   But it is, at the same time, the greatest beer drinking city in the world.   It produced in the year 1876 no less
than 1,198,951 hectoliters=31,772,201 gallons, and its actual home consumption in that year was 956,455 hectoliters
=25,346,057 gallons, which, in a population of 198,000,
gives 128 gallons a year for every individual, costing in all
$6,216,955, or about $31 per head.   The amount paid for
beer is less by $1,363,800 than the amount paid for house
rent.   In the years 1877 and 1878 the amount paid for
beer fell off, but for the current year (1879) it will, according to statistics thus far received, be larger than ever before.
The taxes for the municipal government and city taxes are
less than a tenth of the amount expended for beer—and yet
there is not a more orderly and well behaved city in the

world than this same Munich. All this is indirect evidence of great importance as to the social and intellectual effect that may be expected to follow a free and even a very large use of beer.

Vienna stands in a similar category though it offers a less striking illustration of the case than Munich does. It has, however, one brewer whose operations are extensive enough to deserve special mention. This is the well-known Anton Dreher, whose business, begun at Schwechat in 1836, now comprises large establishments in four Austrian cities, with an annual product of 500,000 barrels, paying a government tax of $750,000.00 or more. The business employs combined water and steam engines of 100 horse power, 400 brewers, 200 teamsters and common laborers, 150 horses, and no less than 250 draught oxen.

Karlsruhe, the capital of Baden is also an important brewing city. Its product is 4,884,350 gallons, and of this amount something over one million gallons is contributed by the Albert Printz brewery alone.

It is, however, useless to attempt any mention of the cities or districts that are distinguished for the quantity or quality of their beer. We can only say that they are very numerous, and add that their character is such as to coroborate all that has been said in this book touching the beneficial effects of a free use of beer in the community.

22

# APPENDIX B.

## ANALYSES OF BEERS.

The following analyses will be found of interest to every student of the beer question.* The first is from Professor Mulder's work on beer.

### 1.—BAVARIAN BEERS.

| | Specific weight at 16° | Water. | Carbonic Acid. | Extract. | Alcohol. | Year. |
|---|---|---|---|---|---|---|
| Young winter beer of Munich, | 1018 | 870.83 | 1.40 | 58.74 | 38.6 | 1849 |
| "        "          " | 1019 | 879.13 | 1.60 | 60.16 | 32.8 | 1853 |
| "        "    Augsburg, | 1013 | 883.30 | 1.80 | 45.30 | 38.9 | 1854 |
| "        "    Bayreuth, | 1013 | 866.90 | 1.80 | 53.60 | 42.8 | 1854 |
| "        "    Landshut, | 1018 | 880.50 | 1.80 | 57.40 | 33.5 | 1854 |
| "        "    Anspach, | 1015 | 889.40 | 1.80 | 51.60 | 32.2 | 1854 |
| Lager (summer) beer of the brewery of the Court of Munich, | 1011 | 880.50 | 1.60 | 39.40 | 43.5 | 1846 |
| "        "        "        of Degelmayer, | 1022 | 867.20 | 1.30 | 66.40 | 36.5 | 1853 |
| "        "        "        of the Court, | 1018 | 870.80 | 1.80 | 51.00 | 42.5 | 1852 |
| "        "        (young) | 1028 | 851.94 | 1.40 | 77.20 | 38.8 | 1850 |
| "        "        of June, 1852, | 1017 | 872.22 | 1.80 | 53.18 | 40.7 | 1852 |
| "        "        (10 months old) of the Franciscan Convent, | 1012 | 854.20 | 1.50 | 50.10 | 51.7 | 1853 |

* Additional analyses may be found in the body of the book, pages 97, 98 and 99.

| | Specific weight at 16° | Water | Carbonic Acid | Extract. | Alcohol. | Year. |
|---|---|---|---|---|---|---|
| Strong beer of Zacherl's brewery, | 1026 | 825.00 | 1.80 | 77.70 | 52.4 | 1853 |
| Salvator beer of " " | 1034 | 820.80 | 1.60 | 94.50 | 46.0 | 1853 |
| Bock beer | 1027 | 830.55 | 1.70 | 92,07 | 42.2 | 1852 |
| Ale of Sedelmaier's brewery, | 1022 | 769.40 | 1.80 | 84.40 | 77.5 | 1850 |
| **II.—FOREIGN BEERS.** | | | | | | |
| Bottom-yeast beer of Wauka (Prague) | 1016 | 869.40 | 1.80 | 46.90 | 48.4 | 1844 |
| Upper " Pstross " | 1017 | 867,20 | 1.50 | 50.70 | 44.6 | 1844 |
| " " Pchowitz, near Prague, | 1013 | 881.90 | 1.60 | 47.70 | 38.5 | 1844 |
| " " Pstross, | 1016 | 876.30 | 1.80 | 50.40 | 39.9 | 1844 |
| " " Berlin, | 1014 | 855.50 | 1.90 | 51.80 | 49.9 | 1851 |
| " " Magdeburg, | 1016 | 884.70 | 1.80 | 50.40 | 35.3 | 1853 |
| Porter of Barclay & Perkins, of London, | 1017 | 840.20 | 1.60 | 60.20 | 53.7 | 1852 |
| Scottish ale of Edinburg, two years old, | 1030 | 730.50 | 1.50 | 109.40 | 84.7 | 1851 |
| Lambick of Brussels, | 1004 | 862.50 | 2.00 | 34.12 | 55.4 | 1841 |
| Faro beer of " | 1004 | 879.16 | 2.00 | 29.58 | 49.1 | 1841 |
| Barley beer of " | 1006 | 868.05 | 1.90 | 38.39 | 50.4 | 1841 |
| Mum of Brunswick, | 1231 | 511 68 | 1.60 | 476.40 | 3 6 | 1854 |

## ACCORDING TO CH. MENE.

| Kind of Barley. | Brewery Firm. | Name of Beer. | Specific weight. | Alcohol. | Residue of evaporation per liter. | Ash per cent. | Nitrogen per cent. |
|---|---|---|---|---|---|---|---|
| S. B. | Detalle & Cie. Ham. (Somme) | Ord. brown beer, | 1.0100 | 3.6 | 50.120 | 1.920 | 0.785 |
| S. B. | " | Ord. pale beer, | 0.9973 | 4.4 | 48.000 | 1.080 | — |
| S. B. | " | Workmen's beer, | 1.0106 | 4.5 | 57.120 | 1.520 | 0.722 |
| S. B. | " | Ladies' beer, | 1.0103 | 4.0 | 48.600 | 1.600 | 0.760 |
| S. B. | Lux & Co., Paris, (Seine) | Light beer | 1.0106 | 3.8 | 42.480 | 1.800 | 0.620 |
| S. B. | Schmidt & Co., " | Young bock, | 1.0225 | 4.3 | 51.400 | 2.600 | 0.770 |
| S. B. | " " | Store beer, | 1.0182 | 4.4 | 57.210 | 2.400 | 0.800 |
| W. B. | Watteblest (Vernelles) Pas de Calais, | Ord. brown beer, | 1.0050 | 4.5 | 39.440 | 1.280 | — |
| W. B. | " " | Ord. pale beer, | 1.0078 | 4.5 | 35.800 | 1.440 | 0.710 |
| W. B. | Meesemaeker (Dunkerque) Nord, | Barley wine, | 1.0130 | 5.5 | 73.120 | 3.700 | 0.840 |
| W. B. | " " | Pale ale, | 1.0127 | 5.2 | 68.960 | 1.200 | — |
| W. B. | Pollet, Courtrai (Belgium) | Export beer, | 1.0080 | 4.5 | 48.160 | 1.195 | 0.750 |
| W. B. | Hauthyssen, Haunut (Liege) | Ord. brown beer, | 1.0115 | 4.7 | 51.105 | 1.310 | 0.715 |

S. B.—Summer Barley.    W. B.—Winter Barley.

## ACCORDING TO HEYDLOFF.

|                                    | Alcohol. | Extract. |
|------------------------------------|----------|----------|
| Beer of Nuremberg,                 | 3.8      | 6.2      |
| "    Erlangen,                     | 3.8      | 6.0      |
| "    Bamberg,                      | 4.1      | 5.8      |
| "    Erfurth, of Treitsokle,       | 3.7      | 5.5      |
| "        "    of Schlegel,         | 4.1      | 6.5      |
| "        "    of John,             | 3.7      | 6.0      |
| "        "    of Buchner,          | 4.2      | 6.5      |
| English porter,                    | 5.1      | 9.2      |

Composition of some Swedish beers :

|                                                        | Percentage of | | |
|--------------------------------------------------------|---------|----------|--------|
|                                                        | Extract. | Alcohol. | Water. |
| Porter of Stockholm,                                   | 6.6     | 6.0      | 87.4   |
| Porter of Goteborg, (Carnezie & Co.)                   | 5.4     | 5.8      | 88.8   |
| Strong beer of Neumiller's brewery in Stockholm,       | 12.4    | 4.6      | 83.0   |
| Swedish beer of Beijnoff (Upsala)                      | 8.9     | 3.0      | 88.1   |
| "          Hillberg      "                             | 8.2     | 2.6      | 89.2   |
| Beer of the Bavarian brewery in Upsala,                | 6.4     | 4.7      | 88.9   |
| Bavarian beer of the Munich brewery in Stockholm,      | 7.4     | 4.0      | 83.6   |
| Erlanger beer,                                         | 6.2     | 4.7      | 89.1   |
| Bavarian beer of Oerebeo,                              | 5.5     | 4.1      | 90.4   |
| Export beer of Stockholm,                              | 5.2     | 4.8      | 90.0   |
| Svagdricke (small beer) of Beijnoff (Upsala),          | 3.2     | 2.1      | 94.7   |
| Svagdricke (small beer) of Hillberg,                   | 3.3     | 2.2      | 94.5   |

## ACCORDING TO C. HIMLEY.

| Names of the Beers.            | Extract of Malt. | Alcohol. | Phosphoric Acid. | Water. |
|--------------------------------|------------------|----------|------------------|--------|
| Double beer of Copenhagen,     | 13.68            | 2.16     | 0.065            | 84.16  |
| (Orp) Salvator,                | 8.20             | 4.10     | 0 084            | 87.70  |
| Waldschlosschen                | 5.50             | 3.84     | 0.088            | 89.66  |
| (Erich) Erlanger beer,         | 6.22             | 3.95     | 0.074            | 89.83  |
| Berliner Actienbier,           | 6.20             | 3.44     | 0.068            | 90.36  |
| (Betz) Eckernforder,           | 6.10             | 3.05     | 0.062            | 90.85  |
| Schluter,                      | 6.09             | 3.60     | 0.074            | 90.31  |
| Scheibel,                      | 6.00             | 3.12     | 0.064            | 90.88  |
| Erlanger,                      | 5.70             | 3 57     | 9.070            | 90.73  |
| (Erich) Erlanger ale,          | 5.62             | 3.04     | 0.076            | 91.34  |
| Hoff's malt extract,           | 5.60             | 3.04     | 0.075            | 91.36  |

| Name of the Beers. | Extract of Malt. | Alcohol. | Phosphoric Acid. | Water. |
|---|---|---|---|---|
| (Eger & Co.) Christiana, | 5.54 | 3.77 | 0.088 | 90.69 |
| (Henniger) Erlanger, | 5.50 | 2.60 | 0.072 | 91.90 |
| Dreiss, | 5.40 | 3.10 | 0.060 | 91.50 |
| Orp, | 5.00 | 3.25 | 0.056 | 91.75 |

## ACCORDING TO HEKMEYER.

| | Alcohol in 100 volumes. | Acetic Acid. | Lactic Acid. | Carbonic Acid. | Extract. | Ash. | Albumen. |
|---|---|---|---|---|---|---|---|
| 1—*Beers of Utrecht.* | | | | | | | |
| Old Brown (uit den boog), | 3.8 | 0.035 | 0.32 | 0.073 | 3.36 | 0.34 | 0.41 |
| Young pale,    " | 4.1 | 0.008 | 0.25 | 0.103 | 2.86 | 0.25 | —— |
| Lambick,    " | 5.4 | 0.016 | 0.35 | 0.159 | 3·49 | 0.36 | —— |
|    " (uit den kraus), | 4.6 | 0.120 | 0.40 | 0.090 | 1.79 | 0.21 | ——— |
| Table beer (uit den aker), | 4.4 | 0.044 | 0.16 | 0.163 | 3.40 | 3.41 | —— |
| 2—*Other Dutch Beers.* | | | | | | | |
| Princessen-bier, | 4.0 | 0.060 | 0.17 | 0.090 | 2.60 | 0.21 | 0 46 |
| Heumens-bier, | 4.2 | 0.012 | 0.27 | 0.135 | 2.79 | 0.28 | —— |
| Bosch-bier(W.Van Heeren), | 5.2 | 0.044 | 0.42 | 0.010 | 4.83 | 0.38 | —— |

## ACCORDING TO LACAMBRE.

| | Alcohol Young Beer. | Alcohol Old Beer. | Extract Young Beer. | Extract Old Beer. |
|---|---|---|---|---|
| London ale, | 7 | 8 | 6.5 | 5 |
| Hamburg ale, | 5.5 | 6 | 6 | 5 |
| London ale, (common,) | 4 | 5 | 5 | 4 |
| Porter, | 5 | 6 | 7 | 6 |
| London porter, (common,) | 3 | 4 | 5 | 4 |
| Munich, Salvator, | 5 | 6 | 12 | 10 |
| Bock, | 3.5 | 4 | 9 | 7 |
| Bavarian beer, (common,) | 3 | 4 | 6.5 | 4.5 |
| Brussels, Lambick | 4.5 | 6 | 5.5 | 3.5 |
|    " Faro, | 2.5 | 4 | 5 | 3 |
| Diest Gulde beer, | 3.5 | 6 | 8 | 5.5 |
| Peeterman, of Louvain, | 3.5 | 5 | 8 | 5.5 |
| White beer, | 2.25 | 3.25 | 5 | 3.5 |
| Double Uitzet of Ghent, | 3.25 | 4.5 | 5 | 4 |
| Single    "    " | 2.75 | 3.5 | 4 | 3 |
| Barley beer of Antwerp, | 3 | 3.5 | 4.5 | 3 |
| Strong beer of Strasburg, | 4 | 4.5 | 4 | 3 5 |
| Strong beer of Lille, | 4 | 5 | 4 | 3 |
| White beer of Paris, | 3.5 | 4 | 8 | 5 |

## ACCORDING TO G. MONIER.

| NAMES OF THE BEER. | ALCOHOL. (in volumes.) | GLUCOSE. | DEXTRINE, ALBUMINOID SUBSTANCES, ETC. | SALTS. |
|---|---|---|---|---|
| | Cubic cntms. | Grammes. | Grammes. | Grammes. |
| Beer of France (Nord), | 40.00 | 7.03 | 31.77 | 1.60 |
| Beer of France (Nord), | 32.50 | 4.80 | 31.00 | 2.10 |
| Beer of France (Nord), | 36.00 | 6.60 | 33.10 | 2.20 |
| Pale ale (Burton), | 60.50 | 8.25 | 39.35 | 2.80 |
| Pale ale (Burton), | 55.00 | 8.30 | 40.10 | 2.65 |
| Munich beer, | 56.25 | 15.10 | 58.40 | 2.52 |
| "        " | 56 50 | 16.20 | 56.45 | 2.40 |
| Amsterdam beer, | 53 75 | 13.55 | 51.50 | 2.20 |
| Paris beer (called Strasburg beer), | 47.00 | 16.30 | 45 00 | 2.65 |
| Paris beer (called Strasburg beer), | 45.00 | 14.35 | 51.30 | 2.05 |
| Paris beer (called Strasburg beer), | 47.50 | 11.60 | 43.40 | 2.00 |
| Vienna beer, | 52.50 | 11.00 | 55.30 | 2.30 |

## ACCORDING TO WACKENRODER.

| | Alcohol. | Extract. | Albumen. | Ash. |
|---|---|---|---|---|
| Beer of Lichtenhain, | 3.2 | 4.5 | 0.05 | 0.2 |
| "    Ilmenau, | 3.1 | 7.1 | 0.08 | 0 2 |
| "    Jena (called of Erlangen), | 3.0 | 6.1 | 0.05 | 0.2 |
| "    Weimar (called of Bamberg), | 2 8 | 6.3 | 0.03 | 0.2 |
| "    Oberweimar, | 2.6 | 7.3 | 0.02 | 0.3 |
| Double beer of Jena, | 2.1 | 7.2 | 0.03 | 0.2 |

## BERLIN BEER—27 SAMPLES.

| | | |
|---|---|---|
| Alcohol, | 4.74 | per cent. |
| Extract, | 4.94 | "   " |
| Malt sugar, | 3.78 | "   " |

## BERLIN WHITE BEER.

| | | |
|---|---|---|
| Alcohol, | 1.48 | per cent. |
| Extract, | 3 65 | "   " |
| Ash, | 0.12 | "   " |
| Original gravity, | 7.94 | "   " |

## NASSAU BEER.

| | | |
|---|---|---|
| Alcohol, | 3.737 | per cent. |
| Free carbonic acid, | 0.285 | "   " |
| Extract, | 6.035 | "   " |
| Phosphoric acid, | 0.072 | "   " |

## BEER OF HANOVER.

|  | Max. | Min. | Mean. |
|---|---|---|---|
| Specific gravity at 17.5°, | 1.0353 | 1.0115 | 1.0165 |
| Water ⎫ ⎧ In beer ⎫ | 91.61 | 85.37 | 89.64 |
| Alcohol ⎬ ⎨ freed from ⎬ per cent., | 5.05 | 0.72 | 4.01 |
| Extract ⎭ ⎩ carbonic acid ⎭ | 13.91 | 4.43 | 6.34 |
| Ash, | 0.28 | 0.19 | 0.24 |
| Phosphoric acid in ash, | 0.093 | 0.024 | 0.069 |
| Original gravity of wort, | 17.37 | 12.33 | 14.36 |

# APPENDIX C.

The brewery of modern times is very different from any-thing conceived of one or two hundred years ago. Not merely its extent but all its appliances are characteristic of this busy, progressive age, that knows how to plant money in extensive outfits and supervision, in order that it may yield a greater return, just as seeds put in rich earth and carefully tended during growth give larger harvests of bet-ter quality than were ever looked for in the old hap-hazard, starving plan. We cannot mention one in fifty of those who deserve notice. Think, for instance, of the great brewery of M. T. Bass, at Burton on Trent, which produces about one million barrels a year; or those of Anton Dreher, turning out five hundred thousand barrels, and see if it is possible to attain such results except by modern processes and modern business energy. No house in the United States has yet reached so great a product, but more than one is on the direct way, and it is not only possible but probable that within fifty years the largest establishments and the finest beer will be found in this country. In the multitude of those who fairly deserve mention it seems almost invidious to select a few, but it has seemed best to give a brief account of some that, in one way or another, may be regarded as typical exponents of this department of American industry. Those mentioned are not always the largest or best known, but they represent different parts of the country and together form a tolerable epitome of the

23

whole brewing business, with its larger and smaller breweries, old and new establishments, and various ways of pro-
cedure, the common feature being that all endeavor to
produce a thoroughly good article, and trust to the merit of
the product for success rather than to any temporary advantages that may be gained by cheapening their brew at
the expense of its flavor or wholesomeness. This is the
noticeable fact in the brewing trade at the present time.

### HISTORICAL SKETCH OF HON. FREDERICK LAUER OF READ-ING, PA.

The brewery of Mr. Frederick Lauer of Reading, Pa.,
is not only among the oldest in the country, but has remained from the beginning in the hands of the Lauer family. It was established in 1823 at Womelsdorf, a few miles
from Reading, by the father of the present proprietor, who
had just arrived from Germany. In 1826 it was removed
to Reading, and the business started on the same spot where
it is now carried on. The elder Lauer was an indefatigable
worker, and is said at this time to have taken no more than
two or three hours regular sleep a day. In 1835 his son
Frederick succeeded to the sole proprietorship of the brewery, and its progress from this time was very rapid. For
several years ale and porter had been brewed, but no lager
beer was made in the country until 1842. In the year 1844
Mr. Lauer began to brew lager beer, and was thus one of
the pioneers in this industry; and since that time ale, lager
beer and porter have been produced constantly. The
brewery is a model of neatness and convenience, perfect in
every appointment and the special pride and pet of its
owner, who would much rather lose a year's profits than

tolerate dirt or disorder or the production of a poor beer. Mr. Lauer has not, however, been constantly occupied with his private business. For at least thirty years he has been one of the prominent men of the city of Reading; has held various important public positions, political and otherwise, and has done great service in securing equable legislation in matters affecting the brewing trade. A man of quick perception and untiring energy, he has again and again accomplished alone, or nearly alone, things that were considered almost impossible, and from whose attempt his associates recoiled. An instance in point is thus described in a recently published sketch of his life: "The way the tax was saved was as follows: Shortly before the adjournment of Congress, he (Mr. Lauer) received a letter apprising him that the Committee on Ways and Means were about advising an increase. He immediately telegraphed to the nearest members of the Brewers' Committee to join him at Washington. They had an interview with the Committee of Ways and Means, but the Committee refused to make any modification in the bill, as it had already passed the first reading in the House. There were ten members of the Brewers' Committee, nine of whom, after the interview, agreed to allow the fifty cents increase and make no further exertion in the matter. Mr. Lauer, the tenth, was not satisfied; and, after gaining the consent of the Committee, he called on a number of members of the House, and urged upon them the ruinous consequences to the brewing business which would follow the passage of the bill as reported. The same day, February 11, 1865, the bill came up in Committee of the Whole, when the desired modification was made by a vote of seventy-three to sixty-eight, and the following week the bill came up for final passage, when the bill, as modified, was passed by a majority of four. The members from Kentucky who had voted against the modification in the first place, voted for the bill when it came up on the third reading, they having been influenced through the exertions of Mr. Lauer. Immediately after its passage, Thad. Stevens, chairman on the Ways and Means, jumped up and exclaimed, ' That d—d Lauer did it.' "

This is only one of many instances in which Mr. Lauer's efforts have been of the greatest value to brewers at large and incidentally to the whole country. He was the first president of the United States Brewers' Association, and has more than once been able in time of scarcity to secure such shipments of malt or hops from foreign countries as to relieve the distress and materially reduce the inflated price of these articles.

### THE JOSEPH SCHLITZ BREWING CO., MILWAUKEE, WIS.

In the year 1849 Mr. August Krug built a small brewery at Milwaukee on Chestnut street, between 4th and 5th streets, and the year after he added vaults of a capacity of 150 barrels, situated on the corner of 3d and Walnut streets. His sale was about 250 barrels. From this small beginning there developed one of the largest breweries in the country.

Mr. Krug died in 1856, and Mr. Joseph Schlitz who had come to Milwaukee during the previous year took the management of the business which at first increased only moderately although managed with skill and energy. In the year 1865 the sales were 4,400 barrels. Five years later he began the erection of the present brewery on the corner of 3d and Walnut streets, the same place where the original vaults

had been situated. The greater part of the present buildings were completed within two years, and the sales for
1871 amounted to 12,283 barrels. The period of rapid development had now been reached, and the advance up to
the present time has been remarkable as may be seen from
the following table of the yearly sales, beginning with the
year 1870.

| | | |
|---|---|---|
| 1870, Barrels, | | 8,707 |
| 1871, " | | 12,283 |
| 1872, " | | 30,868 |
| 1873, " | | 49,623 |
| 1874, " | | 69,624 |
| 1875, " | | 74,813 |
| 1876, " | | 71,017 |
| 1877, " | | 79,538 |
| 1878, " | | 82,068 |
| 1879, " ending April, | | 110,832 |

In 1874 the business was made into a stock company
under the title "Joseph Schlitz Brewing Company," with
Mr. Schlitz as president, the secretary and superintendent
being respectively, Mr. August Uihlein and Mr. Henry
Uihlein. Being thus partially relieved of the immediate
cares of business Mr. Schlitz in the following year sailed
for Germany to visit his native home of Mayence. The
vessel was the Schiller, which, as all readers must remember, was wrecked on the Scilly Islands, May 7, 1875, and
Mr. Schlitz was one of the many victims of that disaster. In
these circumstances the company organization was probably
a fortunate circumstance for the business. The death of a
sole proprietor or even a sole nominal proprietor is apt to
derange a business, no matter how capable the successor

may be, and this difficulty is almost avoided in the case of an established company. The present management is as follows:

President, Henry Uihlein ; secretary, August Uihlein ; superintendent, Alfred Uihlein. The brewery in its present form occupies two whole squares, and still larger accomodations may be needed at no distant day. There is a new ice-house 100 x 124 feet, four stories high, and with a twenty-four foot basement. The cellars have a capacity of 25,000 barrels; the whole storage capacity is 70,000 barrels, and the brewery is already fitted for the production of 200,000 barrels a year. There is a large coopering establishment and the gathering of ice alone occupies 300 men and 90 teams for about twenty days every year. The beer is sent all over the United States and to Brazil, Central America and Mexico, in both barrels and bottles. About one million bottles were sold in 1877, and in the succeeding year the amount was more than two millions. The bottling department alone occupies a building 46 x 150 feet, with basement, and fitted with all conveniences for the work.

The analysis of this beer gives the following result for the percentage of alcohol : ordinary lager beer 4.5 volumetrically, and 5.6 by weight. The bottled lager beer shows as a result of four analyses within six months, six per cent. of alcohol volumetrically, and 4.8 by weight. This is certainly an excellent showing, and calculated to enhance the reputation of any brewery.

THE BREWERY OF MR. GOTTFRIED KRUEGER, NEWARK,
N. J.

The brewery now owned by Mr. Gottfried Krueger was founded in 1851 by Louis Adam and J. Braun, the latter of whom died before the buildings were completed. Mr. Adam at once formed a partnership with John Laible under the firm name of Laible & Adam, and pushed the work so well that within the year brewing was commenced, and a sale of 1,200 barrels for the first twelve months secured.

The property then consisted of six city lots, a small frame house partly used as a saloon, a one-story frame brewery thirty feet square, a stable for two horses and vaults for 500 barrels of beer. The brewing capacity was about twenty barrels.

In 1852 Mr. Gottfried Krueger, the present proprietor, came to this country, and being a relative of Mr. Laible entered the brewery as an apprentice. Here he remained until Messrs. Laible and Adam dissolved partnership in 1855, Mr. Laible building a new brewery and Mr. Adam continuing the old business. Mr. Krueger accompanied Mr. Laible and became foreman in the establishment where he remained until 1865 when in conjunction with Mr. Gottlieb Hill he bought the old brewery of Louis Adam and commenced business under the firm name of Hill & Krueger. During the interval a new brewery had been added and a new stable for six horses, while the sale had increased to 4,000 barrels and the brewing capacity to fifty barrels. This advance, however, was destined to be greatly surpassed by that made under the new management. The first step was the building of two new vaults of a capacity of 5,000 barrels. This together with numerous minor improvements was accomplished during the first year, and within the same time the sale of beer was doubled. The years next succeeding saw a rapid development. In 1866 the firm built a new three-story brick malt and store-house; in 1876 a large building for fermenting rooms; in 1868 stables for twenty horses; in 1869 an ice-house of 4,000 barrels capacity, and also vaults for 2,000 barrels. The result fully justified these preparations for an enlarged business for the sale increased steadily year by year and in 1875 amounted to 25,000 barrels.

At this time Mr. Hill was compelled by the state of his health to retire from business, and on the 16th of February, 1875, Mr. Krueger became the sole owner of the property which then covered the entire block. Adding in 1878 a model office building and in 1879 new stables for forty-five horses, he has now one of the finest breweries in the State. The sale for the current year will be over 40,000 barrels.

In explanation of the cut we may add that the malt and brew-houses are situated on Belmont avenue, the office and stables on West Kinney street, the ice-house on Charlton street, and the yards etc., on Montgomery street.

Every one connected with the establishment, from Mr. Krueger down, is thoroughly fit for his duties and zealous in their discharge. The management is by the proprietor himself, ably seconded by Mr. Theodore C. W. Eggerking who has been long and successfully connected with the business.

# APPENDIX D.

## LIST OF BREWERS WITH PRODUCT FOR THE PAST TWO YEARS, 1878 AND 1879. ALSO, PRODUCT BY STATES.

There is some difference of opinion as to the propriety of publishing such information as the annual product of the various breweries in the country, and it therefore seems proper to explain why it has been decided to give the figures in these pages, and how the information has been obtained.

For some time the particulars were furnished to certain parties in Chicago and New York, by a clerk in the Internal Revenue Department at Washington. In this there was probably an injustice, for what is demanded by the law cannot be withheld by the brewer, and both analogy and general reasoning indicate that this forced information should be considered as confidential, and not exposed to the comment of indifferent persons or business rivals.

This view of the case is the one now held by the Department, as appears from the following correspondence:

*Official.*

FROM THE COMMISSIONER OF INTERNAL REVENUE.

(Copy.)
TREASURY DEPARTMENT, WASHINGTON, D. C.,
September 15, 1879.

HENRY H. RUETER, ESQ.,
*President United States Brewers' Association.*

SIR : Your attention is called to an article in the *Brewers' Gazette* of August 15, ultimo, headed, " Thrown Together ; A Comparative View of the so-called Brewers' Returns," in which are embraced copies of letters from this office in relation to lists of reports of sales of fermented liquors for the years 1878 and 1879, as published by the *Western Brewer* and A. E. Tovey.

Please inform me whether the brewers of the United States desire that such tabulated statements be prepared by this Bureau as therein stated for publication.

Very respectfully,
(Signed) GREEN B. RAUM,
*Commissioner.*

24

REPLY OF THE PRESIDENT OF BREWERS' ASSOCIATION.

(Copy.)

UNITED STATES BREWERS' ASSOCIATION,

BOSTON, September 25, 1879.

GEN. GREEN B. RAUM,

*Commissioner of Internal Revenue, Washington, D. C.*

SIR : In reply to your esteemed letter of the 15th inst., referring to the preparation and publication of tabulated statements of brewers' sales, and asking if, in my opinion, the brewers of the United States desire that such tabulated statements be prepared by the Internal Revenue Bureau—I beg to state, that I have no data which would enable me to answer your question definitely. Many brewers, undoubtedly, feel indifferent in the matter ; some may favor the publication, and others are opposed to it. They argue that there is no parallel case in any other branch of trade ; that individual business affairs should not be thus made public ; that the publication of individual sales leads to undue competition ; and that these lists are a bone of bitter contention between the publishers.

If the inquiry has been addressed to me with reference to the future action of the Department, I beg leave to suggest that the brewers' wishes can be best ascertained at their next yearly meeting, in June, and I would respectfully ask you to delay action in the matter till then.

I am, sir, most respectfully yours,

HENRY II. RUETER.

ANSWER TO ABOVE FROM INTERNAL REVENUE DEPARTMENT.

TREASURY DEPARTMENT,

OFFICE OF INTERNAL REVENUE,

WASHINGTON, September 29, 1879.

HENRY H. RUETER, Esq.

*President United States Brewers' Association, Boston, Mass.*

SIR : Acknowledging the receipt of yours of the 25th instant, in reply to office letter of the 15th instant calling attention to an article published in the *Brewers' Gazette* relative to errors in reports of sales of fermented liquors for the years 1878 and 1879, as published by the *Western Brewer* and A. E. Tovey, and inquiring if such publications were considered desirable by the brewers of the United States, I have to say that I fully concur in your opinion that, while some may favor the publication of such statistics, others would object thereto, and would argue that there is no parallel case in any other branch of trade ;

and that individual business affairs should not thus be made public; that such publications lead to undue competition; and that they become a bone of bitter contention between publishers. For this reason, I have decided to prohibit the furnishing of such lists hereafter to any and all parties.

Respectfully,

R. E. ROGERS.

*Acting Commissioner.*

On the other hand, while it is certain that many brewers are glad to have their product extensively stated, it is at least probable that very few have any real objection. In order to test the question we sent a printed form of inquiry, as to production, to all the brewers in the country. A large majority furnished the desired information, and as many others doubtless failed to answer simply through negligence or indifference, it seemed certain that the number of objectors was so small that this list might be published with propriety and to the satisfaction of far the larger part of those interested. It is to be noticed that this is a very different thing from printing enforced statements, without a shadow of authority from the brewers themselves. In this book the figures are generally furnished by the brewers and for this very purpose. Where no reply has been received, the product has been stated according to the best testimony that could be obtained, and the total result is certainly more accurate than any yet published. This is not because the government returns were incorrect, but because of carelessness in transcription, or errors of the types, or both. Whatever the cause, so many errors have been discovered in the so-called official lists of those who obtained their information through Washington, as to greatly impair the value of those tables, and create much dissatisfaction among those who find an erroneous impression of their business thus disseminated through the country. Without claiming that our own are absolutely free from error, we are prepared to maintain their substantial correctness and their superiority to any yet offered to the public. The product here shown is greater than that stated earlier in this book. The returns on which that statement was made seem to have been incomplete at the time of publication, unless the fault lies in the transfer of figures or in the footings, a kind of defect from which few public documents of a statistical character are wholly free. The number of breweries here given is less than the former statement, owing to the omission of a considerable number of the smaller establishments, concerning which no satisfactory information could be obtained, and the further omission of those whose owners were known to object to a publication of their business. The total product of all so left out is known to be inconsiderable, though it cannot be exactly ascertained.

Those most apt to find fault with a public statement of the amount of their business are the smaller brewers, who sometimes fear that their business will suffer if it is known that they dispose of less beer than some rival. To such it may be said that a good business need not be a large one. There are plenty of men in the country who work on a comparatively small scale, and yet would not be induced to extend their operations. They make enough, as it is, to satisfy their wants, and they are not loaded down by the cares that attend a struggle to sell as much as possible. They fear no injury because their sale is not so large as that of some one else, and they are perfectly in the right, as experience shows. Still again, there are many small breweries to-day, that will be great fifteen or twenty years from now. We have shown in Appendix C something of the possibilities of sudden development in this business, and with the increasing taste for beer these opportunities will be better than ever. It is not against a brewery that it is small. Its product may be of the first quality, and it may be small simply because the owner does not care to have it large.

Other considerations might be adduced, but it seems as if enough had been said to justify the printing of statistics prepared as are those here furnished, especially as they must be interesting to every one who makes a study of the beer question and wants as much and as varied information as he can obtain.

# SUMMARY

## OF THE BEER PRODUCT OF THE UNITED STATES FOR THE YEARS 1878 AND 1879, WITH THE INCREASE OR DECREASE DURING THE SECOND OF THESE YEARS.

| Name of State. | No. of Breweries. | No. of Barrels sold from May 1, 1877-8. | No. of Barrels sold from May 1, 1878-9. | Decrease. | Increase. |
|---|---|---|---|---|---|
| Alabama, | 1 | 184 | 74 | 110 | |
| Arkansas, | 1 | 110 | 72 | 38 | |
| Arizona, | 7 | 713 | 720 | | 7 |
| California, | 195 | 379,373 | 385,839 | | 6,466 |
| Colorado, | 29 | 23,901 | 23,464 | 437 | |
| Connecticut, | 19 | 53,528 | 51,988 | 1,540 | |
| Dakota, | 14 | 4,616 | 4,531 | 85 | |
| Delaware, | 3 | 7,841 | 9,563 | | 1,722 |
| District Columbia, | 10 | 27,506 | 29,126 | | 1,620 |
| Georgia, | 1 | 7,330 | 7,710 | | 380 |
| Idaho, | 12 | 936 | 1,484 | | 548 |
| Illinois, | 115 | 579,888 | 608,627 | | 28,739 |
| Indiana, | 76 | 182,448 | 191,729 | | 9,281 |
| Iowa, | 136 | 186,176 | 169,030 | 17,146 | |
| Kansas, | 34 | 20,995 | 24,709 | | 3,714 |
| Kentucky, | 36 | 127,771 | 143,753 | | 15,982 |
| Louisiana, | 10 | 36,352 | 47,407 | | 11,055 |
| Maine, | 1 | 7,031 | 7 | 7,024 | |
| Maryland, | 63 | 208,228 | 205,042 | 3,186 | |
| Massachusetts, | 39 | 711,166 | 663,978 | 47,188 | |
| Michigan, | 140 | 203,043 | 212,231 | | 9,188 |
| Minnesota, | 114 | 101,916 | 113,529 | | 11,613 |
| Missouri, | 72 | 547,590 | 582,372 | | 34,782 |
| Montana, | 22 | 4,677 | 5,516 | | 839 |
| Nebraska, | 27 | 27,100 | 29,270 | | 2,170 |
| Nevada, | 35 | 12,116 | 13,969 | | 1,853 |
| New Hampshire, | 5 | 127,071 | 116,888 | 10,183 | |
| New Jersey, | 57 | 502,574 | 519,864 | | 17,290 |
| New Mexico, | 2 | 110 | 180 | | 70 |
| New York, | 365 | 3,556,678 | 3,980,716 | | 424,038 |
| North Carolina, | 1 | | 4 | | 4 |
| Ohio, | 186 | 968,332 | 965,480 | 2,852 | |
| Oregon, | 39 | 13,362 | 16,159 | | 2,797 |

| Name of State. | No. of Breweries. | No. of Barrels sold from May 1, 1877-8. | No. of Barrels sold from May 1, 1878-9. | Decrease. | Increase. |
|---|---|---|---|---|---|
| Pennsylvania, | 317 | 1,041,486 | 1,034,082 | 7,404 | |
| Rhode Island, | 8 | 25,210 | 27,831 | | 2,621 |
| South Carolina, | 2 | 778 | 372 | 406 | |
| Tennessee, | 4 | 6,980 | 7,107 | | 127 |
| Texas, | 37 | 10,050 | 7,718 | 2,332 | |
| Utah, | 20 | 9,490 | 11,476 | | 1,986 |
| Vermont, | 1 | 285 | 173 | 112 | |
| Virginia, | 3 | 10,694 | 15,694 | | 5,000 |
| Wash. Territory, | 20 | 7,965 | 7,231 | 734 | |
| West Virginia, | 10 | 23,086 | 23,906 | | 1,036 |
| Wisconsin, | 226 | 508,553 | 585,068 | | 76,515 |
| Wyoming Territory, | 8 | 4,060 | 4,505 | | 445 |
| | 2,520 | 10,279,299 | 10,848,194 | 100,777 | 671,888 |

## List of Brewers in the United States, with the Product for the Years ending May, 1878, and May, 1879.

### ARKANSAS.

| | | Number of barrels sold. | |
|---|---|---|---|
| | | 1878. | 1879. |
| Fort Smith, | Freiseis, Joseph, | 110 | 72 |

### ARIZONA.

| | | | |
|---|---|---|---|
| Alexandria, | Minger, Jos. | 54 | 50 |
| Florence, | Will, P. & Co., | 60 | 60 |
| Globe City, | Medler, Fred & Co., | 41 | 49 |
| Prescott, | Raible, John, | 225 | 269 |
| " | Rodenberg, J. N., | 250 | 211 |
| Rio Verde, | Horn, Wm., | 37 | 34 |
| Tucson, | Levin, Alex., | 46 | 47 |
| | Number of Breweries, 7. | 713 | 720 |

## CALIFORNIA.

| | | No. of barrels sold. | |
|---|---|---|---|
| | | 1878. | 1879. |
| Adin, | Jonas & Bofinger, | —— | —— |
| Alameda, | Alameda Brewery, | 817 | 487 |
| Altaville, | Becker, John, | 350 | 350 |
| Anaheim, | Conrad, Fred, | 145 | 158 |
| " | Goodale, I, | 357 | 281 |
| Auburn, | Grohs, Frederick, | 1,060 | 1,020 |
| Benicia, | Rueger, John, | 622 | 697 |
| Benton, | Partzwick Brewery, | 116 | 87 |
| Bishop Creek, | Munzinger, Philippay & Co., | 57 | 189 |
| Boca, | Boca Brewing Company, | 9,717 | 11,035 |
| Bodie, | Frankenberger & Davidson, | —— | 198 |
| " | Carion, A. A, | —— | —— |
| Boonebar, | Ganser, Benj., | —— | —— |
| Camp Independence, | Star Brewery, | 30 | 61 |
| Castroville, | Lauck, George, | 284 | 404 |
| Cherokee, | Bader, Chs., | 139 | 144 |
| Chico, | Croissant, Chs., | 448 | 563 |
| Chollas Valley, | Doblin, C., | 140 | 150 |
| Cloverdale, | Schaeffer & Auker, | 48 | 159 |
| Colusa, | Kammerer, G. & Co., | 800 | 884 |
| Columbia, | Bixel, Joseph, | 174 | 185 |
| Crescent City, | Mayhoffer, Joseph, | 59 | 81 |
| Davisville, | Faber, Wm., | 74 | 77 |
| Dixon, | Sieber & Oberholzer, | 622 | 586 |
| Downieville, | Bosch, F., | 300 | 321 |
| " | Nessler, L., | 275 | 282 |
| Dutch Flat, | Mitchell, Wm., | 320 | 365 |
| Etna, | Küppler, Chs., | 336 | 394 |
| Eureka, | Harper, I., | 148 | 126 |
| " | Huck & McAllenan, | 210 | 273 |
| Folsom, | Yaeger, Peter, | 320 | 419 |
| Forest Hill, | Andres, Joseph, | 112 | 114 |
| Fort Bidwell, | Fulger, M., | 102 | 159 |
| Fresno, | Erpelding, J. L., | —— | 48 |
| Garrote, | Garrote Brewery, | 125. | 149 |
| Germantown, | Miller, A. & Co., | 162 | 300 |
| Gilroy, | Herold, Adam, | 742 | 718 |
| Grass Valley, | Benkelman, D., | 666 | 699 |

CALIFORNIA—Continued.

| | | No. of barrels sold. | |
|---|---|---|---|
| | | 1878. | 1879. |
| Grass Valley, | Frank, John, | 162 | 183 |
| " | Fritz, Chs., | 465 | 398 |
| " | Hodge, Thomas & Co., | 944 | 10,085 |
| Greenwood, | Muhlback, Nancy, | —— | 35 |
| Gaudalupe, | Togninva, Tomasine, | 32 | 87 |
| Havilah, | Neff, Bernhard, | 34 | 87 |
| Haywards, | Lyon's Brewery, | 483 | 502 |
| " | Booken & Herman, | 1,198 | 1,587 |
| Healdsburg, | Müller, Carl, | 170 | 180 |
| Hormitos, | Lessmann, Henry, | 81 | 61 |
| Hollister, | Narcoe, Henry, | 300 | 366 |
| Hot Springs, | Fantz, Edw., | 661 | 678 |
| Independence, | Fernbach, Jo., | 138 | 139 |
| Ione City, | Raab, C., | 314 | 380 |
| Iowa Hill, | Schmidt, John, | 100 | 87 |
| Jackson, | Beiser & Schroeder, | 241 | 435 |
| Kernville, | Cook, Wm , | 220 | 109 |
| " | Wroesch, R. R., | 149 | 137 |
| Knight's Ferry, | Dolling, Victor, | 221 | 263 |
| Lakeport, | Smith, R. O., | 170 | 188 |
| Livermore, | Livermore Brewery, | 215 | 261 |
| Lone Pine, | Lubken, John, | 115 | 74 |
| " | Munzinger & Dodge, | 155 | 35 |
| Los Angeles, | New York Brewery, | 2,479 | 2,075 |
| " | Philadelphia Brewery, | —— | 1,430 |
| " | U. S. Brewery, | —— | 236 |
| " | Schwarz, Louis, | —— | —— |
| Lower Lake, | Mather & Linck, | 330 | 380 |
| Mariposa, | Weiler, John, | 124 | 115 |
| Marysville, | Lieber, Gottlieb, | 725 | 756 |
| Mayfield, | Ducker & Company, | 950 | 1,056 |
| Mendocino, | Larowskia, J. C., | —— | 93 |
| Merced, | Heinerath & Gossner, | 239 | 290 |
| Middletown, | Munz and Scott, | 180 | 318 |
| Modesta, | Lorensen & Peterson, | 454 | 531 |
| " | Braun, M., | 141 | 260 |
| Mokelumne Hill, | Disbrow & Co., | 224 | 192 |
| "　　　　" | Mokelumne Hill Brewery, | 452 | 382 |
| Monitor, | Scossa, John, | —— | —— |
| Napa, | Pfeiffer, Philip, | 251 | 328 |

## CALIFORNIA—CONTINUED.

| | | No. of barrels sold. | |
| | | 1878. | 1879. |
|---|---|---|---|
| Nevada City, | Blasauf, Mary, | 186 | 157 |
| " | Dreyfuss, L. W., | 833 | 702 |
| " | Fogeli, Casper, | 142 | 163 |
| " | Weiss, Emile, | 385 | 422 |
| North Bloomfield, | Weiss, Valentine, | 39 | 57 |
| " " | Hieronimus, S., | —— | 105 |
| North San Juan, | Koch, G. W., | 356 | 427 |
| Oakland, | Welscher & Westermann, | 2,600 | 3,670 |
| " | Kramm & Dieves, | 7,385 | 9,000 |
| " | Bredhoff & Co., | 4,124 | 4,600 |
| Oleta, | Schroder, Henry, | 459 | 376 |
| Oroville, | Schneider, Wm., | 456 | 439 |
| Pajaro, | Dulla & Werner, | 136 | 249 |
| Petaluma, | Robinson, Geo. & Co., | 818 | 531 |
| " | Michelie' & Griess, | 613 | 666 |
| Pine Grove, | Sass, C. D. F., | 232 | 234 |
| Placerville, | Collins, Fred, | 408 | 424 |
| " | Zeiss, Jacob, | 300 | 281 |
| Point Arenas, | Schlachter, John, | 181 | 105 |
| Quincy. | Schlatter, Wm., | 954 | 94 |
| Red Bluff, | Bofinger, W. F., | 602 | 563 |
| Redwood City, | Eureka Brewery, | 572 | 576 |
| " " | Hadler, C., | 896 | 1,077 |
| " " | Kriess, M., | —— | 418 |
| Sacket's Gulf, | Wolf, John, | 720 | 20 |
| Sacramento, | Borchers & Schwartz, | 2,416 | 2,504 |
| " | Gruhler, E. & C., | 2,885 | 2,675 |
| " | Kerth & Nicolaus, | 3,812 | 4,242 |
| " | Knauer, F. C., | 3,020 | 2,995 |
| " | Scheld, P., | 2,040 | 2,164 |
| " | Ochs, M., | 1,763 | 2,163 |
| Salinas, | Lurz & Menke, | 324 | 478 |
| San Andreas, | Bloom, John, | 124 | 96 |
| San Bernardino, | Anderson, John, | 499 | 424 |
| San Buena Ventura, | Hartman, Fredolin, | 140 | 237 |
| San Diego, | Dobler, C., | 49 | 155 |
| " | Walter, Otto, | 147 | 200 |
| San Francisco, | Albany Brewery, Everett St., | | |
| | Hagerman, F. & Co., props., | 13,815 | 13,000 |
| " | Albrecht, James, 623 Braman St., | —— | 880 |

25

## CALIFORNIA—Continued.

| | | No. of barrels sold. | |
|---|---|---|---|
| | | 1878. | 1879. |
| San Francisco, | Bauer, John, 120 Fillmore St. | —— | 617 |
| " | Buss & Hensler, 209 Treat Ave., | —— | 800 |
| " | Bavaria Brewery, Vallejo and Green Sts. | 3,335 | 3,297 |
| " | Bay Brewery, 612, 614 and 616 7th St., Lumann, G., proprietor, | 6,244 | 1,750 |
| " | Broadway Brewery, 637 Broadway, Adams, Jacob, prop., | 5,225 | 4,045 |
| " | Burnell, J. H. & Bro., Ninth Avenue, | 142 | 400 |
| " | Chicago Brewery, 1420 to 1434 Pine St., Aherns, H. & Co., proprietors, | 22,088 | 20.261 |
| " | Christ, John, 25th St., | 90 | 80 |
| " | Empire Brewery, Chestnut St., Harold, John, proprietor, | 19,535 | 17,014 |
| " | Enterprise Brewery, 2019 Folsom St., Hildebrant & Co., proprietors, | 4,190 | 4,300 |
| " | Eureka Brewery, 235 First St., Schweitzer & Bro., proprietors, | 7,154 | 6,800 |
| " | Golden City Brewery, 1431 Pacific St., Buckle, Geo., proprietor, | 1,610 | 1,500 |
| " | Golden Gate Brewery, 713 Greenwich St., Metzler, Chas., proprietor, | 4,675 | 4,969 |
| " | Hayes Valley Brewery, 612 Grove St., Wahlmuth & Co., proprietors, | 2,901 | 3,000 |
| " | Hensler & Fredericks, | —— | —— |
| " | Hibernia Brewery, Howard St., Nunan, M., proprietor, | 17,250 | 19,546 |
| " | Humbold Brewery, 1839 Mission St., Noethig & Turk, proprietors, | 6,784 | 8,000 |
| " | Jackson Brewery, Mission St., Frederick, Wm. A., proprietor, | 7,522 | 8,008 |

## CALIFORNIA—Continued.

| | | No. of barrels sold. | |
|---|---|---|---|
| | | 1878. | 1879. |
| San Francisco, | Kirby, Thos. J., 528½ Noe St., | —— | —— |
| " | Lafayette Brewery, 725 Green St., Grogan & Austell, proprietors, | 5,462 | 5,649 |
| " | Marks Brewery, Tehama St., Marks, Samuel, proprietor, | 498 | 312 |
| " | Mason's Brewery, 527 Chestnut St., Mason, John, proprietor, | 9,625 | 8,000 |
| " | National Brewery, Fulton and Webster Sts., Gluck & Hansen, proprietors, | 13,270 | 13,200 |
| " | New York Brewery, Shotwell St., Kirby, L. J., proprietor, | 2,457 | 508 |
| " | North Beach Brewery, Powell and Chestnut Sts., Schwarz, Jos., proprietor, | 426 | 360 |
| " | Pacific Brewery, 271 Tehama St., Fortmann & Co., proprietors, | 12,668 | 9,947 |
| " | Philadelphia Brewery, 240 Second St., Wieland, John, proprietor, | 43,407 | 44,276 |
| " | Railroad Brewery, Valencia, between 15th and 16th Sts., Schuster, Fred., proprietor, | 1,647 | 1,300 |
| " | Schultz & Geitner, 26th St., | —— | 1,400 |
| " | South San Francisco Brewery, R. R. Ave. and 14th St., Hoelscher, A. &. Co., proprietors, | 2,192 | 2,200 |
| " | South San Francisco Stock Brewing Co., 2118 Powell St., | 10,420 | 8,900 |
| " | Swan Brewing Co., 15th and Dolores Sts., | 971 | 481 |
| " | Swiss Brewery, 414 and 416 Dupont St., | 765 | 498 |
| " | Union Brewery, Hess & Co., proprietors, | 7,020 | 5,800 |

CALIFORNIA—CONTINUED.

| | | No. of barrels sold. | |
|---|---|---|---|
| | | 1878. | 1879. |
| San Francisco, | U. S. Brewery, Franklin and McAllister Sts., | 15,477 | 13,300 |
| " | Washington Brew'y, 723 Lombard St., | 17,326 | 16,321 |
| " | Wilmot Brewing Co., 324 Green St. | 250 | 100 |
| " | Willows Brewery, Fauss, O. & Co., proprietors, cor. 19th and Mission Sts., | 6,501 | 7,600 |
| San Jose, | Eagle Brewery, | 3,983 | 4,052 |
| " | Herman A,, | 191 | 159 |
| " | Krumbs Brewery, | 938 | 850 |
| " | San Jose Brewery, | 1,343 | 1,864 |
| " | Schramm & Schnabel, | 8,372 | 10,034 |
| San Juan, | Bentler & Beck, | 162 | 96 |
| San Leandro, | Columbia Brewery, | 181 | 239 |
| " | Rantzau, T. H., | 181 | 102 |
| San Luis Obispo, | Lindenmeyer, Julius, | 295 | 122 |
| " | Hauser & Williamson, | —— | —— |
| San Rafael, | Bagen & Goerl. | 1,374 | 1,559 |
| Santa Barbara, | Mueller, H. & Bro ,, | 110 | 144 |
| Santa Clara, | Santa Clara Brewery, | 284 | 480 |
| Santa Cruz, | Bausch, Henry, | 703 | 625 |
| Santa Rosa, | Metzger & Haltinner, | 1,029 | 1,146 |
| Shasta, | Behrle & Litsch | 358 | 379 |
| Sonora, | Baccigalapi, Louis, | 297 | 179 |
| " | Bauman, John, | 640 | 571 |
| South Vallejo, | Deminger, Fred, | 1,706 | 2,534 |
| Stockton, | Boemer & Wirth, | 515 | 612 |
| " | Neistrath, Eliz., | 505 | 716 |
| " | Rothenbush, D., | 384 | 819 |
| Sutter Creek, | Rabolt, L. | 661 | 759 |
| Sutterville, | Theilen, N., | 1,168 | 1,081 |
| Truckee, | Grazer & Stoll, | 245 | 234 |
| " | Menk, Paul, | 76 | 52 |
| Ten-Mile River, | Franz & Bader, | —— | 5 |
| Ukiah, | Wurtenburg, S., | 338 | 250 |
| Vallejo, | Widenmann & Rothenburg, | 1,722 | 1,706 |
| " | Smith, P. & J., | 250 | 1,097 |
| Vallecito, | Vallecito Brewery, | 129 | 113 |

## CALIFORNIA—Continued.

| | | No. of barrels sold. | |
|---|---|---|---|
| | | 1878. | 1879. |
| Visalia, | Mooney's Brewery, | 594 | 581 |
| " | Empire Brewery, | —— | 33 |
| Volcano, | Griesbach, Geo. | 40 | 28 |
| Watsonville, | Kuhlitz, C., | 72 | 118 |
| " | Palmtag, Christian, | 1,495 | 1,721 |
| Weaverville, | Meckel, J , | —— | 34 |
| Woodland, | Schuerley & Miller, | 1,458 | 1,206 |
| " | Wirt, Geo. L., | 200 | 180 |
| Yreka, | Yeters, Chas. | 297 | 305 |
| " | Junker, Chas., | 311 | 298 |
| Yuba City, | Klempp, Fred., | 270 | 305 |
| | Number of Breweries, 189. | 379,373 | 385,839 |

## COLORADO.

| | | | |
|---|---|---|---|
| Black Hawk, | Haubrick, Sam'l, | 791 | 580 |
| Boulder City, | Weisenhorn & Voegte, | 1,410 | 945 |
| Central City, | Lehmkul, Wm., | 890 | 1,175 |
| " | Richards & Wickett, | 777 | 190 |
| " | Staum, Chr., | 903 | —— |
| Colorado City, | El Paso Co. Brewing Co., | 222 | 723 |
| Del Norte, | Bingle & Co., | 170 | 300 |
| Denver, | Denver Brewing Co. | 5,858 | —— |
| " | Colorado Brewing Co., | —— | 59 |
| " | Bendleburg, Geo,, | 40 | 60 |
| " | Melsheimer, Max, | —— | 1,290 |
| " | Oppenlander, G. F., | 1,423 | 1,472 |
| " | Zang, Philip, | 6,110 | 8,408 |
| Fair Play, | Summer, Leonard, | 229 | 344 |
| Georgetown, | Summer, John & Bro. | 694 | 670 |
| Golden, | Schueler & Coos, | 2,857 | 3,004 |
| Granite, | Mesch & Gerter, | 11 | 155 |
| Idaho Springs, | Ullrich, Fred, | 106 | 99 |
| Lake City, | Fisher & Co , | 50 | 182 |
| " | Hirt, Chas., | 135 | 203 |
| Leadville, | Fuernstein. C., | —— | 210 |
| " | Leadville Brewery, | —— | 300 |
| " | Gau, Elizabeth J., | —— | 632 |
| Malta, | Sponagel, V. H., | —— | 300 |

## COLORADO—Continued.

| | | No. of barrels sold. 1878. | 1879. |
|---|---|---|---|
| Ouray, | Geiger, D., | —— | 80 |
| Pueblo, | Merz, Elias, | 850 | 1,062 |
| Rosita, | Townsend, T. D., | 95 | 153 |
| Silver Plume, | Boche, Otto, | —— | —— |
| Trinidad, | Schneider, Henry, | 280 | 868 |
| | Number of Breweries, 29. | 23,901 | 23,464 |

## CONNECTICUT.

| | | | |
|---|---|---|---|
| Bridgeport, | Eckart Bros., | 2,599 | 2,120 |
| " | Kutscher, Louis, | 164 | 162 |
| " | Klaus, Fred, | 3,200 | 3,584 |
| " | Knoedler, Christian, | 66 | 86 |
| " | Loehr, C., | 1,687 | 2,588 |
| " | Stoehr, C., | 1,687 | 2,588 |
| " | Winter, Albert, | 4,170 | 3,362 |
| Hartford, | Herold Capitol Brewing Co., | 2,058 | 2,339 |
| " | Shannon & McCann, | 5,547 | 6,151 |
| " | Sichler, George, | 2,243 | 2,400 |
| Middletown, | Hopke & Wilkins, Jr., | 689 | 1,870 |
| New Haven, | Bassermann, Geo. A., | 4,564 | 3,900 |
| " | Fresenius, Ph., | 8,716 | 8,080 |
| " | Hull, Wm. & Son, | 9,454 | 7,430 |
| " | Nicholas, Chas., | 321 | 233 |
| " | Yastron, Rich., | 22 | 18 |
| Rockville, | Link, Erhardt, | 1,018 | 784 |
| Thompsonville, | Matthewson, John, | 4,967 | 3,791 |
| Waterbury, | Hellman & Kipp, | 356 | 500 |
| | Number of Breweries, 19. | 53,528 | 51,988 |

## DAKOTA.

| | | | |
|---|---|---|---|
| Bismarck, | Walker, J. E., | 684 | 502 |
| " | Walters & Kalberer, | 714 | 404 |
| Central City, | Rosenkranz & Werner, | —— | 264 |
| Custar City, | Parks, Robert, | —— | |
| Deadwood, | Downer & Co., | 12 | 120 |
| " | Nishwitz Wm., | —— | 25 |

## DAKOTA—CONTINUED.

| | | No. of barrels sold. | |
|---|---|---|---|
| | | 1878. | 1879. |
| Deadwood, | Rodebank & Nielson, | —— | —— |
| " | Schuchardt, A., | —— | —— |
| Fargo, | Brokorsch, Jos. W., | —— | 90 |
| Fort Totten, | Brenner, E. W., | 339 | 365 |
| Lead City, | Jentes, Hall, | —— | 19 |
| Sioux Falls, | Knott, G. A. & Co., | 371 | 1,023 |
| Yankton, | Forester John, | 1,621 | 885 |
| " | Roptenscher & Co., | 875 | 834 |
| | Number of Breweries, 14. | 4,616 | 4,531 |

## DELAWARE.

| | | | |
|---|---|---|---|
| Wilmington, | Hartman & Fehrenbach, | 3,871 | 4,700 |
| " | Specht, Carl, | 90 | 308 |
| " | Stoeckle, Jos., | 3,880 | 4,555 |
| | Number of Breweries, 3. | 7,841 | 9,563 |

## DISTRICT OF COLUMBIA.

| | | | |
|---|---|---|---|
| Georgetown, | Duetz, Catherine, 38 and 40 Green St., | 792 | 661 |
| Washington, | Adt. F. J., bet. 13th and 14th Sts., E. and D. and S. E., | 2,509 | 1,960 |
| " | Albert. John, cor. 25th and F. N. W., | 686 | 597 |
| " | Cook, John G., 45 N St , N. W., | 264 | 364 |
| " | Dickson, Chris., 719 4 1-2 St., | 1,373 | 1,309 |
| " | Henrich, Christian, 1229 20th St., N. W., | 7,400 | 10,711 |
| " | Juenemann, Geo., 400 E St., N. W., | 11,341 | 11,151 |
| " | Kernwein, George, No. 124 N St , N. W., | 203 | 261 |
| " | Roth, Jacob, 318 First St., N. W., | 2,258 | 1,674 |
| " | Zanner, Wm., 526 4 1-2 St., S. W., | 620 | 438 |
| | Number of Breweries, 10. | 27,506 | 29,126 |

## GEORGIA.

| | | No. of barrels sold. | |
|---|---|---|---|
| | | 1878. | 1879. |
| Atlanta, | Atlanta City Brewing Co., W. | | |
| | II. Tuller, President, | 7,330 | 7,710 |

## IDAHO.

| | | | |
|---|---|---|---|
| Atlanta, | Wilmer & Motlow, | —— | —— |
| Boise City, | Broadbeck, John, | 6 | 240 |
| " | Lemp, John, | 329 | 492 |
| Bonanza City, | Hepburn, John & Co., | —— | —— |
| Challis, | Albiez, Frederick, | —— | —— |
| Idaho City, | Haug, Nicolas, | 160 | 198 |
| Jordan Creek, | Frank & Gundorf, | —— | —— |
| Lewiston, | Weisgerber Bros., | 307 | 380 |
| Pioneer City, | Stadtmiller, Jos., | 45 | 58 |
| Placerville, | Kohny, Chas., | 25 | 11 |
| Salmon City, | Spahn, Michael, | 31 | 45 |
| Silver City, | Summercamp, W. F., | 33 | 60 |
| | Number of Breweries, 12. | 936 | 1,484 |

## ILLINOIS.

| | | | |
|---|---|---|---|
| Alton, | Jehle & Peters, | 3,183 | 3,995 |
| Aurora, | Knell, John, | —— | —— |
| " | McInhill, J. V., | 651 | —— |
| Beardstown, | Rink, Anton, | 1,645 | 1,284 |
| Belleville, | Hartman Bros., | 11,951 | 13,452 |
| " | Stoegle, Fidel, | 4,300 | 4,022 |
| Belvidere, | Waldeck, J., | 307 | 77 |
| Blue Island, | Bauer, Henry, | 238 | 116 |
| " | Metz & Schwachow, | 2.199 | 680 |
| Bloomington, | Meyer & Wochner, | 4,968 | 5,169 |
| Bowmanville, | Volmer, W., | 1,006 | 1,004 |
| Canton, | Koebel, L., | 182 | 144 |
| Carlinville, | Deibel, G. P. & Bro., | 1,244 | 1,188 |
| Chicago, | Bartholomae & Leicht Brewing Co., 688 to 706 Sedgwick St., | 28,293 | 31,245 |

## ILLINOIS—Continued.

| | | No. of barrels sold. | |
| | | 1878. | 1879. |
| --- | --- | --- | --- |
| Chicago, | Bartholomae & Roesing, 335 W. 12th St., | 12,939 | 10,648 |
| " | Brand, M. & Co., Elston Ave. and River St., | 6,173 | 84,419 |
| " | Busch & Brand Brewery Co., 29 and 31 Cedar St., (May and June, 1878), | 29,941 | 5,070 |
| " | Chicago Union Brewing Co., 27th St. and Johnson Ave., | 6,379 | 4,283 |
| " | Devereaux, J., 432 N. State St., | 250 | 138 |
| " | Downer & Bemis Brewing Co., 91 S. Park Ave., | 56,770 | 66,878 |
| " | Fortune Bros., 138 to 144 W. Van Buren St., | 12,222 | 13,555 |
| " | Funk, Ernst, 44 Willow St., | 362 | 180 |
| " | Gillen, Schmidt & Co., 416 25th St., | 256 | 462 |
| " | Gottfried, M., 166 Archer Ave., | 19,595 | 16,831 |
| " | Hoerber, Jno. L., 220 and 222 W. 12th St., | 1,912 | 2,125 |
| " | Jerusalem, Jos., 307 Rush St., | 312 | 476 |
| " | Keeley Brewing Co., 28th St., near Cottage Grove Ave., | 6,499 | 8,766 |
| " | Schmidt & Glade, 9 to 35 Grant Place, | 21,128 | 26,534 |
| " | Schoenhofen, Peter, 34 to 50 Seward St., | 36,014 | 41,447 |
| " | Seipp, Conrad Brewing Co., foot of 27th St., | 103,787 | 108,347 |
| " | Seiben, Michael, 335 and 337 Larrabee St., | 2,942 | 3,182 |
| " | Wagner, Ludwig, 942 N. Clark St., | 388 | 446 |
| " | Walther, Frank, 408 Paulina St., (March and April, 1879), | —— | 517 |
| Columbia, | Monroe Brewery. | 1,173 | 1,384 |
| Danville, | Stein, John, | 1,861 | 1,587 |
| Decatur, | Harpstrite & Schlanderman, | 4,147 | 3,076 |
| DeKalb, | Corkings, Thos., | 1,013 | 797 |
| Dixon, | Clears, Jas. B., | 510 | 435 |

26

## ILLINOIS—CONTINUED.

| | | No. of barrels sold. | |
|---|---|---|---|
| | | 1878. | 1879. |
| Dixon, | Plein, Nicholas, | 977 | 1,475 |
| East St. Louis, | Heim, F. & Bro., | 11,380 | 14,020 |
| Edwardsville, | Mick, Henry, | 1,026 | 564 |
| Elgin, | Althen, Casper, | 1,350 | 962 |
| Fayetteville, | Luers, P. & F., | 474 | —— |
| Freeburg, | Meyer, Aug., | 675 | 313 |
| Freeport, | Baier & Seyfarth, | 2,134 | 1,954 |
| " | Milner, Jos. & Bros., | 358 | 539 |
| Galena, | Hony & Metzger, | 456 | 488 |
| " | Meller & Haser, | 834 | 628 |
| " | Meller, Math., | 1,550 | 2,066 |
| " | Speier, Rudolph, | 783 | 476 |
| Geneseo, | Gasser, Geo. & Co., | 2,718 | 2,453 |
| Harvard, | Huebner, John, | 630 | 536 |
| Havana, | Dehm & Mack, | 1,590 | 1,192 |
| Highland, | Schott, Martin J., | 3,023 | 3,855 |
| Jacksonville, | Rick, H. & Sons, | 2,144 | 1,177 |
| Joliet, | Eder Henry, | 4,544 | 4,608 |
| " | Porter, Edwin, | 7,494 | 7,467 |
| " | Sehring, Fred., | 4,143 | 4,258 |
| Kankakee, | Radeke, F. K., Brewing Co., | 2 089 | 1,779 |
| Kewanee, | Lee, Frederick, | 590 | 560 |
| Knoxville, | Krotter, John, | 363 | 130 |
| Lacon, | Hochstrasser & Co., | 936 | 652 |
| La Salle, | Eliei, L. & Co., | 13,184 | 12,225 |
| Lebanon, | Hammel, Jacob, | 3,772 | 3,717 |
| Limestone, | Keller, Geo., | 60 | 70 |
| Lincoln, | Mueller, P. & Son, | 1 401 | —— |
| Mascoutah, | Eisele & Koehler, | 1,887 | 1,232 |
| McHenry, | Bailey, G., | 697 | 710 |
| Mendota, | Henning, Christian, | 5,715 | 5,457 |
| Morris, | Bauman & Hahl, | 204 | 318 |
| " | Gabhard, Lewis, | 1,611 | 1,701 |
| Mt. Carroll, | Medlar, Chas., | 114 | 114 |
| Mt. Vernon, | Wetzel & Fuchs, | —— | —— |
| Murphysboro, | Broeg, Conrad, | 565 | 272 |
| Naperville, | Stenger, John, | 4,030 | 2,640 |
| Nauvoo, | Schenk, G. T. | 441 | 288 |
| New Athens, | New Athens Brewery, | 1,023 | 698 |
| Northville, | Rentlinger, Richard, | —— | 141 |

## ILLINOIS—CONTINUED.

| | | No. of barrels sold. | |
|---|---|---|---|
| | | 1878. | 1879. |
| Ottawa, | Rabenstein, C., | 3,278 | 2,857 |
| " | White, Alfred, | 1,441 | 1,594 |
| Pecatonica, | Berridge, Wm., | 251 • | 256 |
| Pekin, | Winkel, Aug., | 2,186 | 2,221 |
| Peoria, | Bitz, Conrad, | 171 | 296 |
| " | Gipps & Co., | 9,526 | 11,019 |
| " | Weber, Aug., | 2,503 | 921 |
| Peru, | Peru Beer Co., | 3,446 | 3,743 |
| " | Union Beer Co., | 2,778 | 2,705 |
| Quincy, | Eber Bros., | 1,556 | 1,386 |
| " | Dick & Bros., | 12,926 | 15,600 |
| " | Koerner, M., | 19 | 85 |
| " | Luther, J., | 483 | 2,100 |
| " | Ruff Bros. & Co., | 3,793 | 4,775 |
| Rockford, | Fisher & Wahl, | 473 | 336 |
| " | Kauffman, Aug., | 398 | 493 |
| " | Peacock, Jonathan, | 982 | 846 |
| Rock Island, | Huber, Ignatz, | 6,758 | 7,308 |
| " | King, J. A. & Co., | 2,826 | 2,856 |
| " | Wagner, Geo., | 10,205 | 9,937 |
| Savannah, | Keller, Jos., | 1,200 | 1,194 |
| Sigel, | Wiedmeier, D. & Co., | 42 | 7 |
| Silver Creek, | Haegeli & Roth, | 345 | 897 |
| Spring Bay, | Eichhorn, Peter, | 630 | 610 |
| Springfield, | Reisch & Bros., | 8,758 | 9,358 |
| Sterling, | Decker, J. & Co., | 737 | 510 |
| " | Hermann, Chas., | 315 | 1,129 |
| Thornton, | Bielfeldt, J. S., | 932 | 1,105 |
| Trenton | Bassler, Paul, | 1,110 | 850 |
| Warsaw, | Popel, Martin, | 58 | 160 |
| " | Schott & Son, | 1,073 | 877 |
| Washington, | Roth, John, | —— | 14 |
| Waukegan, | Besley's Waukegan Brewing Company, | 4,596 | 4,081 |
| West Belleville, | Western Brewing Co., | 10,019 | 11,618 |
| Wheeling, | Periolat Bros. & Co., | 1,875 | 1,889 |
| Wilmington, | Markert & Co., | 2,844 | 3,512 |
| Woodstock, | Arnold, Zimmer & Co., | 4,031 | 3,336 |
| | Number of Breweries, 115. | 579,888 | 608,627 |

## INDIANA.

| | | No. of barrels sold. | |
|---|---|---|---|
| | | 1878. | 1879. |
| Aurora, | Crescent Brewing Co., | 29,037 | 30,731 |
| Bowling Green, | Stucki, Fred, | 420 | 188 |
| Bremen, | Wolff, Hugo, | 471 | 277 |
| Cambridge, | Straub, Cleophas, | 418 | 366 |
| " | Ingerman, Henry, | 477 | 390 |
| Cannelton, | Huber Jacob, | 300 | 373 |
| Centre, | Weckerie, J., | 1,300 | —— |
| Columbia City, | Schaffer, H., | 986 | 1 086 |
| Columbus, | Schreiber, Aug., | 720 | 434 |
| Connersville, | Billan, Valentine, | 190 | 405 |
| Covington, | Miller, Joseph, | 958 | 1,290 |
| Crawfordsville, | Muth, Jacob, | 1,285 | 676 |
| Crown Point, | Korn & Suckfield, | 828 | 515 |
| Decatur, | Rolver, Anna, | 218 | 280 |
| Evansville, | Cook & Rice, | 15,738 | 17,158 |
| " | Uhner & Hoerz, | 1,522 | 6,119 |
| Ferdinand, | Ruhkamp, Henry, Jr., | 665 | 775 |
| Fort Wayne, | Centlivre, C. L., | 2,245 | 3,715 |
| " | Horning, L. J,, | —— | 41 |
| " | Linker, Hey & Co., | 1,310 | 1,616 |
| " | Lutz & Co., | 3,436 | 3,327 |
| German Township, | Pauli, A., | 145 | —— |
| Harmony, | Bauer, John, | 40 | —— |
| Harrison, | Klant, Reinhold, | 385 | 180 |
| " | Krodle, Jno. B., | 453 | 378 |
| Huntington, | Boos, Jacob, | 901 | 889 |
| " | Herrberg, J. & A., | 202 | 106 |
| Indianapolis, | Balz & Co., | 1,452 | —— |
| " | Lieber, P & Co., | 12,000 | 15,000 |
| " | Maus, C., | 5,233 | 7,037 |
| " | Koehler & Co , | 300 | 344 |
| " | Schmidt, Mrs. C. F., | 22,640 | 25,288 |
| Jeffersonville, | Lang Henry, | 533 | 429 |
| Kendallville, | Paul, H. C. | 1,164 | 1 068 |
| La Fayette, | Newman & Bohrer, | 5,537 | 4,872 |
| " | Thieme & Wagner, | 5,076 | 6,524 |
| La Porte, | Puissant, Jno. B., | 1,555 | 880 |
| Lawrenceburgh, | Gamer, J. B., | 3,988 | 2,542 |
| Lawrenceville, | Ritze, Anton, | 368 | 343 |

INDIANA—Continued.

| | | No. of barrels sold. | |
|---|---|---|---|
| | | 1878. | 1879. |
| Logansport, | Mutschler, Jno., | 2,097 | 1,044 |
| Madison, | Belser & Co., | 1,808 | —— |
| " | Greiner, Jno., | 2,202 | 2,523 |
| " | Weber, Peter, | 5,104 | 5,040 |
| Michigan City, | Zorn, Philip, | 2,592 | 3,300 |
| Mishawaka, | Kaume, A., | 3,595 | 3,642 |
| Muncie, | Garst, A. J., | —— | 100 |
| " | Alvery, Ch., | —— | —— |
| Napoleon, | Morbach, Nicholas, | 175 | 280 |
| New Albany, | Buchheit, Barbara, | 3,045 | 3,535 |
| " | Nadorff, Frank, | 105 | 492 |
| " | Reising, Paul, | 3 900 | 3,211 |
| New Alsace, | Meyer, Martin, | 248 | 192 |
| " | Zix, Michael, | 210 | 190 |
| Newburg, | Brizins, Chas., & Co., | 489 | 378 |
| North Vernon, | Schierling, John, | 169 | 156 |
| Oldenberg, | Roell, B., | 988 | 805 |
| Perry, | Hartmetz, John, | 667 | 620 |
| Peru, | Cole, J O., | 5,312 | 4,729 |
| Plymouth, | Weckerle, J., | 1,031 | 928 |
| Richmond, | Martischang, Joseph, | 170 | 197 |
| " | Minck, Emil, | 215 | 217 |
| Rochester, | Metzler, John B., | 437 | 218 |
| Seymour, | Dammrich, Martin, | 396 | 250 |
| " | Kaufman, J. D., | 279 | 288 |
| South Bend, | Muessel Bros., | 1,811 | 2,129 |
| St. Leon, | Biscoff, L., | 20 | 36 |
| St. Peters, | Busold, John A., | 195 | 240 |
| Suhman, | Schneider, P., Jr., | —— | 400 |
| Tell City, | Becker, Chas., | 480 | 430 |
| " | Voelke, Fred, | 765 | 776 |
| Terre Haute, | Mayer, Anton, | 10,043 | 11,753 |
| " | Wheat, N. S., | 351 | 271 |
| Troy, | Thaeny, John, | 595 | 745 |
| Valparaiso, | Hiller Geo., | 798 | 468 |
| Vincennes, | Hack & Simon, | 3,969 | 5,919 |
| Wabash, | Rettig & Alber, | 1,310 | 1,126 |
| | Number of Breweries, 76. | 182,448 | 191,729 |

## IOWA.

| | | No. of barrels sold. | |
|---|---|---|---|
| | | 1878. | 1879. |
| Afton, | Heine, John, | 277 | 64 |
| Anamosa, | Rick, M. F., | 572 | 268 |
| Atlantic, | Fisher, Ernest, | 219 | 1,370 |
| Auburn, | Bilger, Katherine, | 885 | 540 |
| Avoca, | Kampf, Jacob, | 1,300 | 1,250 |
| Bellevue, | Neustatdt, H., | 814 | 892 |
| Belle Plaine, | Michel, Mathias, | 1,258 | 1.258 |
| Boone, | Herman, J. M., | 2,482 | 2,017 |
| Boonsboro, | Zimbelman, L. & Co., | 2,583 | 3,090 |
| Bridgeport, | Walz, Bernhart, | 321 | 408 |
| Brown's Station, | Brown, Henry, | 174 | 147 |
| Buffalo, | Barthberger, John, | —— | —— |
| " | Hoffbauer, Hugo, | 374 | 282 |
| " | Kantz, Theo., | 366 | 286 |
| Burlington, | Bosch Bros., | 2,124 | —— |
| " | Bosch, John, Geo., & Co., | 2,778 | 2,255 |
| " | Heil, Casper, | 1,808 | —— |
| " | Rothenberger, P. P., | 1,670 | 1,091 |
| " | Werthmueller & Ende, | 2,500 | 2,441 |
| Cascade, | May, Francis, | 947 | 757 |
| Cedar Falls, | Lund, Hans N., | 597 | —— |
| " | Pfeiffer, H. & Bro., | 412 | 547 |
| Cedar Rapids, | Magnus, C., | 5,932 | 6,915 |
| " | Williams, Geo. & Co., | 6,237 | 6,166 |
| Charles City, | Andre, Gertrude, | 2,514 | 1,678 |
| Clarinda, | Peterson, B. A., | 495 | 368 |
| Clinton, | Lauer & Allen, | 1,032 | 1,417 |
| Concord, | Sandler, A. Jr., | 10 | —— |
| Council Bluffs, | Geise, Conrad, | 6,006 | 5.740 |
| County of Iowa, | Amana Society, | 1,731 | 1,813 |
| Creston, | Bolig, P., | 118 | —— |
| " | Bolig & Co. | —— | —— |
| Davenport, | Frahm, M., | 6,006 | 6,107 |
| " | Koehler & Lange, | 6,609 | 7,563 |
| " | Lage, J. & Co., | 4,052 | 3,779 |
| " | Lehrkind, J. & Co., | 2,676 | 3,012 |
| " | Noth, G. & Sons, | 2,125 | —— |
| Decorah, | Addicken, Mrs. G., | 1 800 | 1,872 |
| " | Klein, Jos., | 1,395 | 924 |

## IOWA—Continued.

| | | No. of barrels sold. | |
|---|---|---|---|
| | | 1878. | 1879. |
| Des Moines, | Aulmann & Schuster, | 1,646 | 2,185 |
| " | Kinsley, Joseph, | 341 | 362 |
| " | Mattes, Alois, | 3,325 | 2,169 |
| " | Mattes & Jung, | 1,224 | 1,314 |
| De Witt, | Yegge, V., | 1,234 | 1,234 |
| Dorchester, | Tacke, Jos., | 321 | 183 |
| Dubuque, | Glab, Adam, | 3,483 | —— |
| " | Ileeb, A., | 8,327 | 8,072 |
| " | Meuser & Co., | 3,288 | 3,437 |
| " | Peaslee & Co., | 3,497 | 940 |
| " | Peir, John, | —— | 1,410 |
| " | Tschirgi, & Schwind, | 4,171 | 4,348 |
| Dyersville, | Esch & Bros., | 1,198 | 1,432 |
| Elgin, | Shorie & Lehman, | 604 | 532 |
| Elkader, | Schmidt, J. B. & Bro., | 1,644 | 1,145 |
| Fairfield, | Toeller & Suess, | 795 | 482 |
| Fayette, | Moser, Martin, | 119 | —— |
| Fort Dodge, | Koll, Jno., | 882 | —— |
| " | Schmidt, D., | 802 | —— |
| Fort Madison, | Burstor, Anton, | 558 | 476 |
| " | Schlapp, Henry, | 1,584 | 1 316 |
| Franklin Center, | Best, William, | 134 | 150 |
| Garnavillo, | Schumacher, H., | 611 | 563 |
| Grand Meadow, | Koering, Jos., | 1,051 | 736 |
| Guttenburg, | Hassfield, Wm., | 55 | 60 |
| " | Jungk, Aug., | 1,146 | 1,050 |
| " | Roth, John, | 144 | 352 |
| " | Walter, Rudolph, | 100 | —— |
| Hamburg, | Nies, Philip, | 1,984 | 2,095 |
| Independence, | Seeland, Cris., | 429 | 489 |
| " | Wengert, John, | 1,235 | 1,608 |
| Iowa City, | Dostal, Jno. P., | 3,999 | 3,301 |
| " | Englert & Rittenmeyer, | 1,398 | 1.052 |
| " | Hotz, Simon, | 2,945 | 2,452 |
| Iowa Falls, | Althen, John, | 166 | —— |
| Jefferson, | Roth, Peter, | 400 | —— |
| Keokuk, | Anschutez, F. W., | 703 | 580 |
| " | Leisy, Mrs. M. | 2,425 | 2,239 |
| " | Pechstein & Nagel, | 973 | 949 |
| Lansing, | Haas, Jacob, | 1,907 | 1,373 |

IOWA—CONTINUED.

| | | No. of barrels sold. | |
|---|---|---|---|
| | | 1878. | 1879. |
| Lemars, | Diamond, Herbut A., | 58 | —— |
| " | Maning, L. H. & Co., | —— | 45 |
| Lyons, | Tritschler & Tiesse, | 3,414 | 3,187 |
| Marengo, | Knepper, T. C., | 420 | 480 |
| Marion, | Schneider Bros., | 3,588 | 3,916 |
| Marshall, | Roth, Peter, | 276 | —— |
| Marshalltown, | Bowman Bros., | 2,224 | 3,018 |
| " | Vogel, Geo., | . 42 | 265 |
| Mason City, | Brohm & McDevitt, | 210 | 385 |
| Maquoketa, | Dostal & Hoffmann, | 1,713 | 1,782 |
| McGregor, | Hagensick, J. L., | 939 | 773 |
| Montrose, | Spring, Martin, | 169 | 62 |
| Mt. Carmel, | Gram, A. L., | —— | —— |
| Muscatine, | Dold, Chas. J. Brewing Co., | 1,980 | 2,120 |
| " | Dorn, Jacob, | 204 | 108 |
| " | Eegerman, Mary, | 995 | 1,025 |
| " | Schaefe, John, | 1,800 | —— |
| " | Witteman, A., | 2,117 | 1,580 |
| New Hampton, | Gross, A. A. | 1,050 | 1.050 |
| New Vienna, | Baeumle & Ferring, | 754 | 1.238 |
| Nodaway, | Auun & Peterson, | 495 | —— |
| Nora Springs, | Festel, Florian, | 112 | 120 |
| Osage, | Pierce, R. H., | 770 | 600 |
| Osceola, | Jacobs, Chas., | 370 | 480 |
| Oskaloosa, | Blatner & Newbrand, | 975 | 728 |
| Ottumwa, | Hausman & Bauer, | 2,379 | 2.398 |
| " | Hoffman, B., | 2,756 | 3,398 |
| " | Schaefer & Hoffmann, | —— | —— |
| " | The Wm. Kranner Brewing Co., | 2,320 | 4,351 |
| Pella, | Blattner & Herbig, | 372 | 419 |
| Postville, | Koenig, Jos., | 1,051 | —— |
| Red Oak, | Stroh, Charles, | 960 | 550 |
| Rockford, | Marke, S., | 942 | 1.042 |
| Sevastopool, | Munzinger, G., | 1,250 | 1,275 |
| Shell Rock, | Scully, Jas., | 287 | 97 |
| Sherrill's Mound, | Haberkon, Geo,, | 140 | —— |
| Sioux City, | Franz & Co., | 2,148 | 3,120 |
| " | Selzer, R., | 1,512 | 1,522 |
| Spillville, | Nockles, Frank, | 911 | 945 |
| " | Schwela & Glasbrenner, | —— | 288 |

## IOWA—Continued.

| | | No. of barrels sold. | |
|---|---|---|---|
| | | 1878. | 1879. |
| Stacyville, | Huxhold, J. H. C., | 201 | 150 |
| Strawberry Point, | Kleinlein, John, | 921 | 858 |
| Stuart, | Eber, John, | 742 | 1,114 |
| Tama City, | Matthews, A., | 516 | 780 |
| Vail, | Smutney, A., | 220 | 200 |
| Vinton, | Biebesheimer, H. | 168 | 312 |
| Washington, | Jugenheimer, Wm. & Co., | 1,360 | 920 |
| " | Zahm, H., | 410 | 377 |
| Waterloo, | Goldstein & Rainer, | 806 | 840 |
| Waukon, | Mauch, George, | 308 | 270 |
| Waverly, | Foselman, Peter, | 1,632 | 1,671 |
| " | Tabor, S. A., | 43 | 66 |
| Webster City, | Ramharter, A., | 477 | 639 |
| West Mitchell. | Fey, John, | 1,375 | 1,144 |
| West Point, | Lampe, Bernard, | 159 | —— |
| " | Troup, Fritz, | —— | —— |
| Wilton, | Miller, Philip F., | 923 | 890 |
| Winterset, | Schroeder, Morris, | 75 | —— |
| | Number of Breweries, 136. | 186,176 | 169,030 |

## KANSAS.

| | | | |
|---|---|---|---|
| Atchison, | Young, Frank, | 752 | 328 |
| " | Zibold & Haegelin, | 2,079 | 2,700 |
| Beloit, | Pupka & Eberle, | 30 | 214 |
| Carr Creek, | Marsch. Peter, Jr.. | 44 | 78 |
| Cawker City, | Schaaf, Jos., | 208 | 126 |
| Chanute, | Hartman Bros., | 300 | 80 |
| Elinwood, | Hess, John, | 286 | 576 |
| Emporia, | Macke, F. H. & Co., | 400 | 349 |
| Eudora, | Bartusch, Robert, | 101 | 61 |
| Fort Scott, | Schultz & Co., | 2,040 | 2,640 |
| Hanover, | Jockers, Charles, | 128 | 119 |
| Highland, | Weidemaier, Peter, | 66 | 57 |
| Independence, | Hebrank & Truman, | 504 | 253 |
| Iola, | Schindler, R., | 125 | 120 |
| Junction City, | Cammert, Helmon, | —— | 100 |
| " | Frzaskowsky, L. W., | 215 | 257 |

27

KANSAS—Continued.

| | | No. of barrels sold. | |
|---|---|---|---|
| | | 1878. | 1879. |
| Kinsley, | Kinsler, J., | 39 | 44 |
| Kirwin, | Strebel, John, | 100 | 200 |
| Lawrence, | Walruff, John, | 1,965 | 3,491 |
| Leavenworth, | Becker & Link, | 1,532 | 5,329 |
| " | Brandon & Kirmeyer Brewing Co., | 4,403 | 3,774 |
| ' | Kunz, Charles, | 889 | —— |
| " | Peipe, G., | 347 | 274 |
| Leroy, | Schmidt, Albert, | 303 | 209 |
| Manhattan, | Alten, Chas., | 186 | 70 |
| Marysville, | Kalenborn, P. C., | 365 | 483 |
| Ogden, | Weichselbaum, Theo., | 494 | —— |
| Paola, | Hausman, C., | 283 | 292 |
| Salina, | Mugler, Peter, | 266 | 552 |
| Topeka, | Alfeman & Elsner, | 143 | 233 |
| " | Herboldsheimer, A. | 521 | 281 |
| " | Moeser, Philip, | 1,463 | 901 |
| Wichita, | Wiegand, A., & Co., | 418 | 450 |
| Wyandotte, | Hafner, Anna, | —— | 60 |
| | Number of Breweries, 34. | 20,995 | 24,709 |

## KENTUCKY.

| Alexandria, | Meister, August, | 1,169 | 790 |
|---|---|---|---|
| Covington, | Geisbauer, L., | 8,629 | 9,345 |
| " | Lang, Chas., & Co., | 8,708 | 7,986 |
| " | Ruh & Meyer, | 4,258 | 5.248 |
| " | Steinrude, J. H., | 7,446 | 8,651 |
| Frankfort, | Luscher, S., | 2,265 | 2,829 |
| Henderson, | Reutlinger & Eisfelder, | 2,061 | 2,500 |
| Jefferson City, | Antsch & Metzner, | —— | —— |
| Louisville, | Bauer, Elizabeth, | —— | 1,759 |
| " | Bott, Sebastian, | 1,070 | 1,317 |
| " | Christ, M., | 2,280 | 2,475 |
| " | Dierson, A. F., & Co., | —— | —— |
| " | Fehr, Frank, | 17,180 | 22,131 |
| " | Gebhard, Julius, | 2,383 | 357 |
| " | Hartmetz, Charles, | 1,925 | 1.885 |
| " | Huber, Henry, | 1,211 | 1,559 |

## KENTUCKY—Continued.

| | | No. of barrels sold. | |
|---|---|---|---|
| | | 1878. | 1879. |
| Louisville, | Knipers, G., | 790 | 1,437 |
| " | Laux, Peter, | 1,065 | 1,560 |
| " | Loeser, Adam, | 2,259 | 2,668 |
| " | Nadorff, Henry, | 725 | 1,337 |
| " | Sauffer & Brands, | —— | —— |
| " | Schanzenbecker, J. | 140 | 181 |
| " | Senn, M., & Bro., | 2,558 | 4,381 |
| " | Steurer, J., | 422 | 484 |
| " | Stein, J. & Co., | —— | 1,026 |
| " | Senn & Ackerman, | 2,610 | 7,800 |
| " | Templeton, A., | 4,731 | 1,890 |
| " | Weber & Schillinger, | 19,170 | 25,011 |
| " | Walter, Eva, Mrs., | 4,203 | 4,310 |
| " | Walter & Kittinger, | —— | 40 |
| " | Zeller, John, | 7,650 | 5,870 |
| Maysville, | Jaeger, Jacob, | 162 | 152 |
| Newport, | Deppe & Co., | 4,607 | —— |
| " | Schussler & Butcher, | 4,607 | 6,393 |
| " | Wiedemann, Geo., | 11,085 | 9,973 |
| Owensboro, | Breidenbach, A., | 387 | 404 |
| | Number of Breweries, 36. | 127,771 | 143,753 |

## LOUISIANA.

| | | | |
|---|---|---|---|
| New Iberia, | Erath, Aug., | 579 | 783 |
| New Orleans, | Armbruster, Mrs. W., 537 Chartres St., | 1,934 | 2,422 |
| " | Auer, Geo., 540 Tchoupitoulas St., | 8,136 | 9,259 |
| " | Bassemeier, Henry, 1010 New Levee St., | 2,367 | 3,055 |
| " | Blaise, Peter, 5 Prieur St., | 3,973 | 6,775 |
| " | Erath, E., 282 Villeré St., | 5,192 | 6,400 |
| " | Lusse, Henry, 478 Chartres St., | —— | 1,968 |
| " | Soule, Mrs. S. P., 112 & 113 Peter St., | 2,514 | 3,006 |
| " | Sturcken, H. F., 82, 84 & 86 Marais St., | 6,156 | 7066 |
| " | Weckerling, J. J., Magazine & Delerd Sts., | 5,481 | 6,673 |
| | Number of Breweries, 10. | 36,352 | 47,407 |

## MARYLAND.

|  |  | No. of barrels sold. | |
|---|---|---|---|
|  |  | 1878. | 1879. |
| Baltimore, | Bauernschmidt, Jno., 803 W. Pratt St., | 3,573 | 3,778 |
| " | Bauernschmidt, Jno., foot of Ridgley St., | 12,017 | 10,037 |
| " | Bauernschmidt, G.,Belair Ave., | 10,761 | 10,923 |
| " | Beck, Thos., & Son, W. Baltimore St., | 4,209 | 3,875 |
| " | Beck, Henry, 153 East Fayette St., | 113 | 92 |
| " | Beck, Aug., Frederick Road, | 7,706 | 6,935 |
| " | Beh, Jno. G., corner 3d and Lancaster Sts., | 2,083 | 2,311 |
| " | Berger, Bernard, | 197 | 2,113 |
| " | Berger, Jno. M., 317 S. Bond St., | 188 | 2,987 |
| " | Berger, John M., 360 S. Caroline St., | 188 | 115 |
| " | Brehm, George, | 12,656 | 11,836 |
| " | Butterfield & Co., 113 Hanover St, | 2,390 | 1,463 |
| " | Clauss, Jos., cor. Cross & Covington Sts., | 428 | —— |
| " | Dukehart, Thos. M., Holiday St., | 5,925 | 4,750 |
| " | Eigenbrot, Henry, 28 & 30 Wilkens St., | 3,936 | 3,195 |
| " | Extel, N., 360 Pa. Ave., | 174 | —— |
| " | Hecht, Miller & Co., | 9,149 | 9,297 |
| " | Helldorfer, S., cor., Clinton & Lancaster Sts., | 5,358 | 5,063 |
| " | Hertlein, G. C., Belair Road, | 1,406 | 1,102 |
| " | Hœnervogt, Elizabeth, Eastern Ave., | 3,370 | 3,533 |
| " | Kemper, Wm., corner 2d and O'Donnell Sts., | 2,799 | 2,565 |
| " | Kohles, John, 36 S. Wolf St., | 264 | 208 |
| " | Miller, R., 373 Biddle St., | —— | 36 |
| " | Mueller, John, 394 Pa. Ave., | 673 | 732 |
| " | Mueller, Val., 48 Burke St., | —— | —— |

## MARYLAND—CONTINUED.

| | | No. of barrels sold. | |
|---|---|---|---|
| | | 1878. | 1879. |
| Baltimore, | Muth, Louis, Belair Ave., | 7,741 | 6,694 |
| " | Rost, Sophia, Blair Ave., | 10,009 | 8,864 |
| " | Schlaffer, Franz, Belair Road, | 3,701 | 3,640 |
| " | Schreier, Jos., Belair Ave., | 7,198 | 6,664 |
| " | Schultheiss, John, Garrison's Lane, | 2,504 | 1,994 |
| " | Schultheiss & Bros., | 183 | —— |
| " | Schierlitz, Jacob, 413 W. Baltimore St., | 270 | 208 |
| " | Seeger, Jacob, 1053 W. Pratt St., | 10,005 | 7,362 |
| " | Sommerfield & Co., 7 Calverton Road, | 6,063 | 5,193 |
| " | Stab, Lina, 74 Burke St., | 497 | 424 |
| " | Strauss, H. S., Bro. & Bell, Hartford Road, | 10,620 | 12,950 |
| " | Thau & Muhlhauser, | —— | —— |
| " | Von der Horst, J. H., Belair Ave., | 16,298 | 18,300 |
| " | Weber, Fred, Hartford Road, | 3,254 | 2,310 |
| " | Werner & Honig, 370 Penn. Ave., | 1,135 | 1,258 |
| " | Wiessner, Jno. F., Belair Ave., | 12,673 | 14,799 |
| " | Wunder, Fred, cor. McDonnell and 3d Ave., Canton, | 5,899 | 5,275 |
| Barton, | Kolberg & Co., | 500 | —— |
| Canton, | Gunther & Gehl, cor. 3d and McDonald, | 3,901 | 6,851 |
| " | Schneider, Fritz, | 2,500 | 2,696 |
| " | Trost, Jno., O'Donnell St., | 4,459 | 3,973 |
| Carroll P. O., | Stiefel, Ed. W., | 4,253 | 3,568 |
| Carrollton, | Knecht, John, | 20 | 83 |
| Cumberland, | Fesemneier, C., | 279 | 500 |
| " | Himmler, Geo., | 591 | 500 |
| " | Leonard, Wm., | —— | 500 |
| " | Ritter, Paul, | 665 | 500 |
| " | Stucklauser, Gus., | 700 | 500 |
| Frederick, | Hauser, Paul, | 205 | 497 |
| " | Lipps, J. G., | 392 | 457 |
| Frostburg, | Mayer, John, | 240 | 264 |

## MARYLAND—CONTINUED.

| | | No. of barrels sold. | |
| | | 1878. | 1879. |
|---|---|---|---|
| Hagerstown, | Heimel. Justus, | 172 | 149 |
| " | Schuster, Robert, | 150 | 145 |
| " | Wagner, Wm., | 236 | 229 |
| " | Witzenbacher, Wm., | 115 | 126 |
| Lonaconing, | Fredericks & Hanekamp, | 581 | —— |
| " | Honig, C., | 564 | 500 |
| Mt. Savage, | Henckel, H., | 92 | 114 |
| | Number of Breweries, 63. | 208,228 | 205,042 |

## MASSACHUSETTS.

| | | | |
|---|---|---|---|
| Bedford, | Walter, Fred A., | —— | —— |
| Boston, | Boston Beer Co., 249 Second St., | 87,377 | 77.232 |
| " | Burkhardt, G. F., | 45,500 | 39.382 |
| " | Burton Brewing Co., | 29,180 | 24,028 |
| " | Cook, Isaac & Co., | 11,358 | 10.059 |
| " | Decker, Conrad, | 5,878 | 6,748 |
| " | Engle, S. & Co.,* | —— | —— |
| " | Habich, Edward, | 30,486 | 30 853 |
| " | Haffenreffer & Co., | 14,480 | 16.327 |
| " | Houghton, A. J. & Co., | 45,736 | 32,474 |
| " | Hunt, W. P., | —— | —— |
| " | Jones, Cook & Co., | 34,693 | 31,014 |
| " | Kenney, James, | 13,161 | 13.663 |
| " | Kenney & Ballou, | 9,167 | 9.706 |
| " | Kenney, N., | 10,600 | 5,707 |
| " | Lang & King, | †3,420 | 9,822 |
| " | Parsons & Co., | 8,112 | ‡4,530 |
| " | Pfaff, H. & J., | 26,860 | 34,862 |
| " | Roessle, John, | 41,000 | 42.827 |
| " | Rueter & Alley, | 60,156 | 40,509 |
| " | Smith & Engle, | §3,160 | 19,174 |
| " | Suffolk Brewing Co., | 39,409 | 44,055 |
| " | Van Nostrand & Co., | 42,828 | 37,912 |
| Chicopee, | Chicopee Brewery, | —— | —— |

*Leased Houghton & Co.'s Ale Brewery and commenced brewing ale, April, 1879.
† Lang & King, 4 mos.  ‡ Parsons & Co., 10 mos.  § Smith & Engle, 3 mos.

## MASSACHUSETTS—Continued.

| | | No. of barrels sold. | |
|---|---|---|---|
| | | 1878. | 1879. |
| Fall River, | Healy, Thos., Jr., | 166 | —— |
| " | Hurst, J. H., | 2,228 | 4,625 |
| " | Ogden, Henry, | 134 | 130 |
| Lawrence, | Evans & Co., | 2,907 | 3,087 |
| " | Stanley & Co., | 26,035 | 28,184 |
| Newburyport, | Whitmore, W. H., Jr., | 5,119 | —— |
| Pittsfield, | Gimlich, White & Co., | 5,699 | 4,371 |
| Salem, | Walter, F. A., & Co., | 2,459 | 1,794 |
| Springfield, | Kalmbach & Geisel, | 5,093 | 6,407 |
| " | Shaw, Wallace, | 5,813 | 4,405 |
| " | Springfield Brewery, | 1,069 | 1,511 |
| Willimansett, | Brierly, Wm., | 1,543 | —— |
| Worcester, | Hines, N., | 783 | 1,933 |
| " | McNamara, John, | 375 | 285 |
| " | Webster, Esther A., | 1,716 | —— |
| | Number of Breweries, 39. | 711,166 | *663,978 |

## MICHIGAN.

| | | | |
|---|---|---|---|
| Adrian, | Eason, Thos., & Son, | 337 | 256 |
| " | Fischer, Jos., | 1,935 | 1,989 |
| " | Lehmann, Wm., | 1,523 | 1,462 |
| " | Mulligan, Daniel, | 897 | —— |
| Allegan, | Ellinger, Geo. S., | 120 | 117 |
| " | Ely, T. D., | —— | —— |
| Alpena, | Leins, Aug., | 306 | 337 |
| Ann Arbor, | Frey, John, | 2,523 | 2,334 |
| " | Ruck, Frank, | 1,448 | 1,370 |
| Bay City, | Rosa, Thos., | —— | 60 |
| " | Schram, Martin, | 90 | 90 |
| " | Young, Chas. E., | 2,949 | 3,878 |
| Big Rapids, | Erickson & Hoelm, | 198 | |
| Blackman, | Haehnle, Casper, & Co., | 2,246 | 3,358 |
| Charlotte, | Crout & Staudacher, | 750 | 598 |
| Cheboygan, | Heutschel, C., & Bro., | 217 | 83 |
| Clinton, | Miller, Wm., | 271 | —— |

* The Ale Brewers enlarged their barrels during the year, from 27 to 31½ gals.  If 15 per cent. is allowed for enlargement, the number of gallons of Ale sold this year will be equal to last year's sales.

## MICHIGAN—CONTINUED.

| | | No. of barrels sold. | |
| --- | --- | --- | --- |
| | | 1878. | 1879. |
| Coldwater, | Kappler, Geo., | 508 | 793 |
| " | Patsch, Louis, | 865 | 601 |
| Corunna, | Storz, Geo., | 262 | —— |
| Detroit, | Arndt, Henry, | 883 | 1,154 |
| " | Darmstaetter, Jacob, 412 Howard St., | 1,347 | 1,617 |
| " | Darmstaetter, Wm., | 1,944 | 887 |
| " | Dittner & Co., | 4,369 | 7,438 |
| " | East India Brewing Co., 630 Woodridge St., | 2,723 | 2,226 |
| " | Endriss, Charles, | 5,218 | 6,616 |
| " | Fastnacht, D., | 279 | —— |
| " | Goebel, A. & Co., | 8,224 | 9,620 |
| " | Grieser, Eliza, | 153 | 238 |
| " | Hauck, Geo. & C., | 2,163 | 3,127 |
| " | Johnson, E., Jr., Michigan cor. Sixth St., | 565 | 456 |
| " | Kling & Co., | 13,326 | 14,053 |
| " | Koch, John, | 3,694 | 4,248 |
| " | Kuhl, Mrs. A., | 882 | 74 |
| " | Kurtz, J. A., | 473 | 320 |
| " | Lion Brewing Co., Gratiot St., | 5,581 | 9,499 |
| " | Mann, Chris., | 1,441 | 1,341 |
| " | Mann, Jacob, | 5.220 | 5,006 |
| " | Martz Bros., | 5,632 | 5,985 |
| " | McGrath, Thomas, 511 Seventh St., | 1,367 | 2,658 |
| " | Michelfelder, A., | 5,270 | 5,103 |
| " | Miller, Henry, | 1,658 | 308 |
| " | Moloney, Schneider & Co., | 499 | 924 |
| " | Ochsenhirt French, | 1,917 | 2,268 |
| " | Ruoff, Aug., | 4,508 | 4,741 |
| " | Scheu, John, | 21 | 66 |
| " | Seeger, Geo., | 230 | 134 |
| " | Steiner, John, | 2,871 | 3,450 |
| " | Voigt, E. W., 213 Grand River Ave., | 17,358 | 17,552 |
| " | Williams & Co., 232 Woodridge St., | 4,027 | 3.710 |
| Dowagiac, | Horder, Vincent, | 1,058 | 884 |

## MICHIGAN—Continued.

| | | No. of barrels sold. | |
|---|---|---|---|
| | | 1878. | 1879. |
| Eagle River, | Kuvel & Bro., | 888 | 547 |
| East Saginaw, | Darmstaetter, L., | 1,979 | 2,090 |
| " | Mawbray, Wm., | 1,264 | 2,606 |
| " | Raquet, P. & J., | 2,356 | 2,932 |
| " | Ziegner, F., | 1,245 | 1,270 |
| Escanaba, | Nolden, Joseph, | 401 | 234 |
| Fenton, | Hux, C., | —— | —— |
| Flint, | Golden, Wm., | 428 | 437 |
| " | Lewis, William, | 409 | 274 |
| Forestville, | Leonhardt, C., | —— | 16 |
| Frankenmuth, | Geyer, John C., | 608 | 702 |
| " | Rupprecht, John, | 549 | 577 |
| Franklin, | Rublein, Geo., | —— | —— |
| Grand Rapids, | Adrian Bros., | 580 | 444 |
| " | Brandt, George, | 2,447 | 2,971 |
| " | Frey Bros., | 4,519 | 5,608 |
| " | Goldsmith, Jno., | 380 | —— |
| " | Kusterer, C., | 4,648 | 5,752 |
| " | Tusch Bros , | 444 | —— |
| " | Veit, J. & Co., | 2,032 | 2,478 |
| " | Weirich, Peter, | 3,286 | 3,136 |
| Hancock, | Schneuemann, Ph., | 4,231 | 3,620 |
| Highland, | Bentler, J., | 29 | 29 |
| Hillsdale, | Haas, John, | 306 | 630 |
| Holland, | Sutton, E. F., | 423 | 235 |
| Houghton, | Haas, Adam, Estate of | 3,504 | 3,040 |
| " | Hofen, Henry, | 499 | 491 |
| Inverness Township, | Hentschell, Chas., | —— | —— |
| Ionia, | Summ, B. & Co., | 594 | 658 |
| Jackson, | Frey, Gottlieb, | 1,146 | 511 |
| " | Mills, Jas. H., | 489 | —— |
| " | Redmond, John, | 204 | 41 |
| Kalamazoo, | Kinast, L., | 1,230 | 1,078 |
| " | Loescher, B., | 1,298 | 808 |
| " | Neumaier, Geo., | 1,189 | 88 |
| " | Schroder, Henry, | 354 | 378 |
| Lake Linden, | Bosch, J. & Co., | 2,124 | 2,919 |
| Lansing, | Foerster, Adam, | 400 | 1,588 |
| " | Renz, Mary, | 11 | —— |
| " | Schlotter, Geo., | 94 | 82 |

28

## MICHIGAN—Continued.

| | | No. of barrels sold. 1878. | 1879. |
|---|---|---|---|
| Lansing, | Yeiter, F., & Co., | 493 | 581 |
| L'Ance, | McKeman & Steinbeck, | 502 | —— |
| Lapeer, | Burger, J. A., | 578 | 807 |
| Lexington, | Walter, F. L., | 742 | 911 |
| Luddington, | Friedeman & Stoekle, | —— | 7 |
| Manchester, | Seckinger, Jos., | 360 | 195 |
| Marshall, | Central Brewery, | 162 | 484 |
| " | Effinger Bros., | 350 | 320 |
| " | Nonemann & Lutz, | 450 | 450 |
| Marine City, | Bauman, John, | 523 | 497 |
| " | Marshall, Jas., | 273 | 250 |
| " | Meschke & Hoch, | —— | —— |
| Marquette, | Rublein, George, | 855 | —— |
| Mt. Clemens, | Bieber, Aug., | 857 | 856 |
| " | Miller, Wm., | 301 | 180 |
| Menominee, | Leisen & Hencs, | 950 | 1,328 |
| Muskegon, | Muskegon Brewing Co., | 2,025 | 3,095 |
| Monroe, | Roeder, Jacob, | 817 | 719 |
| " | Wahl, John, | 2,300 | 2,576 |
| Negaunee, | Liebenstein, F. A., | 375 | 220 |
| " | Winter, F., | 198 | 285 |
| New Baltimore, | Heuser, A., | 246 | 282 |
| Niles, | Dosch, Aug., | 382 | 455 |
| Oxford, | Findon, Wm., | 120 | 93 |
| Owasso, | Gute Bros., | 747 | 93 |
| Pentwater, | Fricke, C., | 4,291 | 3929 |
| Pontiac, | Dawson, Robt., | 361 | 301 |
| Port Huron, | Kern, Chris., | 2,332 | 1,843 |
| " | Senberg, Chas., | 785 | 778 |
| Rogers, | Bittner, Paul, | 120 | 125 |
| Saginaw, | Rosa, John L., | 386 | 386 |
| " | Schemm & Schoenheit, | 3,238 | 3,708 |
| Saugatuck, | Climpson, Samuel, | 38 | 32 |
| Sebewaing, | Brandle, Sophia, | 110 | |
| St. Clair, | Schlinkert, John, | 496 | 456 |
| " | Schroeder, John, | 102 | 80 |
| Sturgis, | Schlegel, John, | 714 | 410 |
| Three Rivers, | Esslinger & Sulliman, | 170 | —— |
| Traverse City, | Kratockvill, F. W., | 248 | 140 |
| " | Smith, John, | 238 | 217 |

## MICHIGAN—Continued.

| | | No. of barrels sold. | |
| | | 1878. | 1879. |
| --- | --- | --- | --- |
| West Bay, City, | Kohler & Jordan, | 530 | 937 |
| " | Kolb, George, | 1,884 | 2,228 |
| " | Rosa, Thomas, | 530 | —— |
| Westfield, | Kording, H., | 18 | 40 |
| Westphalia, | Arens & Drostle, | 34 | 583 |
| Whitefield, | Rublein, Geo, | 855 | —— |
| Wyandotte, | Marx, Geo., | 809 | 946 |
| Ypsilanti, | Forrester, L. Z. & Co., | 2,156 | 2,473 |
| " | Grob, Jacob, | 190 | 173 |
| | Number of Breweries, 140. | 203,043 | 212,231 |

## MINNESOTA.

| | | | |
| --- | --- | --- | --- |
| Albert Lea, | Weile & Co., R., | 417 | 453 |
| Alexandria, | Volk, Carl, | 210 | 319 |
| " | Wegener, R., | 444 | 629 |
| Arlington, | Klinkers, C., | 93 | —— |
| Austin, | Weisel, Jacob, | 241 | 969 |
| Beaver Falls, | Betz, Andreas, | 16 | 28 |
| Belle Plaine, | Schmidt, C., | 235 | 399 |
| Blue Earth City, | Fleckenstein, Paul, | 228 | 228 |
| Brownsville, | Fetzner, V. & J., | 672 | 680 |
| Canby, | Schmohl, J., | 67 | 59 |
| Carver, | Hertz, B., | 348 | 360 |
| Chaska, | Ittis, Peter, | 820 | 636 |
| " | Karcher, Geo., | —— | 510 |
| " | Liverman, B., | 898 | 844 |
| Caledonia, | Wagner, Philip, | 739 | —— |
| Cold Spring City, | Sarge, M., | —— | —— |
| Corunna Falls, | Kowitz, Ferdinand, | 618 | 650 |
| Crockton, | Burkhard & Co., | —— | —— |
| Duluth, | Fink, Michael, | 1,180 | 614 |
| Fairmount, | Smales, G. S., | 103 | —— |
| Faribault, | Fleckenstein, G., | 1,015 | 1,302 |
| " | Fleckenstein, Ernst, | 485 | 560 |
| " | Shefield, S. A., | 2,389 | 1,919 |
| Fergus Falls, | Brown, Chas. & Co., | 100 | 180 |
| " | Oehlschlager, Peter, | —— | 45 |
| Frankfort, | Weiss, Geo. E., | 272 | 273 |

## MINNESOTA—CONTINUED.

| | | No. of barrels sold. | |
|---|---|---|---|
| | | 1878. | 1879. |
| Frazee, | Carl, G., | —— | 56 |
| Glencove, | Samuel, Ed., | 513 | 618 |
| Granger, | Hasse, Henry, | 536 | 305 |
| Hakah, | Streigel, John G., | 236 | 140 |
| Hastings, | Busch, Fred, | 780 | 682 |
| " | Ficker & Dandelinger, | 1,190 | 1,148 |
| Henderson, | Enes, C., | —— | —— |
| Hutchinson, | Englehorn & Co., | —— | 204 |
| Jackson, | Owens, Evan, | 85 | 67 |
| Jordan, | Gehring, Sebastian, | 1,837 | 1,850 |
| " | Heiland, Fred, | 1,600 | 1,400 |
| Lake City, | Beck, Peter, & Co., | 402 | 387 |
| " | Schmidt & Co., | 503 | 829 |
| Lanesboro, | Frietschel, M., | 207 | —— |
| Lanesburg, | Radly & Chalupsky, | 384 | 691 |
| Le Sueur, | Arbes, Peter, | 229 | 691 |
| Litchfield, | Lenhardt & Roetger, | 318 | 334 |
| Madelia, | Brennis, P. A., | 138 | 233 |
| Mankato, | Bierbauer, W., | 1,391 | 1,489 |
| " | Gassler & Co., | 977 | 1,112 |
| " | Ibach, Joseph, Sen., | 339 | 420 |
| Mantorville, | Maegeli, H., | 483 | 421 |
| Marine, | Wishman & Garner, | 127 | 98 |
| Mazeppa, | Trausch, J., | 131 | 238 |
| Minneapolis, | Mueller & Hendrick, | 7,380 | 8,042 |
| " | Orth, John, | 4,892 | 6,665 |
| " | Zahler & Nohrenberg, | 1,735 | 1,966 |
| Moorhead, | Erickson, John, | 379 | 515 |
| New Munich, | Schmidt, N., | —— | 476 |
| New Ulm, | Bender, Jacob, | 216 | 299 |
| " | Hanenstein, Jno., | 1,017 | 1,523 |
| " | Holl, Aug., | 35 | 173 |
| " | Schell, Aug., | 2,124 | 2,536 |
| " | Schmuker, Jos., | 209 | 296 |
| Northfield, | Grafmueller, A., | 490 | 452 |
| Oshawa, | Veith, Fred A., | 311 | 145 |
| Owatumwa, | Bion, Louis, | 1,138 | 1.018 |
| " | Gauser, Petro, | 781 | 823 |
| Perham, | Schroeder, Peter, | 336 | 307 |
| Pine Island, | Ferber, John, | 100 | 135 |

## MINNESOTA—CONTINUED.

| | | No. of barrels sold. | |
|---|---|---|---|
| | | 1878. | 1879. |
| Red Wing, | Christ, Jacob, | 1,439 | 1,339 |
| " | Hartman, John, | 267 | 167 |
| " | Hoffman, L., | 624 | 607 |
| " | Remmler, A., | 1,456 | 1,428 |
| Reeds, | Voelke, J., | 379 | 180 |
| Reed's Landing, | Burkhard, Samuel, | 520 | 603 |
| Redwood Falls, | Weiss, John, | 32 | 57 |
| Richmond, | Webber, C., | 225 | 122 |
| Rochester, | Bang, Joseph, | 140 | 500 |
| " | Schuster, Henry, | 1,176 | 1,157 |
| Rollingstone, | Vill, Otto, | 378 | 861 |
| Rushford, | Pfeiffer, Jacob, | 355 | 234 |
| Rush City, | Victor, Gustav, | 400 | 595 |
| Sauk Center, | Gruber, Geo., | 40 | 19 |
| Shakopee, | Husmann, A. T., | 1,232 | 1,072 |
| " | Nysson, H., | 1,266 | 952 |
| Sleepy Eye, | Kramer, G. W., & Co., | 237 | 366 |
| St. Anthony, | Gluck, G., | 3,996 | 3,458 |
| St. Charles, | Mueller, F. W., | 944 | 571 |
| St. Cloud, | Brick, John, | 1,688 | 1,444 |
| " | Enderle, Lorenz, | 1,344 | 1,598 |
| " | Thierse & Balder, | 1,196 | 977 |
| Stillwater, | Tepass, Hermann, | 955 | 1,191 |
| " | Wolf, Joseph, & Co., | 2,651 | 3,364 |
| St. Paul, | Bauholzer, Fred, | 1,284 | 1,167 |
| " | Bruggeman, M., | 1,326 | 1,908 |
| " | Drewry & Son, | 641 | 642 |
| " | Emmert, Fred., | 2,760 | 2,800 |
| " | Funk, M., | 1,475 | 1,737 |
| " | Hamm, Theodore, | 5,770 | 7,980 |
| " | Horning, Frank, | 88 | 102 |
| " | Koch, R., & Co., | 1,869 | 2,265 |
| " | Stahlman, Chris., | 8,415 | 10,440 |
| " | Wurm, Johanna, | 210 | 200 |
| " | Yoerg, Anthony, | 2,225 | 2,791 |
| St. Peter, | Engesser, Math., | 358 | 299 |
| " | Stelzer, Jacob, | 327 | 437 |
| St. Vincent, | Raywood & Lemon, | — | — |
| Taylor's Falls, | Schottermuller, J., | 133 | 140 |
| Wabasha, | Leslin, Mary, | 245 | 198 |

## MINNESOTA—CONTINUED.

| | | No. of barrels sold. | |
|---|---|---|---|
| | | 1878. | 1879. |
| Waconia, | Zahler, Michael, | 660 | 652 |
| Waseca, | Kraft, Simon, | 831 | 585 |
| " | Bierwalter, John, | —— | —— |
| Watertown, | Lüders, Fritz, | 734 | 470 |
| Willmar, | Gilger, Wm., | —— | —— |
| Winona, | Becker, John S., | 2,128 | 2,540 |
| " | Bub, Peter, | 2,014 | 2,484 |
| Young America, | Schmasse, A., & Co., | 343 | 389 |
| | **Number of Breweries, 114.** | 101,916 | 113,529 |

## MISSOURI.

| | | | |
|---|---|---|---|
| Appleton, | Ludwig, Casper, | 458 | 378 |
| Boonville, | Gresmeier & Roechel, | 1,170 | —— |
| Cape Girardeau, | Hanney, Ferdinand, | 558 | 624 |
| " | Henniger, Fred., | 364 | 420 |
| " | Uhl, Casper, | 757 | 792 |
| Carrollton, | Schomburg, H. R., | 316 | 274 |
| Carthage, | Beamer, Jas. C., | —— | —— |
| Chillicothe, | Pierson, Peter, | 597 | 257 |
| Edina, | Strohman, F. G., | 51 | 109 |
| Fredericktown, | Gamma, Jacob, | 440 | 340 |
| Fulton, | Lorenz, Edward, | 332 | 316 |
| Glasgow, | Siebel, John, | 292 | —— |
| Hannibal, | Riedel, Geo., | 2,975 | 2,025 |
| " | Schambacher, W. H., | —— | —— |
| Hermann, | Kropp, Hugo, | 495 | 998 |
| Jefferson City, | Franz & Brother, | 1,311 | 1,276 |
| " | Wagner, Geo., & Son, | 2,688 | 2,863 |
| Kansas City, | Kump, F. H., | 8,700 | 8,700 |
| " | Muehlbach, John, | 2,666 | 3,932 |
| Kirksville, | Maloney, A. D., & Co., | 28 | —— |
| " | Sloan, Henry, | 78 | —— |
| Lexington, | Hoffman, Ernst, | 1,060 | 690 |
| Macon City, | Steinbrecher, Geo., | 796 | 204 |
| Maryville, | Niesendorfer & Co., | 909 | 52 |
| Middlebrook, | Seitz, Edward, | 1,097 | 300 |
| Moberly, | Hochberger, G. F., | 1,038 | 332 |
| Palmyra, | Hiner, A., | 225 | 195 |

## MISSOURI—Continued.

| | | No. of barrels sold. | |
|---|---|---|---|
| | | 1878. | 1879. |
| Palmyra, | Menge, Christopher, | 141 | 188 |
| Perryville, | Strobel, F., & Co., | 465 | 420 |
| Princeton, | Antricht, Ferd & Co., | 181 | 136 |
| Rockport, | Hartman, Wm., | 350 | 200 |
| Salt River, | Amesbury & Walker, | 39 | 31 |
| Sedalia, | Siebel & Helm, | 3,692 | 2,731 |
| Springfield, | Dingledein, S., | 936 | 738 |
| St. Charles, | Runge, Theo., | 1,775 | 1,768 |
| " | Schaeffer, E., | 2,308 | 2,200 |
| St. Genevieve, | Rottler, Val., | 1,069 | 700 |
| St. Joseph, | Goetz, M. K., & Co., | 4,651 | 4,299 |
| " | Kuechle, E. J., | 3,813 | 3,804 |
| " | Nunning, Henry & Son, | 6,223 | 5,585 |
| " | Ohnesorg & Co., | 2,270 | 3,570 |
| St. Louis, | Anthony & Kuhn, cor. Sidney and Buel Sts., | 22,018 | 22,970 |
| " | Anheuser-Busch Brewing Association, between Pestallozi and Crittenden, | 61,584 | 83,160 |
| " | Brinckwirth & Nolker, 1820 Cass Ave., | 23,573 | 22,410 |
| " | Cherokee Brewery, Herold & Loebs, props., Cherokee St., Iowa Ave., | 11,151 | 11,432 |
| " | Denber, Geo., s. w. cor. 20th and Dodier Sts., | 104 | 164 |
| " | Excelsior Brewing Co., C. Koehler, president, 2818 So. Seventh St., | 22,865 | 23,284 |
| " | Feuerbacher & Schlossstein, Sidney and Eighth Sts., | 22,350 | 22,121 |
| " | Ferrie, Jos., & Co., 1906 Franklin Ave., | 1,109 | —— |
| " | Griesedieck, A., & Co., Buena Vista and Shenandoah Sts., | 7,904 | 3,519 |
| " | Grone, H., & Co., 2211 Clark Ave., | 27,532 | 27,207 |
| " | Heidbreder, Jno. F., cor. 21st and Dodier Sts., | 7,167 | 8,100 |
| " | Klausman Brewing Co., So. Main St., Carondelet, | 7,970 | 7,638 |

## MISSOURI—CONTINUED.

| | | No. of barrels sold. | |
| --- | --- | --- | --- |
| | | 1878. | 1879. |
| St. Louis, | Koch & Schillinger Brewing Co., 816 to 822 Sidney Sts., | 11,319 | 12,500 |
| " | Lemp, Wm. J., 2d Carondelet Ave. and Cherokee St., | 78,422 | 88,714 |
| " | Milentz, Laura, 1535 Carondelet Ave., | 136 | 175 |
| " | Schnaider, Jos., Brewing Co., 2,000 Chauteau Ave., | 28,589 | 27,960 |
| " | Spengler & Son, 3823 Broadway, | 8,870 | 9,677 |
| " | Stifel, Chas. G., Brewing Co., 1911 N. Fourteenth St., | 26,598 | 30,164 |
| " | St. Louis Brewery Co., Lafayette and 2d Carondelet Ave., | 15,060 | 10,527 |
| " | Uhrig, Jos., Brewing Co., 1800 Market St., | 15,604 | 13,346 |
| " | Wainwright, S. & Co., 727 South Ninth St., | 39,440 | 45,846 |
| " | Weiss, M. & Obert, N. E. cor. State and Lynch Sts., | 10,500 | 11,000 |
| " | Winkelmeyer, J., Brewing Association, from 17th to 18th, and Market to Walnut Sts., | 27,079 | 31,474 |
| " | Young, B. F., 514 So. Second St., | 796 | 808 |
| Stockton, | Gast, M., | —— | 16 |
| Union, | Richenmacher & Gory, | 156 | 84 |
| Warrenburg, | Gross, Philip, | 328 | 199 |
| Washington, | Busch, John B., | 2,228 | 1,912 |
| Wittenburg, | Milster, C. D., | —— | 318 |
| | Number of Breweries, 72. | 547,590 | 582,372 |

## MONTANA.

| | | | |
| --- | --- | --- | --- |
| Bannack, | Harby, James, | 27 | 41 |
| Bozeman, | Spieth & Kugg, | 428 | 332 |
| Butte, | Saile, Buol, | —— | 20 |
| " | Schmidt & Garner, | 299 | 190 |
| Deer Lodge, | Coutaineir & Fish, | 141 | 309 |
| " | Fenner & Co., | 310 | 324 |

## MONTANA—CONTINUED.

| | | No. of barrels sold. | |
|---|---|---|---|
| | | 1878. | 1879. |
| Diamond City, | Rampeck, H. J., | 61 | 42 |
| Fort Benton, | Moersberger & Co., | 73 | 58 |
| Glendale, | Gilg, Frank, | 112 | 151 |
| Helena, | Binzel, B., | —— | 49 |
| " | Foller, August, | 568 | 652 |
| " | Horsky & Kuech, | 889 | 1,003 |
| " | Kessler, Nick, | 1,026 | 912 |
| Miles, | Buch & Rodener, | —— | 115 |
| Missoula, | Hayes, John, | 116 | 203 |
| Phillipsburg, | Guth, Christian, | · 37 | 43 |
| " | Kroger, Chas., | 75 | 76 |
| Radersburg, | Dixon, Thos., | 31 | 28 |
| Silver Bow, | Nissler, Christian, | 267 | 510 |
| Silver Star, | Fullhart, L., | —— | 74 |
| Sun River, | Rohner, John, | —— | 54 |
| Virginia City, | Gilbert, Henry S., | 217 | 330 |
| | Number of Breweries, 22. | 4,677 | 5,516 |

## NEBRASKA.

| | | | |
|---|---|---|---|
| Beatrice, | Coffin & Sonderegger, | —— | 319 |
| Columbus, | Hersenbrock & Hengeler, | 1,127 | 1,117 |
| Colfax, | Jetter & Martin, | 1,037 | 1,069 |
| Fairmount, | Rock, C., | 874 | 151 |
| Falls City, | Brackhahn Bros., | —— | —— |
| " | Brackhahn & Fricke, | —— | 591 |
| Franklin, | Arnold, Ernst, | 106 | 175 |
| Fremont, | Magenan, E., | 2,350 | 2,595 |
| Grand Island, | Boehm, George, | 1,176 | 1,180 |
| Hastings, | Calvert, Alfred, | 170 | —— |
| Kulo, | Borener, Aug., | 79 | 82 |
| Lincoln, | Fitzgerald, J., | —— | —— |
| Nebraska City, | Reyschlag, Fred, | 1,285 | —— |
| " | Roos, A., | 685 | 815 |
| Niohara, | Foerster, Adam, | —— | 47 |
| North Platte, | Distel, Ericksou & Co., | 232 | 558 |
| Omaha, | Bacon, Albert, | 233 | |
| " | Baumann, Mrs. W., | 2,747 | 3,162 |
| " | Engler, E., | 102 | 82 |

29

## NEBRASKA—CONTINUED.

|  |  | No. of barrels sold. 1878. | 1879. |
|---|---|---|---|
| Omaha, | Krug, Fred, 11th St., | 7,298 | 8,065 |
| " | Metz & Bro., | 5,645 | 7,686 |
| Plattsmouth, | Heisel & Rippel, | 617 | 481 |
| Red Cloud, | Bernzen, J., | 201 | 120 |
| West Crete, | Neher, N., | 844 | 739 |
| West Point, | Wala, Jos., | 278 | 218 |
| Wilber, | Kobes, Jno., | 14 | 18 |
| " | Shary, Rob't, | —— | —— |
|  | Number of Breweries, 27. | 27,100 | 29,270 |

## NEVADA.

|  |  | 1878 | 1879 |
|---|---|---|---|
| Aurora, | Stauhler, F., | 281 | —— |
| Austin, | Bauer, G. A., | 324 | 388 |
| Battle Mountain, | Amfahr, John, | 84 | 39 |
| Belleville, | Belleville Brewery, | —— | 93 |
| Carson City, | Berryman, R. A., | —— |  |
| " | Klein, Jacob, | 1,734 | 2,071 |
| Elko, | Bixel, Antonie, | 499 | 355 |
| " | Hawley & Curieux, | 115 | —— |
| Esmerelda, | Stahler, F., | 281 | 644 |
| Eureka, | Bremenkampf, F. J., & Co., | 375 | 495 |
| " | Lautenschlager, C., | 943 | 1,272 |
| " | Mann, H., & Co., | 261 | 993 |
| " | Smith & Mendes, | —— | 237 |
| " | Vosberg, Henry, | —— | —— |
| Gold Hill, | Schweiss, Sylvester, | 1,170 | 1,054 |
| Grantsville, | Koch, Wm., | —— | —— |
| Halleck, | Gruenberg, Chr., | —— | —— |
| Hamilton, | Schmidt, Casper, | 129 | —— |
| Paradise Valley, | Kirchner & Co., | —— | 124 |
| Pioche, | Staler, J. W., | 10 | 5 |
| " | Schustrich & Klein, | 195 | 199 |
| Reno, | Hoffmann, Wm., | 648 | 509 |
| Silver City, | Geyer, Philip, | 155 | —— |
| Tuscarora, | Iwan & Trilling, | 65 | 138 |
| " | Curiaux, F., | 208 | 342 |
| Tybo, | Bohle, H., | 111 | 146 |

## NEVADA—CONTINUED.

| | | No. of barrels sold. | |
|---|---|---|---|
| | | 1878. | 1879. |
| White Pine, | Mezger Bros., | 96 | 124 |
| Winnemucca, | Fink & Hinkey, | 348 | 472 |
| " | Kesler, Charles, | 104 | 132 |
| Virginia City, | Deininger, John P., | 605 | 581 |
| " | Franklin & Schroeder, | 1,400 | 1,516 |
| " | Rapp & Langan, | 1,179 | 963 |
| " | Reich, Louis, | 786 | 840 |
| | Number of Breweries, 35. | 12,116 | 13,969 |

## NEW HAMPSHIRE.

| | | | |
|---|---|---|---|
| Cold River, | Fall Mountain Lager Co., | 4,858 | 8,605 |
| Manchester, | Carney, Lynch & Co., | — | — |
| Portsmouth, | Eldredge Brewing Co., Marcus | | |
| | Eldredge, President, | 40,181 | 33,031 |
| " | Jones, Frank, | 66,398 | 60,105 |
| " | Portsmouth Brewing Co., | 15,634 | 15,147 |
| | Number of Breweries, 5. | 127,071 | 116,888 |

## NEW JERSEY.

| | | | |
|---|---|---|---|
| Clinton, | Krack, J. G., | 271 | 1,109 |
| East Newark, | Hauck, Peter, | 12,705 | 15 243 |
| Egg Harbor, | Schmitz, Henry, | 821 | 919 |
| Elizabeth, | Eckert, P. J., | 90 | 155 |
| " | Wagner, John F., | 832 | 953 |
| Guttenberg, | Biela & Eypper, | 5,850 | 6,027 |
| " | Koehler & Son, | 9,177 | 9,851 |
| Hamilton, | Hetzel, Jacob, | 1,344 | 1,775 |
| Hoboken, | Axtman, John, | 194 | 160 |
| " | Hackenberg, Franz, | 149 | 120 |
| Jersey City, | Freund, H. C., | 137 | 212 |
| " | Hudson City Brewery, | 13,135 | 11,892 |
| " | Lembeck & Betz, | 29,353 | 31,532 |
| " | Marion Brewery, | 3,143 | 4,726 |
| " | Newman, H., | 131 | 106 |
| " | Simon, H. P., | 216 | 222 |

## NEW JERSEY—Continued.

| | | No. of barrels sold. | |
|---|---|---|---|
| | | 1878. | 1879. |
| Midland, | Keeley, James, | 707 | —— |
| Newark, | Abendschoen & Bro., | 142 | 238 |
| " | Ballentine, P., & Sons, | 109,234 | 106,091 |
| " | Ballentine & Co., | 20,494 | 21,979 |
| " | Feigenspan & Co., | 21,366 | 19,074 |
| " | Freche, Gustave L., | 114 | 92 |
| " | Froescher, George, | 140 | 250 |
| " | Griffith, John, & Co., | 1,536 | —— |
| " | Heinnickel, John, | 67 | 144 |
| " | Hensler, Joseph, | 35,560 | 38,638 |
| " | Hill & Piez, | 23,032 | 24,172 |
| " | Kastner, F. J., | 15,349 | 14,637 |
| " | Krueger, Gottfried, | 28,759 | 29,549 |
| " | Laderer, M., | 51 | 93 |
| " | Lyon, D. M., & Son, | 26,560 | 22,994 |
| " | Mander, Jac. | 12,088 | 12,801 |
| " | Morton & Bro., | 20,397 | 18,851 |
| " | Neitzer, Charles, | 93 | 80 |
| " | Neu, John, | 2,969 | 3,403 |
| " | Roesser, Catharina, | 84 | 149 |
| " | Stadelhofer, Max., | —— | —— |
| " | Trant, F. A., | 4,828 | 5,958 |
| " | Trefz, Christiana, | 25,380 | 20,809 |
| " | Wackenhuth, F. C., | 3,188 | 2,682 |
| " | Weidemayer, G. W., | 3,855 | 750 |
| " | Ziehr, Elizabeth, | —— | 248 |
| Paterson, | Graham & Co., | 6,237 | 12,484 |
| " | Braum, C., | 409 | 1,588 |
| " | Katz, Bros., | 129 | 7,062 |
| " | Pfannebecker, P., | 48 | 152 |
| " | Sprattel & Mennel, | 5,768 | 5,027 |
| " | Shaw & Hincliffe, | 22,029 | 22,000 |
| Rahway, | Geyer Bros., | 1,605 | 6,748 |
| Raritan, | Schneider, J., | —— | 1,049 |
| Trenton, | Haas, F. Son's, | 480 | 580 |
| " | Schloetterer, S., | —— | —— |
| Union Hill, | Bromeke, Aug., | 302 | 177 |
| " | Bermus, Daniel, | 14,425 | 17,195 |
| " | Linnewerth, L., | 7,366 | 8,611 |
| " | Peter, William, | 8,967 | 7,862 |

## NEW JERSEY—Continued.

| | | No. of barrels sold. | |
|---|---|---|---|
| | | 1878. | 1879. |
| Union Hill, | Wegenburg, Charles, | 94 | 102 |
| West Hoboken, | Wittig, Catharine, | 1,177 | 543 |
| | Number of Breweries, 57. | 502,574 | 519,864 |

## NEW MEXICO.

| | | | |
|---|---|---|---|
| Golondrinas, | Weber, Frank, | 110 | 180 |
| Silver City, | May, John L., & Co., | —— | —— |
| | Number of Breweries, 2. | 110 | 180 |

## NEW YORK.

| | | | |
|---|---|---|---|
| Albany, | Albany Brewing Co., | 58,201 | 71,568 |
| " | Amsdell Bros., | 40,975 | 57,470 |
| " | Beverywyck Brewing Co., | —— | 25,947 |
| " | Coleman Bros., | 6,593 | 7,585 |
| " | Dobler, John, | 3,305 | 3,897 |
| " | Farun, M. H., | 305 | 463 |
| " | Fulgraff, Wm., estate of, | 1,415 | 1,183 |
| " | Gregory, Alex., | 12,504 | 10,495 |
| " | Hedrick, John F., | 3,407 | 3,766 |
| " | Hinckel, Fred, | 21,267 | 16,448 |
| " | Hoerl & Frank, | 1,051 | 732 |
| " | Kirchner, J., | 4,865 | 4,508 |
| " | Long, A. S., | 1,204 | 1,542 |
| " | Schindler, Wm., | 1,532 | 1,592 |
| " | Schneider, J. G., | 500 | 130 |
| " | Taylor & Son, | 49,512 | 46,001 |
| " | Tzomaski, Julius, | 39 | 35 |
| " | Walker, James, | 10,890 | 6,764 |
| " | Weber, G., & Son, | 342 | 258 |
| " | Quinn & Nolan, | 44,045 | 44,101 |
| Allegany, | Zink, W. F., | 200 | 60 |
| Amsterdam, | Moat, Charles, | 2,550 | 2,990 |
| " | Pabst, Jno. F., | —— | 142 |
| Attica, | Thompson, C. S., Assignee of R. H. Farnham, | —— | 1,083 |

NEW YORK—CONTINUED.

| | | No. of barrels sold. | |
|---|---|---|---|
| | | 1878. | 1879. |
| Auburn, | Burtis & Son, | 1,600 | 2,770 |
| " | Fanning, G. S., | 602 | 918 |
| " | Koenig, Wm., | 3,534 | 1,993 |
| " | Sutcliffe, Wm., | 3,018 | 4,223 |
| Batavia, | Eagar & Co., | 1,266 | 762 |
| " | Millschauer, L., | 867 | —— |
| Binghamton, | West, L., | 1,045 | 1,276 |
| " | White & Fuller, | 3,000 | 2,688 |
| Bleecker, | Ernst, Roman, | 66 | —— |
| Breslau, | Feller, John, | 185 | 139 |
| Buffalo, | Beck, Magnus, | 13,456 | 11,720 |
| " | Driskel, Mrs. F., | 2,836 | 3,183 |
| " | Gecman & Schroeter, | —— | 596 |
| " | Gerber, Charles, | 9,905 | 11,245 |
| " | Haas, David, | 4,428 | 3,262 |
| " | Haberstroh, J. L., | 4,824 | 4,751 |
| " | Hinold, M., | —— | 1,274 |
| " | Jost Brewing Co., | 1,949 | 3,768 |
| " | Kaltenbach, F. X., | 13,843 | 18,115 |
| " | Karn, John, | 2,664 | 2,760 |
| " | Kuhn, Jacob F., | 4,047 | 3,694 |
| " | Lang, Gerhard, | 17,825 | 14,030 |
| " | Luippold, John M., | 6,675 | 9,040 |
| " | Moeller, August, | 460 | 240 |
| " | Moffat & Service, | 5,255 | 6,426 |
| " | Reis, George, | 2,149 | 2,702 |
| " | Rochevot, George, | 10,070 | 9,305 |
| " | Rohrer, Margaret, | 219 | 163 |
| " | Roos, George, | 9,684 | 10,419 |
| " | Schaeffer, Aleis, | 7,600 | 9,520 |
| " | Schanzlin, J. F., | 3,440 | 2,834 |
| " | Schenfele & Co., | 284 | —— |
| " | Scheu, Jacob, | 8,660 | 8,515 |
| " | Schneider, Philip, | 2,250 | 1,872 |
| " | Schuesler, John, | 8,005 | 9,191 |
| " | Scobell & Schub, | 1,503 | 1,610 |
| " | Shoemaker, E. D., | 6,100 | 5,106 |
| " | Sloan, W. W., | 2,223 | 2,554 |
| " | Voetsch, Wm., | 2,481 | 4,150 |
| " | Weyand, Christian, | 7,643 | 10,483 |

NEW YORK—CONTINUED.

|  |  | No. of barrels sold. | |
|  |  | 1878. | 1879. |
| Buffalo, | Ziegele, Albert, | 18,375 | 24,795 |
| Brooklyn, | Burger, Joseph, corner Mese- and Leonard Sts., | 8,215 | 8,400 |
| " | Dahlbender & Greener, 174 Ewen St., | 4,066 | 4,857 |
| " | Devell, J. V., 16 Osmond Place, | 21 | 87 |
| " | Deventhal, Henry, 30 Webster Place, | 108 | 110 |
| " | Epping, Leonard, 32 George St., | 20,300 | 20,800 |
| " | Fallert, Jos., 66 Meserole St., | —— | 845 |
| " | Foster, H. C., Jr., 33 Cranberry St., | 600 | —— |
| " | Gluck & Scharmann, 371 Pulaski St., | 24,000 | 25,520 |
| " | Goetz, Christ'n, Franklin Ave., Bergen and Dean Sts., | 17,960 | 20,990 |
| " | Grass & Co., 435 First St., | 2,574 | 2,838 |
| " | Guenther, Wm., 436 So. Fifth St., | 210 | 250 |
| " | Herrmann, Henry, 14 North Ninth St., | 80 | 92 |
| " | Howard & Fuller, Bridge and Plymouth Sts., | 16,825 | 15,494 |
| " | Huber, Otto, Meserole St. and Bushwick Ave., | 36,911 | 35,356 |
| " | Immen, Henry, 46 Commercial St., | 150 | 185 |
| " | Jones, J. J., 311 Bremen St., | 10,644 | 14,225 |
| " | Kiefer, H., 140 Scholes St., | 14,000 | 19,534 |
| " | Kolb, Charles, Witherspoo: St., | 8,175 | 6,000 |
| " | Leavy & Britton Brewing Co., Jay and Front Sts., | 22,874 | 20,000 |
| " | Liebmann's Sons, Prospect and Bremen Sts., | 52,469 | 57,327 |
| " | Lipsius, Claus, 477 Bushwick Ave., | 14,744 | 20,775 |
| " | Long Island Brewing Co., 81 Third Ave., | 30,029 | 27,142 |

## NEW YORK—CONTINUED.

| | | No. of barrels sold. | |
|---|---|---|---|
| | | 1878. | 1879. |
| Brooklyn, | Malcom, George, cor. Skillman St., and Flushing Ave., | 15,556 | 16,882 |
| " | Mark, John G., 26 Bremen St., | 341 | 242 |
| " | Marquardt Bros., 403 Leonard St., | 50 | 70 |
| " | Marquardt, L., 2 Meserole St., | 111 | 106 |
| | Maupai, Wm., 168 Ewen St., | 5,336 | 6,412 |
| " | Meninger, John, 162 Cook St,, | —— | 6 |
| " | McGoldrich, Daniel, 55 Atlantic St., | 48 | 48 |
| " | Meltzer Bros., Suydam and Myrtle Sts., | 7,000 | 8,000 |
| " | Obermeyer & Liebmann, 71 Bermen St., | 22,242 | 22,238 |
| " | Ochs & Lehnert, Bushwick Ave. and Scholes St., | 3,060 | 5,654 |
| " | Raber, John. 60 Scholes St., | 6,371 | 11,578 |
| " | Raether, Wm., 1089 Myrtle St., | 139 | 151 |
| " | Schmidt, L., 36 Broadway, | 215 | 400 |
| " | Seidler, A., 51st St., between 3rd and 4th Aves., | —— | 65 |
| " | Seitz's, N. Son, Manjer St., | 19,843 | 25,000 |
| " | Streeter & Denison, 84 N. Second St, | 13,455 | 14,238 |
| " | Ulmer, Wm., cor. Beaver and Belvidere Sts., | 27,000 | 22,644 |
| " | Urban & Abbott, Bushwick Ave. | 18,697 | 23,048 |
| " | Weber & Amthor, 182 Graham Ave., | 604 | 2,320 |
| " | Welz, John, Myrtle Ave. cor. Wyckoff Ave,, | 6,982 | 9,744 |
| " | Williamsburg Brewing Co., Wm. Brown, pres't. Humboldt and Meserole St., | 40,284 | 50,287 |
| " | Witte, F. W., 100 Luynier St., | 204 | 200 |
| Canaan, | Losty, Patrick, | 416 | 304 |
| Canajoharie, | Bierbauer, Louis, | 1,346 | 1,309 |
| Canandaigua, | McKechnie, J. & A., | 18,500 | 15,547 |
| Cape Vincent, | Scobell, R. S., | 691 | 422 |

## NEW YORK—Continued.

| | | No. of barrels sold. | |
|---|---|---|---|
| | | 1878. | 1879. |
| Carthage, | Clifford, C., | 678 | 829 |
| Clarkstown, | Schmersahl, J. G. C., | 1,424 | 569 |
| Clifton, (S. I.) | Mayer & Bachmann, | 44,535 | 37,898 |
| Colden, | Miller, Mrs. B., | 1,144 | 401 |
| College Point, (L. I.) | Ochs, Joseph, | 18,990 | 18,717 |
| Concord, | Lutz, Joseph, | 168 | 179 |
| Constableville, | Seigel, Jos., | 208 | 432 |
| Corning, | Haischer, Fred, | 840 | 1,646 |
| Cuba, | Agate, Edward, | 1,766 | 1,730 |
| Dansville, | Klink, John, | 450 | 435 |
| Dobb's Ferry, | Biegen, Peter M., | 16,036 | 16,664 |
| Dunkirk, | Dotterweich, George, | 2,760 | 3,000 |
| " | Finck, Henry, | 1,976 | 2,554 |
| " | Smith, Henry, | —— | 169 |
| East New York, | Atlantic Brewery, | 112 | —— |
| East Williamsburg, | Leicht, Fred, | 3,700 | 3,360 |
| Eden, | Schweikhart, Daniel, | 403 | 640 |
| Elmira, | Arnold, Kolb & Co., | 1,500 | —— |
| " | Briggs, F., & Co., | 7,534 | 7,142 |
| " | Gerber, Chas. Jr., | —— | —— |
| " | Mander, Adam, | 1,682 | 1,172 |
| Esopus, | Staudacher, Fred, | —— | 1,728 |
| Evans' Mills, | Clifford, C., | 900 | 832 |
| Fishkill, | Walshe, J. V., | 973 | 765 |
| Fort Edward, | Durkee & Co., | 6,250 | 5,321 |
| Fort Plain, | Beck, John, | 570 | 595 |
| Fremont, | Kille, Joseph, | 117 | 152 |
| " | Schneider, J., | —— | 74 |
| Geddes, | Mantel, Jacob, | 1,098 | 816 |
| Glens' Falls, | Coney & Sheldon, | 2,928 | 2,581 |
| Gowanda, | Fischer & Garber, | —— | 688 |
| Great Valley, | Forge, L., Jr., | —— | 660 |
| Half Moon, | Wenner. R., | 1 029 | 962 |
| Hall's Corners, | Stokel, Wesley, | 410 | 425 |
| Hamburg, | Fink, Frank J., | 975 | 431 |
| Herkimer, | Goldsmith, Anna M., | 90 | 236 |
| Hicksville, | Becker, Wm., | 223 | 250 |
| Hornellsville, | Leach & Kennedy, | 952 | 1,247 |
| " | Sauter, John, | 796 | 363 |
| Hudson, | Evans, C. H., | 26,441 | 23,606 |

NEW YORK—CONTINUED.

| | | No. of barrels sold. | |
|---|---|---|---|
| | | 1878. | 1879. |
| Hudson, | Waterbury, E., | 1,265 | 1,405 |
| Ilion,. | Speddin, S., | 2,362 | 2,353 |
| Jamestown, | Smith Charles, | 1,160 | 1,610 |
| Kingston, | Barmann, Peter, | —— | 457 |
| " | Cummings, Catherine, | 222 | 139 |
| " | Dressell & Co., | 2,767 | 2,523 |
| " | Scheick, C., | —— | 67 |
| " | Schwalbach, Eliz, | 1,485 | —— |
| " | Stephan, G. F., | 1,573 | —— |
| " | Thiele, Valentine, | —— | —— |
| Lancaster, | Demaugeot, John, | 3,410 | 3,115 |
| " | Hilbert, Sylvester, | 465 | 418 |
| " | Soemann, Chas. J., | 816 | 1,180 |
| Langford, | Kekrer, Henry, | 482 | 374 |
| Lansingburg, | Bolton, Samuel & Sons, | 9,548 | 11,318 |
| Le Roy, | Linxwilder, J. D., | 154 | 68 |
| " | Sellinger, Lorenz, | 483 | 477 |
| Little Falls, | Beattie, W., & J., | 993 | 912 |
| " | Gerhard, N., | 225 | —— |
| Lockport, | Dumville, Joseph, | 948 | 1,320 |
| " | Ulrich, Anton, | 3,292 | 4,240 |
| Lowville, | Siegel, John, | 613 | 400 |
| " | Siegel, Joseph, | 636 | —— |
| Lyons, | Brock, Geo., & Co., | 1,614 | 1,748 |
| Mattawan, | Walsh, J. W., | 1,000 | 884 |
| Medina, | Remde, W., | 420 | 406 |
| Middleton, | Cohalan, T., | 1,132 | 623 |
| " | Herbert, Geo. Ludwig, | 150 | —— |
| Morrisania, | Diehl, Catherine, | 1,211 | —— |
| " | Ebling, P. & W., | 32,438 | 33,471 |
| " | Eichler, John, | 36,356 | 42,701 |
| " | Haffen, J. & M. J., | 13,689 | 12,505 |
| " | Hupfel's, A. Sons, | 15,020 | 14,893 |
| " | Kuntz, J & L. F., | 26,810 | 29,596 |
| " | Rivinius, Chas., | 17,159 | 29,176 |
| " | Zeltner, Henry, | 13,138 | 10,883 |
| Mt. Morris, | White, J. E. & Bro., | 1,058 | 1,000 |
| New Bremen, | Zimmerman, John, | 498 | 446 |
| Newburgh, | Beveridge, T., & Co., | 15,341 | 15,371 |
| " | Leicht Bros., | —— | 179 |

## NEW YORK—Continued.

| | | No. of barrels sold. | |
|---|---|---|---|
| | | 1878. | 1879. |
| New Rochelle, | Jones, David, | 11,736, | 11,140 |
| New York City, | Ahles, Jacob, 155 East 54th St., | 10,581 | 12,578 |
| " | Barry & Bro., 319 East 40th St., | 161 | 171 |
| " | Baur & Betz, 140 East 58th St., | 22,267 | 28,186 |
| " | Beadleston & Woerz, 295 West 10th St., | 78,037 | 78,093 |
| " | Bender, R. & W., 169 Spring St., | 67 | 86 |
| " | Bentle, Chas., 76th St., bet. Ave. A and 1st Ave., | 154 | 115 |
| " | Bernheimer & Schmid, 9th Ave., 107th and 108th Sts., | 51,826 | 56,878 |
| " | Betz, John F., 353 West 44th St., | 28,961 | 34,129 |
| " | Betz, John J , 9th Ave. and 60th St., | 4,725 | 5,833 |
| " | Brecher, Philip, 437 Fifth St., | 60 | 92 |
| " | Clausen & Price, 11th Ave. and 59th St., | 56,786 | 69,271 |
| " | Clausen, H. & Son, 309 East 47th St., | 89,039 | 89,992 |
| " | De La Vergne & Burr, 225 West 18th St., | 28,893, | 42,037 |
| " | Doelger, Joseph, 227 East 54th St., | 19,432 | 20,100 |
| " | Doelger, Peter, East 55th St., bet. Ave. A and First Ave., | 56,215 | 80,000 |
| " | Doemich & Schnell, 291 Broome St., | 92 | 99 |
| " | Doerrbecker, J. H., 188 William St., | 730 | 589 |
| " | Dunton, W. R., 84 Cherry St., | 3,922 | 3,447 |
| " | Eckert & Winter, 218 East 55th St., | 43,322 | 42,866 |
| " | Ehret, Geo., 92d St., bet. 2d and 3d Aves., | 159,103 | 180,152 |
| " | Elias & Betz, 403 East 54th St., | 46,109 | 45,286 |
| " | Englehardt, Jacob, 537 West 54th St., | 42 | 48 |

## NEW YORK—CONTINUED.

|  |  | No. of barrels sold. | |
|---|---|---|---|
|  |  | 1878. | 1879. |
| New York City, | Esselborn, Broadway and 50th St., | 232 | 370 |
| " | Evers, H., 49 Monroe St., | 370 | 338 |
| " | Ferris, H. & Sons, 257 Tenth Ave., | 20,621 | 23,462 |
| " | Feyh, Adrian, 266 William St., | 1,746 | 1,895 |
| " | Finck, A. & Son, 326 West 39th St., | 25,242 | 30,782 |
| " | Flanagan & Wallace, 450 West 26th St., | 82,567 | 84,825 |
| " | Haddock & Langdon, 414 East 14th St., | 21,509 | 23,371 |
| " | Hawkins, C. P., 345 West 41st St., | 5,654 | 6,231 |
| " | Hoertel, G. C., 134 Elm St., | 228 | 296 |
| " | Hoffman, Jacob, 212 East 55th St., | 47,042 | 44,648 |
| " | Hupfel's, A., Sons, 229 East 38th St., | 22,309 | 22,697 |
| " | Jones, David, 638 Sixth St., | 34,297 | 39,551 |
| " | Kirk, William, 15 Downing St., | 7,049 | 8,265 |
| " | Kleinschroth, Fred'k, 89 Sheriff St., | 200 | 287 |
| " | Koch, Andrew, 455 First St., | 301 | 431 |
| " | Koehler, Hermann, 341 East 29th St., | 23,374 | 21,196 |
| " | Kress, John, 211 East 54th St, | 39,448 | 40,015 |
| " | Kerr & Smith, 135 West 18th St., | — | — |
| " | Lincke, G., 124 Forsyth St, | 94 | 67 |
| " | Loehr, Henry, 428 West 55th St., | 10 | 100 |
| " | Loewer, Val., 529 West 41st St., | 1,968 | 2,872 |
| " | Lyman, T. C. & Co., 532 West 33d St., | 41,528 | 42,401 |
| " | McKnight, Mrs. S. M., 159 Sullivan St., | 4,796 | 613 |
| " | Miles, W. A. & Co., 59 Chrystie St., | 13,921 | 13,003 |

## NEW YORK—CONTINUED.

| | | No. of barrels sold. | |
|---|---|---|---|
| | | 1878. | 1879. |
| New York City, | Morse, Michael, 225 East 21st St., | 80 | 90 |
| " | Munch, F., 143 West 30th St., | 27 | 27 |
| " | Neuman, F. A., 233 East 47th St., | 20,257 | 23,500 |
| " | Opperman & Muller, 336 East 46th St., | 21,020 | 26,693 |
| " | O'Reilly, Skelly & Fogarty, 409 West 14th St., | 28,496 | 35,250 |
| " | Otto, F., 58 East 4th St., | 47 | 32 |
| " | Rchberger, V., 101 Broome St., | 99 | 99 |
| " | Ringler, Geo., & Co., 92d St., bet. Second and Third Aves., | 57,984 | 65,658 |
| " | Rottman, J. F., 315 West 47th St., | 14,680 | 13,841 |
| " | Ruppert, Jacob, 1639 Third Ave., | 101,058 | 105,713 |
| " | Schaefer, F.& M , Brewing Co., 4th Ave , bet. 50th & 51st Sts., | 50,842 | 53,565 |
| " | Schaefer, Philip, 310 West 57th St., | 23,022 | 22,489 |
| " | Schmidt & Koehne, 163 East 59th St., | 19,066 | 19,714 |
| " | Schufele, John, 541 First Ave., | —— | 37 |
| " | Schwaner & Amend, 514 West 57th St., | 14,159 | 12,533 |
| " | Seitz, Chas., 240 West 28th St., | 6,443 | 13,187 |
| " | Shook & Everard, 675 Washington St., | 45,171 | 50,005 |
| " | Smith, McPherson & Donald, 242 West 18th St., | 42,316 | 27,131 |
| " | Sorg, Geo., 647 11th Ave., | 21 | 150 |
| " | Spoehrer, H., 75 Norfolk St., | 95 | 119 |
| " | Springmeyer, E., 106 East 88th St., | 158 | 172 |
| " | Stein, Conrad, 528 West 57th St., | 50,642 | 50,145 |
| " | Stengel, F., 48 Ludlow St., | 150 | 169 |
| " | Stevenson, David, Jr., 503 West 39th St., | 13,581 | 25,938 |
| " | Tracy & Russell, 61 to 71 Greenwich Ave., | 40,296 | 33,969 |

## NEW YORK—CONTINUED.

| | | No. of barrels sold. | |
|---|---|---|---|
| | | 1878. | 1879. |
| New York City, | Wallace, James, 70 Madison St., | 13,412 | 20,676 |
| " | Weiland, O., 212 West 30th St., | 232 | 319 |
| " | Werner, Adam, 526 East 12th St., | 48 | 54 |
| " | Werner, Geo., 344 East 105th St., | 41 | 36 |
| " | Wernz, Jacob, 50 Norfolk St. | 50 | 49 |
| " | Wheatcroft & Rintoul, 87th | | |
| " | St., and Fourth Ave., | 5,722 | 7,840 |
| " | Yuengling & Co., 10th Ave. and 128th St., | 47,890 | 58,316 |
| " | Yuengling & Co., 4th Ave. and 128th St., | 27,269 | 29,390 |
| Norwich, | Scott, M. A., | 1,308 | 1,302 |
| Nunda, | Boulton, Geo. E., | 881 | 789 |
| Ogdensburgh, | Arnold, J. H., | 2,391 | 2,344 |
| Olean, | Dotterneich, Chas., | 2,053 | 2,464 |
| Oriskany Falls, | Smith, E., | 3,917 | 4,061 |
| Oswego, | Brosemer, Lewis, | 4,668 | 4,428 |
| " | Millot, J. B., | 2,509 | 2,312 |
| " | Oswego German Brewing Co., | —— | 150 |
| Owego, | Burrows, Caroline, | —— | 69 |
| Palmyra, | Downing Bros., | 1,362 | —— |
| Penn Yan, | Ainsworth, Oliver, | 118 | 321 |
| Peekskill, | McCord, Robt., | 448 | —— |
| " | Meyer & Amott, | —— | 261 |
| Perkinsville, | Didas, N. & Co., | 344 | 181 |
| Plattsburg, | Woerner & Parker, | —— | —— |
| Poughkeepsie, | Biegel, Leonard, | 845 | 556 |
| " | Frank's, V. Sons, | 4,869 | 4,473 |
| " | Gass, John, | 496 | 435 |
| " | Gilman, Fred'k, | 260 | 200 |
| " | Klein, M., | 216 | 2,753 |
| " | Vasser, M. & Co., | 12,261 | 9,511 |
| Ridgewood, | Marquardt, Jacob, | 10.733 | 9,895 |
| Rochester, | Baetzel, J. G. & Bro., | 1,161 | 2,226 |
| " | Bartholomay Brewing Co., George Arnoldt, Sec'y, | 42,921 | 61,824 |
| " | Enright, Patrick, | 3,243 | 3,333 |
| " | Genesee Brewing Co., | —— | 9,579 |
| " | Hathaway & Gordon, | 9,795 | 9,504 |
| " | Marburger & Spies, | 2,439 | 2,805 |

## NEW YORK—Continued.

| | | No. of barrels sold. | |
|---|---|---|---|
| | | 1878. | 1879. |
| Rochester, | Meyers & Loebs, | 880 | 1,195 |
| " | Miller, Fred'k, | 5,220 | 5,805 |
| " | Nunn, Joseph, | 789 | 742 |
| " | Rochester Ale Co , G. W. Archer, Pres't, | 929 | —— |
| " | Rochester Brew'g Co., G. Mannel, Pres't, | 32,693 | 43.000 |
| " | Warren, E. K., | 6,290 | 6,546 |
| " | Weinmann, Margaret, | 132 | 128 |
| " | Yaman & Nase, | 416 | 384 |
| " | Zimmermann, Geo., | 370 | 235 |
| Rome, | Kelly & Gaheen, | 2,471 | 2,333 |
| " | Smith, Julius, | 493 | 403 |
| " | Evans, Edward, | 1,650 | 3,050 |
| Saratoga Springs, | Eheman, George, | 245 | 203 |
| Saugerties, | Loerzel, M., | 270 | 317 |
| Schenectady, | Dickson, Virginia, | 327 | 156 |
| " | 'Engle, Peter, | 1,710 | 1,420 |
| " | Meyers, Jos. S., | 2,067 | 2,025 |
| Seneca Falls, | Weiss Bros., | 150 | 93 |
| Sheldon, | Battendorf, Thos., | 216 | 264 |
| Southfield. | Kaltenmeir, Jos., | 495 | 425 |
| Stapleton, (S. I.,) | Bechtel, Ceo., | 44,535 | 45,000 |
| " | Bischoff, Chas., | 10,317 | 10,311 |
| " | Eckstein, Munroe, | 13,495 | 13,402 |
| " | Korner, Gotlied, | 68 | —— |
| " | Menken, Fred., | 60 | 80 |
| " | Ruebsam & Horrman, | 39,500 | 26,360 |
| Strykersville, | Glaser, Frank, | 880 | 633 |
| Suspension Bridge, | Hager, Theo., | 975 | 1,158 |
| Syracuse, | Ackerman & Stuben, | 2,306 | 2,485 |
| " | Becker, Jacob, | —— | 61 |
| " | Greenway Brewing Co., | 43,695 | 43,058 |
| " | Haberle & Son, | 6,080 | 4,607 |
| " | Kearney, Wm., | 9,072 | 9,689 |
| " | Pfohl, Jacob, | 1.186 | 1,291 |
| " | Zett, Xavier & Son., | 1,230 | 1,764 |
| Tonawanda, | Zent, George, | 3,520 | 3,146 |
| Troy, | Conners, P., | 1,934 | 2,012 |
| " | Daly & Stanton, | 18,854 | 16,136 |

## NEW YORK—Continued.

| | | No. of barrels sold 1878. | 1879 |
|---|---|---|---|
| Troy, | Fitzgerald Bros., | 26,409 | 24 649 |
| " | Gaffigan, Julia, | 50 | 58 |
| " | Isengart & Voigt, | 3,875 | 3,650 |
| " | Kennedy & Murphy, | 27,841 | 34 288 |
| " | Potter, W. H., | 9,206 | 9,221 |
| " | Quandt, A. & A., | 665 | 1,825 |
| " | Ruscher, A. L , | 3,325 | 2 727 |
| " | Stoll, Jacob F., | 3,450 | 3,875 |
| Utica, | Bierbauer, Chas., | 880 | 392 |
| " | Gulf Brewery, | 7,473 | 6,918 |
| " | Hutton, Chas., | 2,064 | 2,393 |
| " | Myers, Jno. & Co., | 7,912 | 8,331 |
| " | Ralph, Geo., Jr., & Co., | 6,001 | 6,035 |
| Watertown, | Kellogg, Alonzo, | 600 | —— |
| " | Seibert, Peter, | 571 | —— |
| Watervliet, | Weinbender, A., | 449 | 384 |
| Waterville, | Peck, E. S., | 1,299 | 480 |
| Wawarsing, | Kuhlmann, John, | 1,174 | 1.002 |
| Weedsport, | Brewster & Becker, | 4,379 | 4,155 |
| Westfield, | Rorig, A., | 62 | 77 |
| Westmoreland, | Brockett, J. A., | 822 | 463 |
| West Seneca, | Messner, Mrs. A., | 1,056 | 1,150 |
| West Troy, | Reilly & McGrath, | 5,644 | 5,124 |
| Williamsville, | Batt, J. & Co. | 2,715 | 3.108 |
| Yonkers, | Krafft, Chas., | 31 | —— |
| " | Underhill's, E., Sons, | 9,906 | 8,840 |
| | Number of Breweries, 365. | 3,556,678 | 3,980,716 |

## NORTH CAROLINA.

| Fayetteville, | Lancashire J, W., | —— | 4 |
|---|---|---|---|

## OHIO.

| Akron, | Burkhardt, Wm., | 1,840 | 1,855 |
|---|---|---|---|
| " | Horix, F., | 2,275 | 2,312 |
| Alliance, | Knam, Floriva, | 408 | 484 |
| Amherst, | Braun, Wm., | 429 | 471 |
| Archbold, | Walder, A., | 48 | 576 |
| Arnwell, | Rich, Peter, | 1,313 | 1 091 |

## OHIO—Continued.

| | | No. of barrels sold. | |
|---|---|---|---|
| | | 1878. | 1879. |
| Bryan, | Hahn, Jacob, | 1,400 | 1,800 |
| Bucyrus, | Donnenworth & Bro., | 2,470 | 2,303 |
| Canal Dover, | Bernhardt, F., | 994 | 270 |
| Canal Fulton, | Rusch, Christian, | 796 | 660 |
| Canton, | Balser, Louisa, | 287 | 429 |
| " | Giessen, Otto, | 2,774 | 2,985 |
| " | Knobloch & Hermann, | 1,880 | 2,340 |
| Celina, | Ott, A., | 919 | 721 |
| Chagrin Falls, | Goodwin, A. A., | 18 | 33 |
| Chasetown, | Gines, N., | 347 | —— |
| Chillicothe, | Knecht & Muehling, | 2,331 | 2,833 |
| " | Wissler, R., | 2,070 | 2,037 |
| Circleville, | Kruemmel & Hoover, | 1,255 | 1,308 |
| Cincinnati, | Bruckmann, John C., Ludlow Ave., | 5,347 | 6,003 |
| " | Darusmont, M.. 184 Hamilton Road, | 7,222 | —— |
| " | Foss & Schneider, 259 Freeman St., | 17,871 | 28,060 |
| " | Gambrinus Stock Co , (C. Boss, Pres't,) cor. Sycamore and Abrigal Sts., | 29,995 | 33,350 |
| " | Hauck, John, 1 to 39 Dayton St., | 32,457 | 34,458 |
| " | Herancourt, G. M.. Harrison Ave., | 24,574 | 26,100 |
| " | Kauffmann, John, 598 'to 606 Vine St., | 41,357 | 43,228 |
| " | Kinsinger, C., assignee for Klotter's Sons, Brown St., | 8,824 | 12,304 |
| " | Lackmann, Herman, 443 and 445 W. 6th St., | 17,622 | 20,272 |
| " | Moerlein, Chris., 712 Elm St.. | 98,191 | 93,337 |
| " | Mueller, M., 652 to 658 Main St., | 7,425 | 6,471 |
| " | Nichaus & Klinckhammer, cor. 13th and Race Sts., | 10,667 | 18,407 |
| " | Schaller & Gerke, cor. Plum St. and Canal, | 39,276 | 39,723 |
| " | Schmidt & Bro., 45 McMicken Ave., | 8,014 | 11,165 |

31

## OHIO—CONTINUED.

| | | No. of barrels sold. | |
|---|---|---|---|
| | | 1878. | 1879. |
| Cincinnati, | Sohn, J. G. & Co., 330 Mc-Micken Ave., | 18,986 | 20,045 |
| " | Walker, J. & Co., 385 to 393 Sycamore St., | 5,152 | 4,318 |
| " | Weber, George, 284 McMicken Ave., | 57,086 | 16,709 |
| " | Weyand & Jung, 771 Freeman St., | 25,163 | 31,121 |
| " | Windisch, C., Muhlhauser & Bro., Miami Canal, bet. Wade and Liberty Sts., | 66,794 | 62,157 |
| Cleveland, | Aenis & Fenelich, 557 Columbus St., | 4,380 | 4,806 |
| " | Allen A. L., 127 Vermont St., | 793 | 20 |
| " | Baehr, Mrs. M., 225 Pearl St., | 4,331 | 4,072 |
| " | Beltz & Mueller, 59 Cyprus St., | 3 | 41 |
| " | Bishop, J. A., 371 Broadway, | 1,640 | 1,193 |
| " | Fovargue, D., 30 to 36 Irving St., | 2,543 | 2.778 |
| " | Gehring, C. E., 19 Brainard St., | 15,783 | 19,500 |
| " | Grabel, P., 529 Columbus St., | 793 | 988 |
| " | Griebel, Mrs. M., 52 Columbus St., | 793 | 1,003 |
| " | Haley, J. P., cor. Seneca and Canal Sts., | 2,728 | 2,405 |
| " | Hoffman Henry, 155 Walton St., | 2,118 | 2,594 |
| " | Hodge, Clark R., 7 Briggs St., | 2.131 | 1,107 |
| " | Hughes, J. M., 15 West St., | 10,789 | 7,509 |
| " | Koestle, Mrs. J., 38 Freeman St., | 2,363 | 1,592 |
| " | Leisy, Isaac & Co., 135 Veger St, | 22,855 | 20,042 |
| " | Lloyd & Keyes, 19 St. Clair St., | 3,629 | 2.781 |
| " | Mack, J. M., 239 Broadway, | 581 | 470 |
| " | Mall, Jacob, 9 Davenport St., | 6,510 | 5,868 |
| " | Mueller, Rudolph, 483 Pearl St., | 2,529 | 2,659 |
| " | Muth & Son, 10 Burckley St., | 4,439 | 4,554 |
| " | Opperman, A.W., cor.Columbus Wiley Sts., | 5,455 | 5,091 |
| " | Schlather, L., cor. York and Carroll Sts., | 23,087 | 27,298 |

## OHIO—CONTINUED.

| | | No. of barrels sold. | |
|---|---|---|---|
| | | 1878. | 1879. |
| Cleveland, | Schmidt & Hoffman, Ansell Ave., | 7,616 | 7,736 |
| " | Schauerman, L., 39 Broadway, | 6,191 | 3,875 |
| " | Schneider, C., 2 Ash St., | 3,916 | 4,042 |
| " | Schneider, Wm. & Co., | —— | —— |
| " | Stoppel, Joseph, cor. Ohio and Canal Sts., | 6,675 | 5,538 |
| " | Strieberger, Jacob, cor. Seneca and Canal Sts., | 2,728 | —— |
| " | Stumpf, M., Lake St., | 845 | 290 |
| Columbus, | Biehl, Henry & Co., cor. Front and Schiller Sts., | 2,588 | 2,924 |
| " | Born & Co., 449 South Front St., | 6,905 | 12,706 |
| " | Hoster, L., Sons & Co., 371 So. Front St., | 15,268 | 18,520 |
| " | Say, Charles, | | |
| " | Say, Joseph, 50 East Third Ave., | 48 | 40 |
| " | Schlee, N., 667 South Front St., | 7,180 | 8,176 |
| " | Schlegel, Geo. & Bro., 404 So. Front St., | 2,572 | —— |
| Crestline, | Westnitzer, B., | —— | 60 |
| Dayton, | Buchenen, A. & F., 45 Broome St., | —— | 443 |
| " | Bergman & Tettman, | 22 | 43 |
| " | Braum, Anton, 1st and Beckel Sts., | 1,484 | 1,460 |
| " | Euchenhoefer, F., 3495 Third St., | 2,010 | 1,694 |
| " | Hecker, George, 751 Van Cleve St.. | 124 | 115 |
| " | Poock & Senbert, | —— | 128 |
| " | Schwind, Mrs. Agnes, 345 So. Main St., | 820 | 632 |
| " | Schwind, C., River Side, | 6,150 | 5,977 |
| " | Schimmel, M., Wayne St., | 2,313 | 3,351 |
| " | Stickle, Jacob, Warren St., | 4,037 | 3,960 |
| " | Wilke & Saubert, | —— | —— |
| Defiance, | Bauer & Co., | 2,450 | 2,525 |
| Delaware, | Anthoni, F., | 1,523 | 1,578 |
| " | Wittlinger, C. H., | 138 | 263 |

## OHIO—Continued.

| | | No. of barrels sold. | |
|---|---|---|---|
| | | 1878. | 1879. |
| Delphos, | Dephos Brewery, | 2,280 | 3,598 |
| Eaton, | Fastnacht & Rau, | 593 | 424 |
| Elyria, | Plocher, Andrew, | 28 | 115 |
| Franklin, | Katlein & Co., | 144 | 113 |
| Fremont, | Fremont Brewing Co., | 2,939 | 2,999 |
| Gallipolis, | Hankel, F., | 381 | 343 |
| Greenville, | Wagner, J., Assignee, | 1,078 | 1,208 |
| Hamilton, | Engert, Casper, | 2,729 | 3,382 |
| " | Schwab, P. & Co., | 13,891 | 11,524 |
| Harrison, | Schneider, J. & Bro., | 933 | 994 |
| Ironton, | Ebert, Leo, | 3,136 | 2,742 |
| " | Mayer Jacob, | 540 | 494 |
| Jackson Township, | Kropf, Christian, | 758 | 497 |
| Kenton, | Kayser, Anton, | 190 | 180 |
| " | Ruffer, John, | 880 | 757 |
| Laetoria, | Haller, B. F., & Bro., | 227 | —— |
| Lancaster, | Becker & Co., | 2,813 | 3,127 |
| Lawrence, | Homig & Schneider, | 1,029 | —— |
| Lima, | Duvel, Chas., | 960 | 1,029 |
| " | Zimmermann Bros., | 252 | 402 |
| London, | Weber, Peter, | 625 | —— |
| Louisville, | Dilger & Menegay, | 2,018 | 1,855 |
| Mansfield, | Frank & Weber, | 1,601 | 1,128 |
| " | Reiman & Aberle, | 2,376 | 2,568 |
| Marietta, | Shneider, John, | 1,844 | 1,719 |
| Marysville, | Schlegel, Paul, | 130 | 160 |
| Massillon, | Baummerlin. L., | 1,029 | 472 |
| " | Halbysan Emma, | 1,747 | 1,625 |
| McConnellsville, | Burckhalter & Reed, | —— | 109 |
| Miamisburg, | Nuss, Wm., | 1,174 | 949 |
| Middleburg, | Davis, E., & Son, | 1,228 | 393 |
| Middletown, | Sebald, W., & L., | 4,790 | 5,866 |
| Milan, | Herb, Anton, | 46 | 25 |
| Minster, | Lange, Frank, | 1,790 | 2,144 |
| Monroeville, | Rapp, U., & Co., | 858 | 1,808 |
| Morrow, | Scheer, Thompson & Co., | 1,961 | 1,433 |
| Napoleon, | Roessing, F., | 838 | 955 |
| Newark, | Bentlitch Bros., & Eichhorn, | 281 | 285 |
| " | Kassenbom, Chas., | 1,171 | 787 |
| " | Rickrich, Philip, | 303 | 265 |

## OHIO—Continued.

| | | No. of barrels sold. | |
|---|---|---|---|
| | | 1878. | 1879. |
| New Bremen, | Meyer & Schwers, | 320 | 321 |
| New Philadelphia, | Hasenbrock, M., & Seibold, | 1,727 | 1,530 |
| New Richmond, | Baumann, Chas., | 307 | —— |
| New Springfield, | Seeger, John, | 66 | 36 |
| N. Robinson, P. O., | Gerhard, Jacob, | 212 | 146 |
| Norwalk, | Fletcher & Ott, | 1,842 | 2,023 |
| " | Lais, Anthony, | 1,064 | 940 |
| Painesville, | Carfield & Warner, | 560 | —— |
| Perry Township, | Sommers, J., & Co., | 1,488 | —— |
| Piqua, | Butcher & Mittler, | 1,200 | 1,254 |
| " | Keifer, L., | 842 | 863 |
| " | Schneyer, J. L., | 677 | 564 |
| Polk, | Roth, Daniel, | —— | 867 |
| Pomeroy, | Wildermuth, G., | 2,609 | 2,401 |
| Portsmouth, | Kleffner & Mair, | —— | 1,548 |
| Reading, | Kroger, J. B., & Co., | 636 | 946 |
| Rome, | Kropf, C., & Co., | 910 | 570 |
| Roscoe, | Mayer, Conrad, | 311 | 228 |
| Salem, | Muff, Wm., | 300 | 450 |
| Sandusky, | Anthony & Ilg, | 4,998 | 5,070 |
| " | Bender, Lena, | 5,735 | 5,996 |
| " | Kuebler, J., & Co., | 11,302 | 11,611 |
| Sidney, | Wagner, John, | 4,126 | 3,752 |
| Springfield, | Engert & Dinkel, | 6,609 | 7,160 |
| " | Vorce & Blee, | 5,561 | 2,565 |
| Steubenville, | Butte, J., Jr., | 1,138 | 696 |
| " | Basler, J., Jr., | 389 | 611 |
| Strasburg, | Seikel, Jacob, | 146 | 132 |
| Tiffin, | Hubach, H., | 737 | 2,816 |
| " | Mueller, C., | 5,294 | 4,337 |
| Toledo, | Findlay & Zahm, | 24,061 | 34,208 |
| " | Grasser & Brand, | 21,691 | 18,910 |
| " | Jacobs, Coughlin & Co., | 14,294 | 15,471 |
| " | Toledo Brewing Co., | 16,255 | 17,910 |
| Troy, | Henne, Joseph, | 1,895 | 2,046 |
| Tuscarora, | Heim, Louis, | 73 | 316 |
| Upper Sandusky, | Allstaeller & Bechler, | 1,719 | 1,662 |
| Wapakoneta, | Kotter, C., & Bro., | 1,040 | 1,119 |
| " | Schuman Bros., | 278 | 260 |
| Warren, | Clement, Geo., Jr., | 719 | 765 |

## OHIO—CONTINUED.

| | | No. of barrels sold. | |
|---|---|---|---|
| | | 1878. | 1879. |
| Waynesburgh, | Grubel, C., | 480 | 600 |
| Willoughby, | White, O. F., | —— | 5 |
| Williamsburgh, | Bools, John, | 21 | 37 |
| Winesburg, | Wiegand, L., | 189 | 77 |
| Woodville, | Keil, Jonas, | 283 | 289 |
| " | Lang, M., | 90 | 121 |
| Wooster, | Mongey & Graber, | 2,311 | 2,204 |
| Xenia, | Farrell & Co., Assignees, | 1,441 | 1,585 |
| Youngstown, | Knott & Klas, | 703 | 1,043 |
| " | Seeger, Mat, | 2,576 | 2,624 |
| " | Smith, John's Sons, | 3,299 | 3,261 |
| Zanesville, | Achauer, C. F., | 84 | 97 |
| " | Bohn, Sebastian, | 79 | 117 |
| " | Brenner, J. A., & Co., | 1,194 | 1,042 |
| " | Fisher Bros., | 2,123 | 2,373 |
| " | Merkle Bros., | 2,813 | 2,791 |
| Zoar, | Zoar Society, | 362 | 315 |
| | Number of Breweries, 189. | 968,332 | 935,480 |

## OREGON.

| | | | |
|---|---|---|---|
| Albany, | Bellanger, E., | 267 | 345 |
| " | Keifer, Charles, | 160 | 135 |
| Astoria, | Meyer, M., | 866 | 801 |
| " | Hahn, John, | 440 | 483 |
| Baker City, | Rust, Henry, | 158 | 196 |
| " | Kastner, N., | 275 | 249 |
| Brownsville, | Cloner, B., | —— | —— |
| Canyon City, | Sels, F. C., | 126 | 126 |
| Canyonville, | Stenger, L., | 27 | 33 |
| Corvallis, | Hughes, Henry, | 183 | 132 |
| Coquette City, | Mehl, G., | 43 | 38 |
| Eugene City, | Miller, M., | 114 | 103 |
| Gardner, | Varrelman, F., | 21 | 21 |
| Gervais, | Glaser & Kirk, | —— | 129 |
| Jacksonville, | Schutz, Val, | 138 | 171 |
| " | Wetterer, Joseph, | 150 | 159 |
| Junction City, | Braun & Seeger, | —— | —— |
| Marshfield, | Reichert, Wm., | 280 | 303 |

## OREGON—CONTINUED.

| | | No. of barrels sold. | |
|---|---|---|---|
| | | 1878. | 1879. |
| McMinnsville, | Ahrens, Anton, | — | — |
| " | Bachman, W. R., | — | — |
| Oakland, | Robinson, A. D., | 25 | — |
| " | McGregor & Freyer, | 25 | 50 |
| Oregon City, | Rehfuss, H., | 1,412 | 1,269 |
| Pendleton, | Stang, Adam, | 140 | 127 |
| " | Lang, Adolph & Co., | — | — |
| Portland, | Feuer, L., | 181 | 1,089 |
| " | Molson & Sons, | — | 181 |
| " | U. S. Brewing Co., | 1,506 | 1,557 |
| " | Weinhard, Henry, | 5,280 | 6,242 |
| Roseburgh, | Rast, John, | 257 | 258 |
| " | Kreutscher, Th. F., | — | — |
| Salem, | Adolph S., & Co., | 478 | 545 |
| " | Westacott, L, | 258 | 434 |
| " | Westacott & Son, | — | — |
| Scottsburgh, | Rumelhort, L. H., | — | — |
| St. Paul, | Ahrens, A., | 94 | 83 |
| The Dalles, | Buechler, Aug., | 438 | 881 |
| Union, | Washburn, S. N., & Co., | — | — |
| Wilderville, | Closner, David, | — | 17 |
| | Number of Breweries, 30 | 13,362 | 16,159 |

## PENNSYLVANIA.

| | | | |
|---|---|---|---|
| Allegheny City, | Booth, Thomas, | 10,427 | 8,612 |
| " | Dippel, Henry, | 634 | 394 |
| " | Eberhardt & Ober, | 11,905 | 11,480 |
| " | Herdt, Mrs. D., | 824 | 947 |
| " | Lion Brewing Co., | 8,678 | 11,221 |
| " | Lutz, D. & Son, | 13,414 | 12,990 |
| " | Mueller, John M., | 5,046 | 6,272 |
| " | Ober, Frank L., | 4,541 | 6,073 |
| " | Straub, J. N., & C, | 10,008 | 9,387 |
| Allentown, | Benedict, Nuding, | 2,706 | 2,675 |
| " | Daenfer, Jacob, | — | 507 |
| " | Kern, Leopold, | 990 | 326 |
| " | Lieberman & Co., | 2,706 | 1,931 |
| Altoona, | Ensbronner, Geo., | 355 | 474 |

PENNSYLVANIA—CONTINUED.

| | | No. of barrels sold. | |
|---|---|---|---|
| | | 1878. | 1879. |
| Altoona, | Haid, Chas., | 316 | 342 |
| " | Hoelle, Martin, | 1,297 | 1,007 |
| " | Klemert, Gustav, | 516 | 531 |
| " | Stehle, John B., | 524 | 358 |
| " | Wahl, Christ, | 336 | 298 |
| Beaver Falls, | Anderton, James, | 789 | 756 |
| " | Holmes & Timmins, | —— | —— |
| " | Volk, John, | 786 | 826 |
| Bellefonte, | Haas, Louis, | 504 | 618 |
| Bennett's Station, | Baeurlein, C., Bro. & Co., | 4,715 | 5,484 |
| " | Gast & Bro., | 1,236 | 946 |
| " | Hoehl, Henry, | 366 | 319 |
| Benzinger, | Straub, Peter, | 656 | 475 |
| Bethlehem, | Uhl, Mathias, | 1,483 | 971 |
| Blossburg, | Plummer, Elijah, | 49 | 53 |
| Braddock's, | Schulz, G. | 159 | 201 |
| " | Schafer, N. | 397 | 340 |
| Bridgewater, | Weisgerber, Conrad, | 317 | 283 |
| Brookville, | Allgeier, M., | 464 | 449 |
| " | Christ, S. C., | 319 | 367 |
| Cambria, | Goenner, Jacob, | 573 | 592 |
| Carbondale, | Nealon, John, | 320 | 1,096 |
| Carlisle, | Faber, C. C., | 51 | 96 |
| " | Krause, E. J., | 723 | 293 |
| Carrollton, | Blum, Henry, | 287 | 229 |
| " | Eger, F. & C., | 224 | 184 |
| Catasauqua, | Kostenbader, H., | 1,598 | 1,660 |
| " | Stockberger, M. J., | 510 | 720 |
| Centerville, | Dluzer, John, | —— | —— |
| Chambersburg, | Kurtz, L. B., | 465 | 451 |
| " | Klenzing, H. A., | —— | 167 |
| " | Ludwig, Charles | 1,033 | 766 |
| " | Richter, Henry, | 229 | 170 |
| Chartiers, | Schmelz, Henry, | 276 | 301 |
| Clarion, | Hartle, George, | 101 | 79 |
| " | Sandt, H. J., | 521 | 418 |
| Clearfield, | Leipoldt, C., | 91 | 110 |
| " | Sell, Thomas, | —— | —— |
| Coal Township, | Markle, M , | 630 | 1,126 |
| Columbia, | Brink, A. H., & Co., | 543 | 671 |

PENNSYLVANIA—Continued.

| | | No. of barrels sold. | |
|---|---|---|---|
| | | 1878. | 1879. |
| Columbia, | Desch, J., | 1,625 | 2,200 |
| Condersport, | Zimmerman, C., | —— | —— |
| Conemaugh, | Kost, Lawrence, | 434 | 538 |
| " | Lambert & Kress, | 2,120 | 3,083 |
| Corry, | Morris, Hiram, | 491 | 380 |
| " | Spreter, Gustave, | 1,512 | 1,260 |
| Danville, | Fraudenberger, G., & Co., | 1,012 | 1,073 |
| " | Gerstner, Mrs. M, A., | 466 | 238 |
| Easton, | Borman & Kuebler, | 6,179 | —— |
| " | Seitz Bros., | 3,195 | 2,957 |
| " | Veile, Xavier, | 1,988 | 1,527 |
| East Mauch Chunk, | Gerste, Mathilde, | 184 | 208 |
| East Stroubsburg, | Burt, John, | 124 | 105 |
| Emans, | Kling, Fred, | 997 | —— |
| Emlenton, | Kreis, Sebastian, | 872 | 485 |
| Emporium, | Blummle, F. X., | 167 | 186 |
| Erie, | Conrad, C. M., | 6,360 | 8,200 |
| " | Downer & Howard, | 2,140 | 2,092 |
| " | Kalvelage, Henry, | 3,236 | 2,795 |
| " | Koehler & Bro., | 7,365 | 8,388 |
| " | Vogt, Anton, | 245 | 295 |
| Etna, | Metzger. Michael, | 175 | 231 |
| Exeter, | Hughes, H. R., & Co., | 1,760 | 1,373 |
| Farmers' Valley, | Schott, E., | —— | 108 |
| Franklin, | Crossman, Philip, | 870 | 761 |
| Gallitzen, | Ankenbaber & Gaegler, | —— | 61 |
| Germania, | Meixner, Frank, | 35 | 62 |
| " | Schwarzenbach, J., | 26 | 53 |
| Gettysburg, | Henning, John, | 49 | 35 |
| " | Bartel, J. F. | 250 | 196 |
| Greensburg, | Hagel, John, | 349 | 332 |
| Green Township, | Schnell, J. L., & Bro., | 167 | 97 |
| Hanover P. O. | Neiderhofer, John, | 108 | 108 |
| Hamburg, | Buckman, Jacob, | 347 | 138 |
| Harrisburg, | Bynre & Ogden, | 18 | 155 |
| " | Doehn, George, | 3,147 | 2,646 |
| " | Dressell, C. A., | 3,979 | 826 |
| " | Fink, Henry, | 3,794 | 3,220 |
| Harrison, | Brewer, John, | 73 | 83 |
| Hazelton, | Bach, Henry, | 3,543 | 3,230 |

32

PENNSYLVANIA—Continued.

| | | No. of barrels sold. | |
|---|---|---|---|
| | | 1878. | 1879. |
| Heidelburg, | Schmidt, Ambrose, | 183 | 63 |
| Hollidaysburgh, | Buckberger, A., | —— | 48 |
| " | Springer, J. J., | 6 | 12 |
| Indiana, | Stadmiller, Geo., | 55 | 119 |
| Jefferson, | Werner, John, | 1,418 | 832 |
| Jersey Shore, | Hauser, Chas., | 135 | 146 |
| Johnstown, | Baemiy, W. H., | 251 | —— |
| " | Emmerling, John, | —— | 111 |
| " | Heubach, Max, | 509 | 371 |
| " | Wehn, Charles, | 363 | 392 |
| Kittanning, | Biehl, Louis, | 1,564 | 877 |
| Lancaster, | Effinger, Jas., Agt., | 2,872 | 2,154 |
| " | Knapp, Lawrence, | 962 | 1,085 |
| " | Knapp, Lawrence, | 1,938 | 1,916 |
| " | Koehler, Casper, | 2,828 | 1,240 |
| " | Laudis, D. B., | 504 | 488 |
| " | Richman, G. E., Agt., | 422 | 576 |
| " | Rieker, Frank A., | 2,816 | 3,063 |
| " | Schwenberger, W. A., Agt., | 602 | 635 |
| " | Sprenger, J. A., | 2,104 | 1,890 |
| " | Wacker, S. V. S. Bros., | 2,112 | 1,790 |
| Lebanon, | Hoezle, Joseph, | 240 | —— |
| " | Leubert, F. A., | 1,425 | 1,393 |
| Lewistown, | Bossinger, H., | 495 | 446 |
| " | Haeben, Theo., | 367 | 143 |
| Liberty, | Zeifle, John, | 63 | 69 |
| Lock Haven, | Fable, Charles P., | 456 | 443 |
| " | Flaig, Matthew, | 230 | 348 |
| " | Pfeffert, Mary, | 144, | 164 |
| Loretto, | Bengele, Jos., | 106 | 28 |
| Lower Saucon, | Benz, Edward, | 910 | 628 |
| Lykens, | Bueck, H., | 2,252 | 2,905 |
| Manheim, | Loerher, Fred'k, | 545 | 810 |
| Marietta, | Manlick, Fred, | 381 | 388 |
| Mauch Chunk, | Weysser & Ziuzer, | 154 | 273 |
| McKreesport, | Reichenbach, Ernest, | 640 | 558 |
| Mead, | Smith, E. A., | —— | 650 |
| Mill Creek, | Voigt & Platz, | 730 | 8 6 |
| Minersville, | Aapf, Charles, & Co., | 730 | 826 |
| " | Kear, F. J, & Co., | —— | —— |

## PENNSYLVANIA—Continued.

| | | No. of barrels sold. | |
|---|---|---|---|
| | | 1878. | 1879. |
| Mount Joy, | Bube, Alvis, | 394 | 316 |
| Muncy, | Harp, Wm., | 100 | 103 |
| Newcastle, | Knock, C., | 500 | 500 |
| " | Tresser, Adam, | 1,410 | 1,400 |
| Norristown, | Cox, A. R., | 2,376 | 2,228 |
| " | Schiedt, | 720 | 699 |
| North East, | Bannister, James, | 134 | 134 |
| North Huntington, | Hufnagel, Conrad, | 63 | 58 |
| Oil City, | Wurster, Chas., | 1,500 | 810 |
| Philadelphia, | Ambrou, Adam, 338 Dillwyn St. | 28 | 37 |
| " | Amrhein, L., 6th and Clearfield Sts., | 1,774 | 1,858 |
| " | Archby, McLean & Co., 309 and 311 Green St., | 13,555 | 10,620 |
| " | Baltz, J. & P., 31st and Thompson Sts., | 23,619 | 23,915 |
| " | Bander, Jehn, 400 Lynd St., | —— | 150 |
| " | Bergdoll, Louis, 29th and Parish Sts , | 47,514 | 46,410 |
| " | Bergner & Engel, Brewing Co., cor. 32d and Thompson Sts., | 120,187 | 124,860 |
| " | Betz, John F., 401 New Market St., | 52,891 | 44,653 |
| " | Bower, John, estate of, 33d near Master St., | 4,724 | 4,617 |
| " | Cary, Geo. & Co., 934 N. 3d St., | 16,753 | 13,579 |
| " | Conrad, Jacob, 27th and Parish Sts., | 3,714 | 4,709 |
| " | Connor, James, 819 Carpenter St., | —— | 68 |
| " | Christmas, Chas., 1605 Cabot St., | 185 | 145 |
| " | Class, Charles, 1732 Mervine St., | 2,570 | 2,160 |
| " | Dauterich, H., 341 N. 4th St., | 1,407 | 534 |
| " | Eble & Herter, 32d and Thompson Sts , | 12,280 | 9,990 |
| " | Eisele, Franz, 2630 Girard Ave., | 90 | 329 |
| " | Engelke, Mathias, 835 St. John St., | 1,551 | 1,272 |

PENNSYLVANIA—CONTINUED.

| | | No. of barrels sold. | |
| | | 1878. | 1879. |
|---|---|---|---|
| Philadelphia, | Enser & Theurer, 2d and Ontario Sts., | 6,628 | 5,490 |
| " | Erdreig, Andrew, 142 Ash St., | 2,916 | 2,400 |
| | Esslinger, George, 1012 Jefferson St., | 494 | 783 |
| " | Feil, F., 2204 Lairhill St., | —— | 405 |
| " | Fielmeyer, Joseph, 2325 N. Broad St., | 2,707 | 1,975 |
| " | Finkenauer, Theo., 31st St., above Master, | 1,278 | 1,624 |
| " | Finkenauer, Theo., 1716 Germantown Ave., | —— | —— |
| " | Fisher, Albert, 2900 Frankford Road, | 48 | 72 |
| " | Fritch, John, 4224 Edward St., | 1,910 | 2,014 |
| " | Gamdler & Co., 715 North 3d St., | 861 | 596 |
| " | Gardner, J. & Co., 21st and Washington Sts., | 31,516 | 37,471 |
| " | Gindele, Geo., 1024 W. Girard Ave., | 5,040 | 4,934 |
| " | Gindele, Joseph, 1205 Darien St., | 1,542 | 1,445 |
| " | Grauch, John, 4228 Edward St., | 3,240 | 2,599 |
| " | Gross, Louis, estate of, 2421 N. St., | 32,807 | 393 |
| " | Guckes, Riehl & Co., 824 St. St., | 8,469 | 6,477 |
| " | Guckes, Philip, School Lane, | 2,427 | 2,278 |
| " | Haisch, Christian, 1748 Mervine St., | 5,355 | 4,728 |
| " | Henzler & Flach, 32d and Thompson Sts., | 12,741 | 10,000 |
| " | Jocobi, Otto, 913 N. 4th St., | 62 | 67 |
| " | Jeckel, Geo., | —— | —— |
| " | Kasper, Charles, 606 N. 4th St., | 990 | 499 |
| ' | Keller, George, 31st, near Jefferson St., | 5,866 | 1,624 |
| " | Kumpf, Wm. & Co., 2610 Frankford Road, | 1,464 | 951 |

## PENNSYLVANIA—Continued.

| | | No. of barrels sold. | |
|---|---|---|---|
| | | 1878. | 1870. |
| Philadelphia, | Klopfer, Christian, 2427 N. Broad St., | 1,437 | 1,458 |
| " | Kohnle, J., 321 Fairmount Ave., | 1,850 | 1,700 |
| " | Leibert & Obert, 156 Oak St., | 1,591 | 1,971 |
| " | Leimbach, Eliza F., 1751 Bodine St., | 875 | 1,008 |
| " | Loescher, John, 1735 Walter St. | —— | —— |
| " | Maass, Charles, 1214 Germantown Ave., | 233 | 243 |
| " | Magee, Richard, 731 Vine St, | 15,833 | 30,631 |
| " | Massey, Wm. & Co., 10th and Filbert Sts., | 58,214 | 57,667 |
| " | Manz, Gottleib, 6th and Clearfield Sts., | 3,722 | 3,433 |
| " | McCaffrey & O'Rielley, 407 Lynd St., | —— | 65 |
| " | McKenney & Co., 614 S. 6th St., | 1,024 | 1,528 |
| " | Miller, Adams, 929 N. 5th St, | 470 | 399 |
| " | Miller, John C., Ashmead and Wakefield Sts., Germantown, | 22,852 | 20,716 |
| " | Moore, James L., 1314 Fitzwater St., | 5,137 | 4,488 |
| " | Mueller, Henry, Agent, 31st and Jefferson Sts., | 15,225 | 18.040 |
| " | Mueller, Charles, 2107 German-Ave., | 123 | 186 |
| " | Muellerschoen, C., 495 N. 3d St., | —— | 74 |
| " | Narr, Minnie, 242 N. 4th St., | 48 | 49 |
| " | Ohse, Henay, 1423 Germantown Ave., | 258 | 353 |
| " | Ortleib, Trubert, 1248 N. 3d St., | 73 | 32 |
| " | Otterbach, L., | —— | 1,062 |
| " | Otto & Layer, 518 Locust St., | 1,593 | 1,235 |
| " | Pfaehler, Mary, 931 St. John St., | 141 | 175 |
| " | Philadelphia Brewing Co., Falls of Schuylkill, | —— | 1,920 |

## PENNSYLVANIA—Continued.

| | | No. of barrels sold. | |
|---|---|---|---|
| | | 1878. | 1879. |
| Philadelphia, | Poth, F. A., 31st and Jefferson Sts., | 23,049 | 34,178 |
| " | Presser, Charles, Jr., 35th and Aspen Sts., | —— | 79 |
| " | Reiger, Jos., 4th and Cadwalader Sts., | 1,037 | 1,623 |
| " | Rothacker, G. F., 31st St., below Master, | 6,872 | 6,755 |
| " | Ruoff, Moritz, 1230 Frankfort Road, | 330 | 493 |
| " | Salber, Jno., 520 Richmond St., | 80 | 104 |
| " | Salomon, J., 1514 N. Front, | 17 | 65 |
| " | Schaal, Caroline, 627 Carpenter St., | 94 | 114 |
| " | Schaefer, F., 1220 Mosher St., | 515 | 2,187 |
| " | Schaufler, Chas., 1742 North Forth St., | 300 | 478 |
| " | Schaufler, J. F., 2551 N. 2d St., | 1,166 | 776 |
| " | Schemm, Peter, 25th and Poplar Sts , | 11,135 | 9,697 |
| " | Schillinger, G., 1020 E. Cumberland St., | —— | 17 |
| " | Schick, Jacob, 118 Master St., | 1,804 | 1,945 |
| " | Schmid, Gottlieb, 715 S. 7th St., | 125 | 357 |
| " | Schmidt, Christian, 113 Edward St., | 13,981 | 13,211 |
| " | Schintzer, J., 1148 N. 3d St., | 14 | 624 |
| " | Seitz, George, 2327 N. 7th St., | 2,048 | 1,819 |
| " | Smith, Robert, 20 S. 5th St., | 15,000 | 14,711 |
| " | Specht, C. L., 1033 W. Girard Ave , | 2,678 | 2,774 |
| " | Staubmiller, J , 1441 N. 10th St., | 97 | 181 |
| " | Stein, John, 3365 Ridge Ave., | 3,338 | 2,515 |
| " | Strobele, Anton, | 943 | 902 |
| " | Theis, C. & Co., 32d and Master Sts., | 14,716 | 7,372 |
| " | Straubmueller, Jos., 33d and Thompson Sts , | 8,904 | 8,086 |

## PENNSYLVANIA—Continued.

| | | No. of barrels sold. | |
|---|---|---|---|
| | | 1878. | 1879. |
| Philadelphia, | Weihmann, John, 815 Callow-hill St., | 1,792 | 2,150 |
| " | Wolf, Christian, 212 North Third St., | 90 | 217 |
| " | Wolters, Charles, 11th and Oxford Sts., | 3,431 | 15,158 |
| " | Wurster, Wm., 1325 German-town Ave., | 24 | 141 |
| " | Zann, Philip, 620 N. Third St., | 168 | 321 |
| " | Zierfuss, Fritz,422 Diamond St., | 142 | 270 |
| Pittsburgh, | Auen, Philip, | 84 | 102 |
| " | Darlington & Co., | 6,013 | 7,346 |
| " | Frauenheim & Vilsak, | 15,030 | 18,933 |
| " | Friedel, Henry, | 547 | 484 |
| " | Gangwisch, John, | 4,384 | 4,725 |
| " | Hauch, E., | 1,720 | 1,490 |
| " | Kaltenhaeusser, V., | 197 | 120 |
| " | Lauer, Philip, | 218 | 163 |
| " | Nusser, John, | 2,349 | 1,834 |
| " | Pier, Dannels & Co., | 9,404 | 6.261 |
| " | Reichenbach, John, | 1,176 | 1,509 |
| " | Rhodes, Joshua, | 6,090 | 4,752 |
| " | Schaler, John, | 159 | 203 |
| " | Spencer, McKay & Co., | 15,651 | 14,350 |
| " | Stirm, John G., | 258 | 433 |
| " | Straub & Son, | 6,457 | 9,400 |
| " | Wainwright, Z., & Co., | 9,229 | 10,888 |
| " | Weber, Frank, | — | — |
| " | Wilhelm, Henry, | 2,200 | 2,318 |
| " | Wood, H. T., & Bro., | 957 | 3,058 |
| Pittston, | Bishop, George, | 2,794 | 332 |
| " | Hughes, H. R., & Co., | 1,760 | 1,373 |
| " | Hughes, H. R., & M., | 4,569 | 4,526 |
| Plumer, | Brecht, Christian, | 337 | 99 |
| Pottsville, | Rettig, Chas., | 1,980 | 1,904 |
| " | Schmidt, Lorenz, | 5,220 | 4,707 |
| " | Yuengling, D. G., & Son, | 13,404 | 13,688 |
| Railroad P. O., | Helb, Fred, | 315 | 429 |
| Reading, | Barbey, Peter, | 6.211 | 8,152 |
| " | Felix, N. A., Estate of, | 3,991 | 4,333 |

## PENNSYLVANIA—Continued.

| | | No. of barrels sold. | |
|---|---|---|---|
| | | 1878. | 1879. |
| Reading, | Keller, Samuel C , | 2,595 | 2.010 |
| " | Lauer, Fred'k, (No. 1,) | 3,990 | 3,648 |
| " | Lauer, Fred'k. (No. 2,) | 15,157 | 18,793 |
| " | Peltzer, Abraham, | 114 | 198 |
| Renevo, | Binder, Luke, | 232 | 277 |
| Reynoldsville, | Kingsley & Co., | —— | —— |
| Roxborough, | Nagle, Sebastian, | 490 | —— |
| Saucon, | Rennig. George, | 895 | —— |
| Scranton, | Morton & Briggs, | 651 | 764 |
| " | Robinson, Elizabeth, | 5,830 | 6,800 |
| Shenandoah, | Tunnah, J., | 27 | 34 |
| Spring Garden, | Pfeiffer, Abraham, | 570 | 322 |
| St. Mary's, | Geier, William, | 399 | 155 |
| " | Luhr, Chas. & Co., | 732 | 825 |
| " | Vogel, Lorenz, | 105 | 97 |
| Tamaqua, | Adam, Joseph, | 135 | 86 |
| " | Haffner. Jos., | —— | 723 |
| Texas, | Hartung & Krantz, | 2,716 | 2.802 |
| " | Lauer, Jacob, | 735 | 738 |
| Tioga, | Ochs, G. F., | 34 | 44 |
| Titusville, | Schwartz, Chas., | 3,798 | 3,064 |
| " | Theobold, John, | 3,373 | 2,566 |
| Towanda, | Loder, Anton, | 681 | 753 |
| Tyrone, | Hewel, Jos., | 422 | 393 |
| Union City, | Wager, Theresa. | 235 | 286 |
| Unity, | Benedictine Society, | 2,457 | 2,644 |
| Upper Augusta, | Moeschlin. J., & A., | 932 | 1,066 |
| Vernon, | Dudenhoeffer, N., | 2,487 | 1,775 |
| " | Schwab, Frank, | 2,427 | 3,044 |
| Warren, | Loenhart, Philip, Jr., | 1,973 | 1,679 |
| Washington, | Ditz, Andrew, | 299 | 171 |
| " | Schnarderer, G. J., | 395 | 384 |
| " | Zelt, Louis & Bro., | 370 | 291 |
| Walker, | Hagle, George, | 157 | 96 |
| Wellsborough, | Ochs, John, | 52 | 59 |
| " | Scheffer, Christian, | 61 | 41 |
| Weissport, | Geisel, Catherine, | 322 | —— |
| Wilkesbarre, | Reichards & Son, | 5,020 | 3,588 |
| " | Stegmaier, C., & Son, | 3,908 | 4,362 |
| Williams, | Bennann & Kuebler, | 6,033 | 5,566 |

## PENNSYLVANIA—Continued.

| | | No. of barrels sold. | |
| | | 1878. | 1879. |
|---|---|---|---|
| Williamsport, | Flock, Jacob, | 3,013 | 2,465 |
| " | Koch, A., & Bro., | 2,302 | 2,465 |
| " | Schroeder, Wm., | 115 | 127 |
| Woodward, | Weikman, R., | 284 | 226 |
| York, | Helb, Theo. R., | 770 | 1,045 |
| " | Ulrich, F. W., | 800 | 1,009 |
| Young, | Haag, Christian, · | 324 | 264 |

Number of Breweries, 317.  1,041,486 1,034,081

## RHODE ISLAND.

| | | 1878. | 1879. |
|---|---|---|---|
| Newport, | Cooper, W. S., | 284 | 838 |
| Providence, | Gartner, Herman, | 77 | 94 |
| " | Gauch, Chas., | —— | 140 |
| " | Hanley, J., & Co., | 16,221 | 3,092 |
| " | Herrman, Henry, | —— | —— |
| " | Kiely Bros., | 8,588 | 6,207 |
| " | Molter, N., | —— | 17,460 |
| " | Nauman & Gaush, | 40 | —— |

Number of Breweries, 8.   25,210   27,837

## SOUTH CAROLINA.

| Columbia, | Seegers, John C., | 739 | 328 |
|---|---|---|---|
| Walhalla, | Bush, Chr., | 39 | 44 |

Number of Breweries, 2.    778    372

## TENNESSEE.

| Jackson, | Kunz & Co., | —— | 33 |
|---|---|---|---|
| Knoxville, | Knoxville Brewing Co., | 103 | 228 |
| Memphis, | Memphis Brewing Co., Henry Luchmann, Pres't, 33 Munroe St., | 6,877 | 6,810 |
| Nashville, | Maus, C. A., & Bros., | —— | —— |

Number of Breweries, 4.    6,980   7,107

## TEXAS.

|  |  | No. of barrels sold. | |
|---|---|---|---|
|  |  | 1878. | 1879. |
| Austin, | Pressler, Paul, | 431 | — |
| Belleville, | Frank, F. J., & Bro., | — | 54 |
| Ben Ficklin, | Wolters, H, & Co., | 121 | 156 |
| Boerne, | Hammer & Buelle, | 153 | 237 |
| Brackett, | Weidlich Bros., | — | — |
| Brenham, | Giesecke, G. F., & Bro, | 1,137 | 1.255 |
| " | Zeiss, Lorenz, | 746 | 882 |
| Castroville, | Kieffer, Blaise, | 281 | 300 |
| Cleburne, | Guffee, John, | 200 | — |
| Cuero, | Buschick, Hugo, | 121 | 120 |
| Cypress Creek, | Jugenhutt, T. & M., | 120 | 202 |
| Dallas, | Arnoldi, E., | 595 | — |
| Fayetteville, | Janak, Jos., | 85 | 141 |
| Flatonia, | Amsler & Co., | — | 319 |
| " | Richter, Vincent, | 346 | 390 |
| Fort Concho, | Hubert, Walter, | — | — |
| Fredericksburg, | Maner, John, | 66 | 81 |
| " | Probst, Fred, | 208 | 228 |
| Giddings, | Umlang, Theo., | 130 | 311 |
| High Hill, | Richtel & Kinshel, | 433 | 484 |
| Houston, | Wagner & Hermann, | 270 | 152 |
| Industry, | Walter, J. W., | 90 | 80 |
| Lagrange, | Kreisch, H. L., | 774 | 780 |
| Lando, | Knott, J. J., | — | — |
| Millheim, | Galler, H., | 107 | 101 |
| New Braunfels, | Rennert, Julius, | 589 | 261 |
| New Ulm, | Hagemann, W., | 157 | 125 |
| San Antonio, | Esser, William, | 498 | 390 |
| " | Hutzler, Joseph, | 573 | — |
| " | Lareoda & Beau, | — | — |
| " | Menger, Mrs. W. A., | 1,166 | — |
| Seguin, | Krause, C. P., | 84 | 59 |
| " | Leber, F. F., | 107 | 164 |
| Victoria, | Mack, L. F., | 168 | 233 |
| " | Weber, M., | 181 | 152 |
| Weatherford, | Both, W. F., & Co., | 49 | — |
| Yorktown, | Cellmer, M., | 56 | 55 |
|  | Number of Breweries, 37. | 10,050 | 7,718 |

## UTAH.

|  |  | No. of barrels sold. | |
|---|---|---|---|
|  |  | 1878. | 1879. |
| Alta, | Schmidt, P., | 91 | 18 |
| Beaver, | Fischer, A. A., | 59 | 134 |
| Bingham, | Wehrsitz, B., | 166 | —— |
| Corinne City, | Amsler, N., | 386 | 237 |
| Frisco, | Savior, John, & Co., | —— | 6 |
| Hot Springs, | Crossley, James, | 265 | 275 |
| Logan, | Worley, Henry, | —— | —— |
| Minersville, | Kiescle, G., | —— | —— |
| Nephi City, | Coulson, Samuel, | 59 | 67 |
| Ogden, | Brickmiller & Wells, | 784 | 876 |
| " | Richter & Fry, | 649 | 666 |
| Salt Lake City, | Burns, James, | 630 | —— |
| " | Keyser & Monitz, | 1,360 | 3,315 |
| " | Margetts, R. B., | 486 | 479 |
| " | Wagener, Henry, | 3,979 | 4,590 |
| Sandy, | Schueler, Maria, | 220 | 233 |
| Silver Reef, | Noebling, B, | —— | 61 |
| " | Welte, P., | 166 | 185 |
| Springville, | Dallin, John, | 16 | 16 |
| South Cottonwood, | Winkler, R., | 174 | 318 |
|  | Number of Breweries, 20. | 9,490 | 11.476 |

## VERMONT.

|  |  |  |  |
|---|---|---|---|
|  | One Brewery, | 285 | 173 |

## VIRGINIA.

|  |  |  |  |
|---|---|---|---|
| Alexandria, | Engelhardt, H., | 328 | 480 |
| " | Portner, Robert, | 10,366 | 12.192 |
| Richmond, | Robson, G. W., | —— | 3,022 |
|  | Number of Breweries, 3. | 10,694 | 15,694 |

## WASHINGTON TERRITORY.

|  |  |  |  |
|---|---|---|---|
| Colfax, | Erford & Palmday, | —— | 159 |
| Dayton, | Rumpf & Dunkel, | 87 | 66 |
| Mukilteo, | Cantrini, Geo. & Co., | 240 | 432 |

## WASHINGTON TERRITORY—CONTINUED.

| | | No. of barrels sold. | |
|---|---|---|---|
| | | 1878. | 1879. |
| Olympia, | Wood, J. C. & J. R., | 175 | 264 |
| Palama, | Schauble, J., | 105 | 72 |
| Pomeroy, | Scholl Bros., | —— | 36 |
| Port Colville, | Hosstetter, J. M. | 126 | 186 |
| Port Townsend, | Roesch, W. | 55 | 77 |
| Seattle, | Mehlhom, Aug., | 1,804 | 868 |
| " | Slorah & Co., | 1,652 | 1,111 |
| Spoken Falls, | Peterson, M. & Co., | —— | —— |
| Steilacoom, | Schafer & Howard, | 1,810 | 1,559 |
| " | Furst & Baumeister, | —— | 83 |
| Vancouver, | Young, Anton, | 218 | 243 |
| " | Dampfhoffer, L., | —— | 30 |
| Walla Walla, | Betz, Jacob, | 216 | 222 |
| " | Kleber, F. E., | 172 | 281 |
| " | Scott, Benj., | 360 | 649 |
| " | Stahl, J. H., | 851 | 811 |
| Yakima, | Schanne, Chas., | 94 | 97 |
| | Number of Breweries, 20. | 7,965 | 7.231 |

## WEST VIRGINIA.

| | | | |
|---|---|---|---|
| Charlestown, | H., Slack, | —— | —— |
| Fairmount, | Berns, W. F., | 88 | 72 |
| Lubeck, | Hebrank & Rapp, | 1,911 | 1,752 |
| Martinsburg, | Rossmarck, F. T., | 253 | 237 |
| Wellsburg, | Hebrank, Andrew, | 83 | 93 |
| Wheeling, | Balzer, Mauras, Twenty-Fifth St., | 488 | 408 |
| " | Kinghorn & Smith, 840 Market St., | 36 | 252 |
| " | Kress, Kilian, 1425 Smith St., | 1,265 | 1,207 |
| " | Nail City Brewing Co., Peter Weltz, Pres't, 33d and Wetzel Sts., | 6,395 | 7,630 |
| " | Reymann, A., Wetzel St., | 12,557 | 12,255 |
| " | Smith & Co., 1700 Chapline St., | —— | —— |
| | Number of Breweries, 10. | 23,086 | 23,906 |

## WISCONSIN.

| | | No. of barrels sold. 1878. | 1879. |
|---|---|---|---|
| Algonga, | Gatz & Elser, | 1,530 | —— |
| Allonez, | Hochgrave, A., | 1,384 | 1,417 |
| Alma, | Briggeboos, Wm., | 531 | 614 |
| " | Hemrich, John, | 680 | 630 |
| Alnapee, | Alnapee Brewing Co., | 448 | 631 |
| Appleton, | Munch, Carl, | 1,493 | 1,907 |
| " | Wing & Fries, | 496 | 320 |
| Arcadia, | Ferlig, John N., | 500 | 450 |
| Ashland, | Schottmiller, F. X., | 179 | 171 |
| Bangor, | Hussa, Joseph, | 540 | 490 |
| Baraboo, | Bender, Anna, | 356 | 539 |
| " | Ruland, Geo., | 467 | 470 |
| Beaver Dam, | Binzel, Philip, | 1,004 | 1,034 |
| " | Goeggerle, John, | 1,055 | 848 |
| " | Steil, F. X., | 112 | 181 |
| Beloit, | Schleuk & Co., | 381 | 279 |
| Berlin, | Schmidt & Schunk, | 490 | 473 |
| Berry, | Esser, George, | 975 | 915 |
| Black River Falls, | Oderbolz, Ulrich, | 684 | 540 |
| Bloomer, | Wendland, John, | 300 | —— |
| Boscobel, | Ziegelmaier, Geo., | 270 | 418 |
| Branch P. O., | Zunz, Elizabeth, | 1,512 | 1,620 |
| Burlington, | Finke, W. J., | 498 | 650 |
| Carlton, | Langenkamp, A. & Bro., | 228 | 227 |
| Cassville, | Scherr & Alrath, | 250 | 223 |
| Cedarburg, | Weber, John, | 1,556 | 1,270 |
| Centreville, | Scheibe, C., | 1,392 | 1,470 |
| Chilton, | Becker, Phil, | 1,092 | 1,056 |
| " | Gutheil, F. R., | 340 | 320 |
| Chippewa Falls, | Huber & Neher, | 634 | |
| " | Leinenkugel & Miller, | 1,880 | 1,700 |
| Christiana, | Mehels, Henry, | 166 | —— |
| Columbus, | Fleck, Stephen, | 30 | 42 |
| " | Kurth, Henry, | 132 | 231 |
| De Sota, | Eckhardt, George, | 261 | 245 |
| Dodgeville, | Treutzech John G., | 244 | 228 |
| Durand, | Lorenz, Philip, | 234 | 288 |
| " | Stimger, John, | 105 | —— |
| Eau Claire, | Hautzsch, Emily M., | 340 | 270 |
| " | Leinenkugel, Theresa, | 740 | 1,260 |

## WISCONSIN--Continued.

| | | No. of barrels sold. | |
|---|---|---|---|
| | | 1878. | 1879. |
| Eau Claire, | Leinenkugel Caroline, | 625 | —— |
| " | Sommermeyer, Henry & Co., | 239 | 712 |
| Farmington, | Jaehnig, L., | 1,051 | 741 |
| Fond du Lac, | Bech & Bros., | 2,158 | 2,556 |
| " | Frey, J. & C., | 1,645 | 1,692 |
| " | Sander, A., | 748 | 726 |
| " | Schussler, Jos., | 1,056 | 904 |
| " | Ziegenfus, John S., | 268 | —— |
| Fountain City, | Fiedler, Henry, | 420 | 357 |
| " | Koschitz, John, | 288 | 276 |
| Fort Atkinson, | Klinger, N., | 414 | .236 |
| " | Dalton, A. & Co., | —— | 62 |
| Fox Lake, | Regelein, John C., | —— | —— |
| " | Shlep, John, | 91 | 150 |
| Franklin, | Gross, Philip, | 323 · | 382 |
| " | Koellner, A., | 370 | —— |
| Germantown, | Steben, John, | 387 | —— |
| " | Staats, John, | 637 | 724 |
| " | Van Dycke, O., | —— | —— |
| Golden Lane, | Link, John, | 368 | 238 |
| Grafton, | Klug & Co., | 168 | 1,116 |
| Grand Rapids, | Schmitt, Nicholas | 190 | 188 |
| Green Bay, | Hagemeister, F., | 2,525 | 2.688 |
| " | Rahr, Henry, | 3,669 | 3,473 |
| Hartford, | Portz, Jacob, | 700 | 710 |
| Highland, | Schaffer, John, | 316 | 203 |
| Hillsborough, | Schnell, Fred'k, | 590 | 396 |
| Horicon, | Deierlein, Paul, | 76 | 73 |
| " | Groskopf, John, | 70 | 76 |
| Hudson, | Moutman, Wm., | 40 | 120 |
| " | Yoerg, Louis, | 666 | 711 |
| Humbird, | Eilert, Ernest, | 498 | 512 |
| Janesville, | Buob, John & Bro., | 2,046 | 3,151 |
| " | Rosa, C. & Co., | 650 | 610 |
| " | Todd, John G., | 1,516 | 1564 |
| Jefferson, | Breuning, Jacob, | 1,180 | 1,312 |
| " | Danner & Heger, | 580 | 714 |
| " | Neuer & Georgelein, | 191 | 317 |
| Kenosha, | Gottfredson, J. G. & Son, | 910 | 1,010 |
| " | Muntzenberger & Co., | 2,041 | 1,965 |

## WISCONSIN—CONTINUED.

| | | No. of barrels sold. | |
|---|---|---|---|
| | | 1878. | 1879. |
| Kewaunee, | Brandes, Chas., | 408 | 458 |
| " | Deda, Chas., | 264 | 286 |
| Kilbourne City, | Leute, Julius, | 139 | 190 |
| Kossuth, | Chloupek, A., | 192 | 96 |
| La Crosse, | Gund, John, | 4,370 | 6,250 |
| " | Heilman, J., | 2,880 | 2,360 |
| " | Hofer, J. & J., | 289 | —— |
| " | Michel, C. & J., | 6,348 | 7,504 |
| " | Zeisler, Geo., | 1,425 | 2,350 |
| Leroy, | Weidig, Nic., | 193 | 166 |
| " | Schmidt, Geo., | —— | —— |
| Lincoln, | Loux, Geo. E., | 138 | 166 |
| Lisbon, | Boots, Ephraham, | 301 | 463 |
| Madison, | Breckheimer, M., | 1,880 | 1,580 |
| " | Fauerbach, Peter, | 1,170 | 1,375 |
| " | Hausmann, Jos., | 4,255 | 5,836 |
| " | Hess & Moser, | 1,640 | 1,670 |
| " | Rodermund Brewing Co., F. Briggs, Manager, | 1,653 | 1,557 |
| Manitowoc, | Dobert, Chr., | —— | —— |
| " | Fricke, Carl, | 320 | —— |
| " | Pautz, F., | 926 | 1,345 |
| " | Rahr, Wm., | 3,050 | 4,150 |
| " | Richter, J., | 580 | —— |
| Marshfield, | Bourgevis, M., | 923 | 941 |
| Mauston, | Runkel, Maria & Co., | 496 | 496 |
| Mayville, | Darge, Wm, | 428 | 385 |
| " | Mayville Brewing Co., | —— | —— |
| " | Zeigler, M., | 320 | 331 |
| Mazomanie, | Tinker & Slough, | 496 | 528 |
| Megnon, | Zimmerman, Franz & Co., | 1,154 | 973 |
| Menasha, | Mayer, Joseph, | 1,095 | 1,091 |
| " | Merz & Behre, | 868 | 615 |
| Menomonee, | Fuss, Christian, | 454 | 386 |
| " | Roleff & Wagner, | 450 | 920 |
| Merton, | Frederickson, R., | 108 | 94 |
| Milwaukee, | Allpeter, Phillip, 601 3rd St., | 495 | 436 |
| " | Best, Ph. Brewing Co., Empire Brewery, Chestnut St., | 87,527 | 121,980 |
| | Best, Ph. Brewery Co., So. Side Brewery 425 Virginia St, | 38,286 | 45,994 |

## WISCONSIN—CONTINUED.

| | | No. of barrels sold. | |
|---|---|---|---|
| | | 1878. | 1879. |
| Milwaukee, | Blatz, V., 609 Broadway, | 49,168 | 53,907 |
| " | Borchert, F. & Son, Ogden and Milwaukee Sts. | 8,250 | 10,025 |
| " | Ennes, John & Co., 810 State St., | 3,640 | 94 |
| " | Falk, Franz (Wauwatosa), | 22,205 | 34,009 |
| " | Gettelman, A., (Wauwatosa,) | 4,780 | 4,539 |
| " | Gipfel, Charles, 417 Chestnut St., | 45 | 45 |
| " | Grisbaum & Kehrein, 91 Knapp St., | 148 | 163 |
| " | Liebscher, L., 189 Sherman St., | 337 | 410 |
| " | Miller, F, J., Wauwatosa,) | 10,677 | 16,293 |
| " | Milwaukee Brewing Association, 7th and Cherry Sts., | 3,629 | 4,674 |
| " | Obermann, J. & Co., 502 Cherry St., | 6,416 | 7,282 |
| " | Powell's Ale brewing Co., 222 Huron St., | 1,034 | 562 |
| " | Schlitz, J., Brewing Co., 3rd and Walnut Sts., | 96,913 | 110,832 |
| Mineral Point, | Argall, James, | 600 | 595 |
| " | Gillmann, C., | 2,071 | 1,731 |
| Mishicot, | Linstadt, J. | 656 | 720 |
| Mt. Pleasant, | Wolf, Charles, | 350 | 341 |
| Munroe, | Hefty, Jacob, | 1,354 | 1,600 |
| " | Luenberger & Co., | 1,080 | 1 365 |
| " | Pastel & Huppler, | 1,260 | 1,570 |
| Neenah, | Ehrgott Bros., | 410 | 360 |
| Neilsville, | Neverman & Sontag, | 637 | 424 |
| Neosha, | Binder, J., | 319 | 410 |
| Newburg, | Schwalbach, R., | 99 | 132 |
| New Cassel, | Husting, J. P., | 203 | 224 |
| New Glarus, | Hefty, Jacob, | 346 | 306 |
| New Lisbon, | Bierbauer, Henry, | 642 | 618 |
| New London, | Becker, Edward, | 557 | 531 |
| " | Knapstein, T., & C., | 830 | 898 |
| Oconomowoc, | Bingel, Peter, | 1,320 | 905 |
| Oconto, | Pahl, Louis P., | 810 | 849 |
| Onalaska, | Moore, M. G., | 648 | 660 |
| Oshkosh, | Glatz & Elser, | 1,530 | 1,646 |
| " | Horn & Schwalm, | 1,366 | —— |

## WISCONSIN—CONTINUED.

| | | No. of barrels sold. | |
|---|---|---|---|
| | | 1878. | 1879. |
| Oshkosh, | Kaehler, Christian, | 140 | 178 |
| " | Kinzl & Walter, | 470 | 480 |
| " | Rahr, August, | 310 | 315 |
| Pewaukee, | Schock, Mathias, | 395 | —— |
| Pheasant Branch, | Bernard, H., | 485 | 760 |
| Pierce, | Vaser, John, | 110 | 47 |
| Platteville, | Rheinstedt, F., | 724 | 532 |
| Plymouth, | Schneider, A., | 435 | —— |
| " | Weber, G., | 380 | 313 |
| Portage, | Epstein, Henry, | 178 | 190 |
| " | Haertel, Chas., Estate of, | 2,940 | 3,064 |
| Port Washington, | Dix, H., & Co., | 1,632 | 1,114 |
| " | Wittmann, John, | 610 | 590 |
| Potosi, | Hail, G., | 1,373 | 1,187 |
| " | Meerke, Henry, | 1,016 | —— |
| Priarie du Chien, | Schumann & Menges, | 3,216 | 2,779 |
| Prescott, | Husting, N. P., | 734 | 696 |
| Racine, | Dienken & Schad, | 167 | —— |
| " | Engle & Co., | —— | 194 |
| " | Heck, Fred, | 2,033 | 1,725 |
| " | Schelling & Klenkerl, | —— | 1,856 |
| Reedsburg, | Reedsburg Brewing Co., | 494 | 213 |
| Ripon, | Haas, John, | 1,274 | 1,268 |
| River Falls, | Hickey & Meyer, | 307 | 189 |
| Sauk City, | Drossen, Anna, | 420 | 476 |
| " | Leinkugel, F. L., | 130 | —— |
| " | Lenz, Wm., | 620 | 382 |
| " | Zapp, Robert, | —— | 300 |
| Schleisingerville, | Stork & Hartig, | 497 | 792 |
| Schleswig, | Gutheil & Bro., | 406 | 670 |
| Sevastopol, | Lindemann, L., & Bro., | 225 | 207 |
| Shawano, | Dengel, Geo. | 250 | 292 |
| Sheboygan, | Gustsch, L., | 2,887 | 2,608 |
| " | Kull, Martin, | 412 | —— |
| " | Schlachter, Thos., | 490 | 212 |
| " | Schrerer, K., | 4,615 | 5,455 |
| Sheboygan Falls, | Durow, D., | 248 | 176 |
| Sherman, | Mayer, Jos., | 234 | 207 |
| " | Seifert, Julius, | 672 | —— |
| Shullsburgh, | Schultz & Lauterbeck, | 303 | 159 |

31

## WISCONSIN—CONTINUED.

| | | No. of barrels sold. 1878. | 1879. |
|---|---|---|---|
| Stevens Point, | Kuhl, Adam, | 441 | 624 |
| " | Lutz, A., & Bro., | 705 | 975 |
| Sturgeon Bay, | Wagner Bros., | 288 | 469 |
| Theresa, | Quast, John, | 350 | 347 |
| " | Weber, Gebhard, | 1,387 | 1,042 |
| Tomah, | Goudrezick, I., | 192 | 221 |
| Trempeleau, | Melchoir J., | 120 | 172 |
| Trenton, | Schwalbeck, R., | 132 | 142 |
| Two Rivers, | Mueller, R. E., | 1,156 | 1,145 |
| Waterford, | Beck, John & Bros., | 168 | 201 |
| Waterloo, | Schwager, Wm., | 94 | 64 |
| Watertown, | Bursinger, Joseph, | 5,237 | 4,992 |
| " | Fuermann, Aug., | 10,287 | 8,065 |
| Waukesha, | Weber, Stephan,, | 1,170 | 1,363 |
| Waupaca, | Arnold, L., | 53 | 39 |
| Waupun, | Seifert, Peter, | 926 | 976 |
| Wausau, | Mathie, Frank, | 791 | 916 |
| " | Ruder, George, | 768 | 824 |
| Wayne, | Kreutzer & Groeschel, | —— | 59 |
| " | Pies, P., | 193 | 159 |
| West Bend, | Kuehlthau, Adam, | 1,470 | 1,360 |
| " | Mayer, S. F. & Co., | 2,460 | 2,192 |
| West Depere, | Schmidt, A. P., | 348 | 408 |
| Westford, | Justin, Jos., | 88 | 19 |
| West Lindo, | Gross, John & Son, | —— | —— |
| Weyauwega, | Duerr, J. A., | 338 | 415 |
| " | Griel & George, | 570 | —— |
| Whitewater, | Klinger, N., | 1,440 | 1,297 |
| Winneconne, | Yaeger, Theo., | 78 | 83 |
| Wista, | Ede, Peter, | 90 | 74 |
| Wrightstown, | Gutbier & Miller, | 203 | 64 |
| | Number of Breweries, 226. | 508,553 | 583,068 |

## WYOMING TERRITORY.

| | | | |
|---|---|---|---|
| Atlantic City, | Macomber & Huff, | 102 | 136 |
| Cheyenne, | Braun, J., | 750 | 808 |
| " | Kabis, L., | 580 | 343 |
| " | Kapp. C., | 902 | 1,605 |

## WYOMING TERRITORY—Continued.

|  |  | No. of barrels sold. | |
|---|---|---|---|
|  |  | 1878. | 1879. |
| Green River, | Brown, Adam, | 76 | 29 |
| Lander, | Hart & Marcum, | 45 | 26 |
| Laramie, | Bath, Fred., | 1,605 | 1,462 |
| Rawlins, | Fischer, G. & Co., | —— | 52 |
|  | Number of Breweries, 8. | 4,060 | 5,505 |

# INDEX.

———•◦•———

35

www.ingramcontent.com/pod-product-compliance
Lightning Source LLC
Chambersburg PA
CBHW031409270326
41929CB00010BA/1390